THE
NATIONAL GUARD
AND
NATIONAL DEFENSE

THE
NATIONAL GUARD
AND
NATIONAL DEFENSE

The Mobilization of the
Guard in World War II

ROBERT BRUCE SLIGH

Foreword by Roger Beaumont

New York
Westport, Connecticut
London

Library of Congress Cataloging-in-Publication Data

Sligh, Robert Bruce.
    The National Guard and national defense : the mobilization of the
Guard in World War II / Robert Bruce Sligh ; foreword by Roger Beaumont.
        p.   cm.
    Includes bibliographical references and index.
    ISBN 0-275-94056-X (alk. paper)
    1. World War, 1939-1945—United States. 2. United States—
National Guard—Mobilization—History. 3. United States—Militia—
Mobilization—History—20th century. I. Title.
    D769.2.S55   1992
    940.54'0973—dc20   91-28770

British Library Cataloguing in Publication Data is available.

Library of Congress Catalog Card Number: 91-28770
ISBN: 0-275-94056-X

First published in 1992

Praeger Publishers, One Madison Avenue, New York, NY 10010
An imprint of Greenwood Publishing Group, Inc.

Printed in the United States of America

The paper used in this book complies with the
Permanent Paper Standard issued by the National
Information Standards Organization (Z39.48-1984).

10 9 8 7 6 5 4 3 2 1

Dedicated to
First Sergeant Freddie Charles Sligh (Ret)
Company A, 3d Battalion, 153d Infantry Brigade
Arkansas Army National Guard

Contents

List of Tables   xi

Foreword by Roger Beaumont   xiii

Preface   xv

Acknowledgments   xvii

1. Introduction: The Last Battle for Control   1

2. A Wall of Paper   5

     War in Europe   5
     Roosevelt's First Priority   7
     The Isolationist Challenge   8
     Immediate Action   11
     Adding Flesh to Skeletons   16
     Streamlining the Army   18
     Fighting for Repeal   20
     Avoiding a Fight   22
     The Baltimore Convention   29

3. Funding, Feuds, and a Common Front   41

     The Campaign for Federal Funds   41

The Guard Leadership Meets   44
Planning for the Guard   46
Dissent within the Guard   49
The Guard Requests a Meeting   52
The Two Sides Meet   53
The AGA and NGA Hold Council   54
Before the Committee   57
Congressional Cuts   60

4. Europe Blazes, Washington Debates   67

War in the West   67
Mobilizing the Guard?   70
Searching for Alternatives   71
Congressional Reaction   74
Planning a Mobilization   75
The June 17 Meeting   78
Grenville Clark and a Peacetime Draft   79
The War Department Moves toward a Draft   80
The Guard's Reaction to the Draft Bill   82
Roosevelt's Reluctant Moves   84

5. Setting the Terms   93

Senate Joint Resolution 286   93
Public Opinion   96
The Press and Guard React   97
The Senate Debates   99
The House Debates   110
Conference and Compromise   118

6. Mobilization   125

Induction Planning   125
Induction   126
Equivocation over Extension of Service   128
Aid Short of War   132
Extension Legislation   135
Trouble with the Guard   145
Demobilization Plans   150

7. Conclusion　　　　　　　　　　　　　　　　　　　　　157

    The Successful Lobby　　　　　　　　　　　　　157
    The Congress　　　　　　　　　　　　　　　　　160
    Roosevelt　　　　　　　　　　　　　　　　　　161
    The Army　　　　　　　　　　　　　　　　　　163
    The States　　　　　　　　　　　　　　　　　165
    The Law　　　　　　　　　　　　　　　　　　166

Bibliography　　　　　　　　　　　　　　　　　　　171

Index　　　　　　　　　　　　　　　　　　　　　181

List of Tables

2.1 Army Divisional Strength, 1939   12

2.2 Air Corps Units, 1939   13

3.1 Proposed New Guard Units   47

5.1 National Guard Discharges   99

Foreword

Shortly after I joined the Wisconsin Thirty-second "Red Arrrow" Division thirty years ago, we were called to active duty in the Berlin Crisis. I had only completed my obligated service as an ROTC graduate a year and a half earlier and prior to that had served in the Army Reserve. Many of those experiences and some subsequent academic research on such matters came back to me as I reviewed Robert Sligh's dissertation. As sometimes happens, it proved upon completion to be more pertinent to "real world" concerns than any of us thought at the outset. Many concerned citizens, as well as military historians, political scientists, makers and shapers of defense policy, service professionals, and Guardsmen will find Robert's rigorous and workmanlike tracing of the evolution of the oldest major institution in American society, inter-threaded through the lives of American communities in peace and war since the early seventeenth century.

As one follows the events of 1940 and considers the subsequent effects, especially at a moment in which the Gulf War, hemispheric low-intensity conflict, and imminent reductions and reforms all bring Regular-militia relations under scrutiny, it is not wholly comforting to consider the implications of Robert's study. Those classical models in clear view of the Founding Fathers are no longer touchstones of American elites, especially the transition from a citizen-based to a standing army that marked the fall of the Republic and the rise of Empire.

Whether this is a relevant anecdote or not, the complexities of militia and Regular forces marched close on the tracks of the American Republic's evolution, generating paradoxes and anomalies along the way. This study examines some of those as a critical point, and underscores the lack of clear definitions and of shared vision. The wave of reconstituting of State Guard forces in the 1980s reflected the unresolved dilemma regarding the role of the

Guard as a constabulary *versus* a component in the Total Force. The sharp discontinuity between the expectations of some Guardsmen called to federal service and what they encountered on active service and the tensions over readiness and discipline seen in the Gulf War echoed discordancies heard in 1917-18, 1940, 1950-51, and 1961-62.

It seems safe to predict that these problems will not be wholly solved in the near future. In any event, those looking to the record of history for guidance will find, in this work, a solid guidepost and perspective on the question of the people-in-arms that stands as much a challenge to framers of American defense policy now as it did when the colonial frontier was being traced. If it is true, as students of cycles have averred, that America swings from a predisposition to interventionism to isolationism, then this study will be of special value to those concerned for the national weal, foreign and domestic, for a very long time.

Roger Beaumont
College Station, Texas
May 1991

Preface

In September 1939, as Europe went to war, the United States had an Army rated seventeenth in the world. The National Guard was a force, although partially equipped and trained, that could augment it. The Army quickly won presidential approval to increase both the Guard's size and its training but not to the levels the Army wished. President Franklin D. Roosevelt was hesitant to take too large a step for the predominantly isolationist populace. The Army, too, moved cautiously in its efforts to train and reorganize the National Guard. The National Guard Association represented the Guard's officer corps and possessed one of the most effective lobbies at that time. It had long sought an increased national defense and funds without incurring substantial federal control. From 1939 through 1941, the Association, at the behest of Milton A. Reckord, its able lobbyist, set aside its concerns over federal control, if only briefly, and cooperated with the Army, but only if the federal government paid for more troops and equipment.

While the Association attempted to balance its state and national concerns, Congress grappled with the political costs of mobilizing citizen soldiers. Isolationists in particular faced the dilemma of strengthening national defense and restricting the growth of presidential power. Public Law 96 passed in August 1940 provided for the mobilization of the National Guard for one year, but restricted its use to U.S. possessions and the Western Hemisphere. In 1941 Roosevelt requested Congress to retain Guardsmen, Reservists, and draftees. While retention of the Guard was not in serious doubt, it was tied to keeping draftees beyond one year. Passage of retention legislation by one vote denoted the nation's division over the nation's possible evolvement in the war.

The Acts of 1940 and 1941 tested the National Guard as an instrument of national defense and expanded the federal government's powers over the

Guard. Federalized units served as training grounds for draftees and effective combat units. Mobilization brought another result. Congress had expanded its power to use the Guard as a federal reserve force, effectively removing it from the states' hands, a point finally clarified in 1990 by the Supreme Court.

Less than two months after the Court rendered its decision the Guard faced its greatest test since Vietnam. On August 2 Iraqi forces invaded neighboring Kuwait. President George Bush reacted by dispatching American forces to Saudi Arabia. While Guard support elements were in evidence, the bulk of the Guard's combat forces were conspicuously absent. With the Court decision in hand, the Regular military establishment could use, or not use, the Guard as it saw fit. In the wake of the hundred hour ground campaign, many, including Secretary of Defense Dick Cheney, began to question the Guard's combat mission.

The ghosts of 1940 were returning to haunt the Guard. Whether this visitation is cyclical or the beginning of the National Guard as a dual mission force is yet to be seen.

Acknowledgments

Researching the National Guard mobilization of 1940-1941 has led down many paths and along the way I received help, advice, and encouragement from those I met. The education I gained at Texas A&M was the beginning of my journey. Particular thanks goes to Dr. Larry D. Hill, Chairman of the History Department, whose advice and patient editing of this manuscript introduced me to the Roosevelt era. Dr. Roger Beaumont's instruction in military history made me appreciate political influence on the military while Dr. Claude Hall's practical lessons in diplomatic history demonstrated how world affairs affect domestic issues. Completing the historical circle was Dr. Arnold Krammer, whose vivid depiction of Nazi Germany helped frame the back drop of world events. The ghastly picture he painted will remain with me forever. To all of you gentlemen, my sincere thanks.

The path of research was eased by the advice, and on occasion a patient ear, from the late Dr. Richard Morse and Dr. Robert Johnson of the United States Air Force Historical Research Center, Maxwell AFB, Alabama. Ms. Anita M. Weber, formerly of the George C. Marshall Foundation, Lexington, Virginia, provided substantial help in locating documents vital to my work. Likewise, the staffs of the National Archives and the National Guard Association Library rendered invaluable service in completing the documentary picture.

Finally, and most importantly, I wish to thank my family and especially my wife, Chuan-Hwa. Without their love, commitment, and encouragement this work would never have gone forward.

1

Introduction:
The Last Battle for Control

On June 11, 1990, the Supreme Court of the United States handed down a unanimous decision that ended decades of legal doubt. In the case of *Perpich v. Department of Defense*, Minnesota Governor Rudy Perpich challenged the federal government's authority to send National Guard troops outside the United States during peacetime without their governor's consent. In reality, the case revolved around the power of the state to control the Guard in peacetime.[1]

The challenge arose as a result of President Ronald Reagan's Central American policy and the use of National Guardsmen in the area. Sending Guardsmen overseas for training was not new. In 1973 the Forty-seventh Infantry Division, Minnesota Army National Guard sent a platoon-sized unit to Norway as part of an exchange program. Three years later the Army formally established an overseas training program where Guard units and their NATO counterparts traded visits. Members of the Guard enthusiastically embraced the program, as did their governors. Support changed to criticism when the deployment was to troubled Latin America rather than scenic Europe. Administration critics charged President Reagan with using Guardsmen in a show of force against Nicaragua's Sandinista government. Several governors began to question the wisdom and legality of sending state troops to "tindery parts of the world."[2]

In 1986 the controversy came to a head when Governors Michael Dukakis of Massachusetts and Joseph Brennan of Maine refused to allow their Guard units to participate in Honduran exercises.[3] Dukakis, a Democratic presidential hopeful, and Brennan were soon joined by the governors of New York, Vermont, Washington, Arizona, and Kansas. To forestall the governors' protest, the Reagan Administration proposed a law to circumvent state controls granted by the Armed Forces Reserve Act of 1952. The proposal encountered immediate resistance from members of both political parties. Arizona's Democratic Governor Bruce Babbit contended the Pentagon was "trying to . . . duck a political problem." A spokesman for Republican Governor Robert D. Orr of Indiana characterized the prospect of a change in the law as "a bit of an over-reaction."[4]

The Administration quickly retreated from separate legislation preventing governors from standing in the way of sending Guardsmen on training exercises but not from the idea. In the fall of 1986, Representative Gillespie V. "Sonny" Montgomery of Mississippi successfully amended the Fiscal Year 1986 Defense Authorization Act to prevent governors from withholding units from training outside the continental United States.[5]

Governor Rudy Perpich of Minnesota, supported by Dukakis and other governors, filed suit in federal court to have the "Montgomery Amendment" declared unconstitutional. On August 4, 1987, Federal Judge Donald Alsop ruled that "Congress may exercise plenary authority over the training of the National Guard while the Guard is on active federal duty."[6] Perpich appealed the decision and won a favorable opinion from a three-judge panel of the Eighth U.S. Circuit Court of Appeals.[7]

While Perpich pursued his challenge to the Montgomery Amendment, Governor Dukakis pressed another case before federal courts. On May 6, 1988, U.S. District Court Judge Robert Keeton upheld the constitutionality of the Montgomery Amendment and Congress's power to regulate the National Guard.[8] In October 1988 Dukakis appealed the case to the First U.S. Circuit Court of Appeals. But once again Judge Keeton, speaking for the court, rebuffed the suit in a one-sentence ruling: "Having examined the briefs of the parties . . . and having had the benefit of oral argument, we affirm the judgment on the basis stated in the district court's well-reasoned opinion."[9] Having lost in two federal courts, Dukakis took his case to the last legal avenue, the United States Supreme Court. The High Court, however, refused to hear the case thus upholding the lower courts' rulings. Without a word, the Supreme Court affirmed the place of the National Guard in the nation's defense structure and limited state governors' authority over the Guard.[10]

The Dukakis/Perpich suits resurrected old issues of state control of the National Guard and to what extent the federal government could use the Guard as an instrument of foreign policy. The *Providence (Rhode Island) Journal* asked the question, "Whose Guard is it, anyway?"[11] Syndicated columnist Neal Peirce queried, "National Guard: Will the real commander stand up?"[12]

When Iraq invaded Kuwait the real commander stood up. Within days of the invasion, U.S. forces were headed to the Persian Gulf region to protect the kingdom of Saudi Arabia. Guardsmen went to the troubled area--largely in support roles--and many of these were found wanting. Combat forces were for the most part left out of the grand strategy. After the stunning hundred hours ground campaign, the Guard's role as a combat arm came under serious question. The fact that the Department of Defense could cast such aspersions on the Guards' readiness and combat usefulness with only a weak response by leading Guardsmen denotes the depth of change in the nature of the National Guard Association (NGA).

In reality, these events marked the last battle over control of the National Guard, of which the Perpich and Dukakis suits and the Gulf War were only the last skirmish. The National Guard Association's insistence on a federal role for the Guard prompted the creation of dual status for Guardsmen by means of the National Defense Act of 1933. From that point on, Guardsmen were soldiers not only of the state, but also of the nation. The first test of the Guard's new status came as the world plunged into World War II. The compromises, conflicts, emotions, and legal precedents involved in the 1940-41 mobilization were to affect the National Guard and national defense strategy for many years to come. Yet, this important aspect of American history has been largely ignored. In most works on the Roosevelt era, the federalization of eighteen Guard divisions, which doubled the size of the Army, is given one or two lines. Guard historians such as John K. Mahon, Jim Dan Hill, and Elbridge Colby paid attention to Guardsmen entering federal camps but glossed over the politics of Army-Guard maneuvering prior to mobilization. It is the purpose of this work to demonstrate the importance of the political situation between these two defense establishments and their consequences on later defense policy and legislation.

NOTES

1. U. S. Supreme Court, Rudy Perpich, Governor of Minnesota, *et al.*, Petitioners v. Department of Defense, *et al.*, June 11, 1990.

2. "The Guard in Honduras: Innocent Maneuvers?" *Newsweek*, February 17, 1986, p. 36.

3. Ibid.

4. *New Orleans Times Picayune*, April 26, 1986, p. A-3.

5. *New York Times*, May 6, 1986, p. 24; *Christian Science Monitor*, February 20, 1987, p. 5.

6. *New York Times*, August 5, 1987, p. 4.

7. *Washington Times*, December 15, 1988, p. 2.

8. *Washington Post*, May 7, 1988, p. 19.

9. *Washington Post*, October 26, 1988, p. A-14.

10. "Supreme Court Rejects Dukakis Appeal, Upholds Montgomery Amendment on OCONUS Training," *National Guard*, June 1989, p. 10.

11. *Providence (Rhode Island) Journal*, December 12, 1988, p. 8.

12. *New Orleans Times Picayune*, February 2, 1987, p. 9.

2

A Wall of Paper

The maintenance of our peace and neutrality in the midst of the present troubled world demands that our agencies for national defense be immediately placed in a higher state of efficiency.
—Secretary of War Harry H. Woodring[1]

WAR IN EUROPE

On the morning of September 1, 1939, Adolf Hitler unleashed the forces of Nazi Germany against Poland. Europeans, who had long feared the eruption of yet another war, held their breath while awaiting Great Britain and France's actions. The two nations had given in to Hitler's demands and threats before; however, after Hitler's violation of the Munich Agreement the Allies were determined to stand behind their pledge to support Poland. Their declaration of war on September 3 heralded the beginning of World War II.

The start of Europe's second war in the twentieth century came as no surprise to Americans. For two decades isolationists proclaimed the inevitability of another European war. Most Americans believed that European antagonists, with their old feuds and internal political strife, would eventually indulge in violence. However, the war that confronted the world in 1939 did not comfort its prognosticators. Isolationists deeply dreaded American involvement in the war.[2] Disillusionment with American entry in World War I began in the 1920s and culminated in the 1934 *Fortune* article "Arms and the Men," which laid the blame for American involvement on the arms and munitions industries. Revisionist historians strengthened the isolationists and the pacifists by claiming that British propaganda and powerful U.S. financial houses seeking to protect loans to the Allies drew the nation into an unnecessary war. Radical pacifist organizations such as the

National Society for the Prevention of War and the Women's Inter-national League for Peace and Freedom staged effective Congressional lobbying efforts, believing that economic pressure could prevent war. Older pacifist organizations such as the American Peace Society, the World Peace Foundation, and the Carnegie Endowment for International Peace believed that only collective security through world bodies such as the League of Nations could ensure peace.[3]

Isolationists in Congress fell into broad-based groups that maintained the United States had no stake in a European war and thus should remain neutral. Some isolationists, notably Senator Gerald P. Nye of North Dakota,[4] believed that the United States should remain neutral no matter the cost. A second more traditional faction, led by Senators William Borah and Hiram Johnson, believed that the U.S. should protect the rights of neutrals, even at the risk of war. Although the two factions disagreed on this point, both held the common belief that a new war threatened the fabric of American society. Senators Burton K. Wheeler, Hiram Johnson, and others well remembered the repression of civil liberties during World War I and feared the consequences a new war could bring.

Events in Europe also deeply concerned President Franklin D. Roosevelt. During his first term, President Roosevelt had concentrated on national problems; however, by the late 1930s events in Europe and Asia distressed him. The rise of Italy, Germany, and Japan convinced him that the United States would inexorably become involved in the struggle. Faced with an isolationist Congress and public, the President set a cautious course toward rebuilding the nation's defenses while also aiding the opponents of Hitler, thus walking a political tightrope. As historian Robert A. Divine noted, Roosevelt shared the isolationist desire to keep the United States out of armed conflict, yet he also followed a seemingly interventionist policy of rendering aid to anti-fascist nations.[5]

For the United States Army and its newly installed chief of staff, General George Catlett Marshall, the pressing question was how to acquire the men and material needed to defend the United States and the Western Hemisphere from an expansion of the European war. Born in 1880, Marshall was a graduate of the Virginia Military Institute. During World War I, he served as First Army chief of operations and Eighth Army chief of staff where he helped plan the St. Mihiel and Muese-Argonne campaign. From 1919-24 he was General John Pershing's aide; three years later, Marshall moved to Fort Benning, Georgia, where he was the assistant commandant of the Infantry School. After five years at Fort Benning, General Douglas MacArthur sent him to the Illinois National Guard as an advisor. Despite MacArthur's assurances that the post was an important one, Marshall thought this tour with the Guard spelled the end of his career and his chance at a star. Happily for Marshall, his career was still very much alive. By 1938 he was the chief of the War Plans Division and the whispered candidate for chief of staff. A year later General Pershing and others used their influence with Roosevelt to have Marshall selected as the new chief of staff.

Like the President, Marshall faced opposition from a Congress strongly influenced by isolationism, conservatism, and partisan politics. His task was not made easier by a semi-independent, politically strong military force, the National Guard Association of the United States (NGA). As the voice of Guard officers, the Association aggressively sought more Federal dollars and a larger role in national defense. Neither Marshall nor the NGA leadership realized that the isolationists would be right in at least one regard about the war in Europe: World War II would change the way America society raised and maintained its armed forces for the next forty years; the Army and the National Guard would ever be quite the same.

ROOSEVELT'S FIRST PRIORITY

Roosevelt learned of the Nazi invasion of Poland in an early morning call from William Bullitt, United States Ambassador to France. The news saddened but did not surprise the President. Since the mid-1930s Roosevelt had become increasingly concerned over the rise of aggression in both Europe and Asia. On October 5, 1937, Roosevelt addressed the world's ills, if only in vague terms, with a call for a quarantine of aggressor nations by implied collective security. Isolationist reaction to the idea of America policing the world came swiftly, but Roosevelt gained support from such newspapers as the *New York Times* and the *Washington Post*. Whether a political trial balloon or a search for policy, the President had already begun to build collective security, at least in the Western Hemisphere. Roosevelt's 1933 Good Neighbor policy toward Latin America had by the Buenos Aires Conference of 1936 turned into an attempt at hemispheric solidarity in the face of "Old World" intervention.[6]

In Europe, Roosevelt had hoped that the 1938 Munich Agreement had satiated Hitler's demand for more territory. But Hitler's violation of that pact made a new war seem inevitable. When news of the war reached the President he found the situation reminiscent of his days of as Assistant Secretary of the Navy during the Great War. The President told the Cabinet:

I was almost startled by a strange feeling of familiarity—a feeling that I had been through it all before. But after all it was not strange. During the long years of the World War the telephone at my bedside with a direct line to the Navy Department in the night—the same rush messages were sent around—the same lights snapped on in the nerve centers of government. I had *in fact* been through it all before. It was *not* strange to me but more like picking up again an interrupted routine.[7]

Of immediate concern to Roosevelt was the position that Great Britain and France would take in regard to Germany's aggression against Poland.

Roosevelt, long convinced that America's defense rested in large part on the protection provided by the British fleet, waited intently for the British government's reaction. Although both Great Britain and France demanded German forces leave Polish soil by September 2, neither nation backed up its pledges to Poland by immediately declaring war. Roosevelt publicly stated that he had not lost all hope that war could be averted; however, behind the closed doors of the Oval Room of the White House the President informed his poker companions that the Allies would declare war by noon on September 3.[8]

Shortly after Great Britain and France declared war on Germany, Roosevelt addressed the American people by radio. He told the nation:

When peace has been broken anywhere, the peace of all countries everywhere is in danger. . . . This nation will remain a neutral nation, but I cannot ask that every American remain neutral in thought as well. Even a neutral cannot be asked to close his mind or his conscience. . . . As long as it remains within my power to prevent there will be no blackout of peace in the United States.[9]

Roosevelt, however, was already working to negate some of the provisions of the Neutrality Act of 1937. Though the President assured the nation that "at this moment there is being prepared a proclamation of American neutrality," he was delaying the implementation of the embargo provision of the Neutrality Act to allow Britain and France to hurriedly purchase war supplies. He also planned to call Congress into special session to repeal the embargo provision, a move that would surely bring on a wave of partisan recriminations and stiff opposition from isolationists.[10]

THE ISOLATIONIST CHALLENGE

The Roosevelt Administration faced several challenges in its attempt to formulate foreign policy. In Congress the President encountered a small but vocal group of isolationists who believed the nation should remain politically separate from European affairs. Although not a new philosophy in American political history, post-World War I disillusionment enhanced isolationism's appeal. The rise of popular isolationism, accentuated by the Great Depression, compelled Roosevelt to refrain from taking actions that gave the impression that he supported political cooperation with foreign nations. His course through the early days of his presidency was quite understandable; any policy that detracted from, or threatened, the New Deal was quickly dropped. This policy was clearly evident in Roosevelt's sudden abandonment of both the London Economic and the Geneva Armaments Conferences. He turned from the internationalist's path, finding it a poor source for solutions to the nation's ills.[11] Roosevelt's respect for the isolationists stemmed not from their numbers in Congress, for they were no more than a handful; their strength, and therefore Roosevelt's wariness, came from the American public's desire to remain out of any foreign war.

The onset of the Great Depression encouraged the image of businessmen as the "devils" who had needlessly taken the nation to war in 1917. This unflattering portrait was further colored by the 1934 publication of articles and books that told how corporations schemed to prolong World War I for profit. For years many isolationists believed and preached the evils of the so-called "merchants of death." The idea that greed prompted America's entry into the Great War consumed Senator Gerald P. Nye of North Dakota; he believed that by exposing the causes of the last war America could keep out of another. With support from leading pacifists, the Senate formed a committee, popularly known as the Nye Committee, to study the munitions industry and its part in taking the nation to war. Although it accomplished little of substance during its two-year existence, the committee heightened national isolationist feelings. Congress noted the rise in the public's concern and acted accordingly.[12]

Isolationists tended to paint the President as wanting to lead the nation to war. Roosevelt, however, was himself worried about the United States becoming involved in yet another world war. In letters and speeches he "reiterated his belief that the United States should avoid all future conflicts."[13] Since 1933 he had wanted to enact neutrality legislation that gave him discretionary power to embargo arms and munitions. In 1935, the President proposed to Nye and other senators the enactment of a neutrality law that would keep American out of future wars. Although the isolationists and their allies in the anti-war movement, the pacifists, had long endorsed such a law, their idea of a neutrality act differed markedly from that of the President. Roosevelt sought a flexible law giving him the ability to impose sanctions against aggressor nations. While isolationists wanted a neutrality law, they believed both sides in a war should be embargoed, without regard to aggressor or victim. The differences between the President and the isolationists produced the Neutrality Act of 1935, which pleased no one completely. Under the Act Roosevelt had no other discretionary power than to determine when a state of war existed between two nations. Once a war erupted, as it did between Italy and Ethiopia in 1935, the United States treated both victim and aggressor the same. The circumstances of the Ethiopian War, however, served the aims of Roosevelt and the isolationists; the United States severed trade in war materials with both nations. Since Ethiopia had no real trade with the United States, the embargo gave the Administration a moral weapon against Italy.

Yet dissatisfaction on both sides of the neutrality issue insured a renewal of the issue in 1936. As before, Roosevelt sought presidential discretionary powers to curb the rising tide of German, Italian, and Japanese aggression. Isolationists resisted Roosevelt's attempt to, as they saw it, grab power at Congress' expense.[14] Yet the isolationists were less united in the second round of the embargo battle. Nye wanted to extend the law to non-munitions war material and to loans to foreign nations, a logical progression from the ideas of the Nye Committee. Isolationists such as William Borah and Hiram Johnson viewed Nye's proposal as a threat to the traditional rights of neutral trade. However, both isolationist factions remained united in their determination to deny Roosevelt discretionary powers. As a result neither side gained a clear victory, and the 1936 struggle ended in by extending the 1935 Neutrality Act.[15]

The inadequacies of the neutrality law became appaient during the Spanish Civil War. At first the Administration attempted to avoid imposing the embargo, citing Secretary of State Cordell Hull's logic that the 1936 Act did not pertain to civil wars. In a reversal of his 1935 policy, Roosevelt preferred a moral embargo against the belligerents rather than a policy that would aid one side against the other. His concern, which mirrored that of Britain and France, was that the Spanish Civil War might spread to the remainder of Europe. The isolationists in Congress did not share this opinion. They sponsored and passed their own embargo against both sides in the civil war. The effects of Congress' policy became quickly apparent. As Francisco Franco's Nationalists captured ports, the Loyalists were cut off from sources of supply. The Congressional embargo worked to the fascist's advantage. As a result, the embargo became increasingly unpopular among Americans, most of whom sympathized with the Loyalists. Even Senator Nye began to talk against the embargo imposed by Congress.

The question by 1937 was how to remain neutral yet retain trade rights. Roosevelt continued to seek discretionary powers over the imposition of the embargo. In the wake of his failed attempt to reorganize the Supreme Court, the so-called "Court packing scheme," Congress was in no mood to grant the President additional power. Indeed, the rising tide of conservatism in the nation, reflected in Congress, pointed to a possible decline in presidential power. The solution to the question came from Bernard M. Baruch, head of the World War I War Industries Board. He proposed a cash-and-carry provision, which maintained American trade but did not expose the nation to a *casus belli*, such as the sinking of an American ship. Although Baruch's proposal did not end the debate, it offered a temporary fix.[16]

Hardly had the ink dried on the new act when war flared in Asia; Japanese and Chinese forces clashed outside Peking during the summer of 1937. Roosevelt privately favored the Chinese and declined to invoke the Neutrality Act because it would work to Japan's advantage. China, which lacked a merchant marine, would be denied access to American exports. Japan, with its naval superiority, would have no trouble obtaining war material. Yet pressure from the isolationists over arms to China carried on American ships and Roosevelt's own concern over a possible international incident, forced the President to restrict trade in war materials to China.

Events in Asia and growing tensions in Europe at last compelled Roosevelt to issue a statement. In his October 5, 1937, "Quarantine Speech" Roosevelt called, in vague terms, for international action to curb the acts of aggressor nations. Whether Roosevelt meant the speech to be a "trial balloon" or, as Dorothy Borg maintained, a statement of his own ambiguous feelings about American noninterventionism, from that time on, although cautious, he took a more internationalist stand. Yet events in Asia did not cause him to press for reform of the neutrality law as he had during the Spanish crisis. Roosevelt did not make another attempt to win discretionary powers until after Hitler had violated the Munich Agreement by overrunning the remnant of Czechoslovakia in 1939.[17]

In March 1939, Roosevelt had Senator Key Pittman, the chairman of the Foreign Relations Committee, introduce a proposal to repeal the embargo provision of the 1937 Act. Roosevelt distanced himself from the bill, allowing Pittman to face the isolationists. Pittman's inept management of the bill, Roosevelt's low popularity in the wake of the attempted party purge of 1938, and strong isolationist opposition led to a Congressional deadlock on the issue. With no hope of victory, Roosevelt withdrew the legislation and awaited another international crisis before attempting to remake the 1937 Act closer to his own design. Hitler's invasion of Poland provided the necessary catalyst for neutrality "reform."[18]

IMMEDIATE ACTION

Like the President, Acting Chief of Staff General George Marshall learned of the German invasion of Poland from an early morning telephone call—the morning Marshall was to become the Army Chief of Staff. His predecessor, Lieutenant General Malin Craig, had tried to bring the Army to a higher state of readiness, but the political pressure exerted by isolationists and an economy-minded Congress kept the Army at a low manpower level. Beyond that, internecine warfare between Roosevelt's isolationist Secretary of War Harry H. Woodring, and interventionist Assistant Secretary of War Louis Johnson, damaged department morale and efficiency. Marshall, who was friendly with both men, was caught in the middle. This delicate and disruptive situation persisted until Woodring's resignation in 1940. After 1937, however, Roosevelt's shift toward interventionism had already pushed Woodring into the background. With a Secretary of War who was becoming politically unreliable, the President increasingly bypassed him and communicated directly with the Chief of Staff.

The Army that Marshall inherited from General Craig was at a low ebb. By its own accounts, it ranked seventeenth in the world. Although Roosevelt pressed Congress for more defense spending, by June 30, 1939, the Army numbered only 187,893 officers and men. Fifty thousand troops served outside the continental United States in Hawaii, the Philippine Islands, and the Panama Canal Zone. Units stationed in the continental United States were scattered among 130 posts—mostly relics of the Indian wars. Combat units consisted of nine infantry and two cavalry divisions. Yet these units were little more than paper organizations. No division was near its authorized peacetime strength. The Second Division came nearest the mark with 10,000 men—still 4,000 short. As Table 2.1 shows, the Army was 76,900 men short of peacetime strength.

Table 2.1
Army Divisional Strength, 1939

Division	Actual Strength	Peace Strength Shortage
1st	8,800	5,200
2nd	10,000	4,000
3rd	8,500	5,500
4th	4,400	9,600
5th	3,800	10,200
6th	3,400	10,600
7th	3,500	10,500
8th	4,200	9,800
9th	2,500	11,500

Source: Marvin A. Kreidberg and Merton G. Henry, *History of Military Mobilization in the United States Army, 1775-1945* (Department of the Army, 1955), p. 550.

During the previous year, the Army Air Corps had received increasing attention from the President, who envisioned it as a major force to defend the United States from sea borne attack. Roosevelt pushed through Congress a plan for the manufacture of 10,000 planes a year in an attempt to "influence" Hitler.[19] However, he made no provisions for increasing the number of officers and men or improving training, a point the Army stressed. On September 1, 1939, the Army Air Corps numbered roughly 26,500 men and 2,200 planes.[20] Like the infantry, the Air Corps suffered severe shortages of men and outdated equipment. (Table 2.2 provides a summary of the units contained within the Army Air Corps.)

The two reserve organizations of the Army, the Army Reserve and the National Guard, had fared little better than the regulars. In 1939 the Army Reserve contained a total of 119,773, with 104,228 in the Active Officer

Reserve Corps and 12,408 inactive reserve officers. The Enlisted Reserve Corps contained slightly over 3,000 men. However, the Army Reserve contained only men, not units; officers and men would be used as fillers in an expanded Army.[21]

The National Guard and the Regular Army were roughly equal in strength. Unlike the Reserve, the Guard maintained eighteen infantry and four cavalry divisions. But the Guard, too, had suffered during the postwar period and the Great Depression. As part of the National Defense Act of 1920 Congress set the Guard's authorized strength at 400,000; however, inadequate funding limited it to 199,491 officers and men.[22] Few, if any, of its units maintained peacetime strength.[23]

Table 2.2
Air Corps Units, 1939

Unit	Number
Air Force Headquarters	1
Wing Headquarters	5
Group Headquarters	14
Squadron (Heavier-Than-Air)	55
Bombardment	15
Reconnaissance	8
Pursuit	15
Attack	7
Observation	10
Squadron (Lighter-Than-Air)	3

Source: Maurer Maurer, *Aviation in the U.S. Army, 1919-1939* (Washington, DC, 1987), p. 473.

The condition of the Army, the Reserve, and the National Guard stemmed from both a reaction to the idealism of World War I and the catastrophe of the Great Depression. Isolationist sentiment among the American people increased in the years that followed the war. Feeling betrayed, the public turned inward and against militarism. In the prosperity of the twenties, Congress responded to the mood of the nation and repeatedly trimmed the defense budgets. Although the onset of the Great Depression stimulated enlistment, the Army's material base did not improve and in some cases worsened.

Faced with severe budget reductions, the Army chose a course of action that would preserve its structure while sacrificing strength. In time of crisis, the theory went, the Army would expand, based on the preserved skeletal structure. Secretary of War John C. Calhoun (1817-1825) first offered the idea of an expandable army. In the late nineteenth century, Major General Emory Upton revised Calhoun's plan of an expandable army based on a cadre system. Each formation within the Army would be organizationally complete, every element necessary for a fighting force present but manpower was reduced to the bare minimum. When needed, these formations would be quickly fleshed out with volunteers or reservists. Army professionals theorized that a fleshed out army could be ready for duty in six months to a year. General Leonard Wood in particular believed that an army could be raised in six months.[24]

The "Uptonian" (for General Upton) idea of an expandable army encountered criticism from several sources. Civil War General John A. Logan, stressing the value of the citizen soldier over that of the professional, believed that a well trained citizenry could adequately defend the nation. The Army's role, he believed, was that of teacher rather than sole defender of the nation. Following World War I, Colonel (later Brigadier General) John M. Palmer, a vocal proponent of the citizen soldier, objected to the Uptonian solution. He believed that citizen soldiers were cheaper to train and maintain than regulars. Yet neither side looked to the growing state National Guard units as the solution to the manpower problem.[25]

Although the Army reluctantly accepted the Uptonian principle of an army cadre system, budget cutbacks in the 1920s and early 1930s forced further reductions, eventually eliminating some units in order to conserve more important ones. The result was an army that, in time of need, had to recreate important units from scratch, a point Palmer stressed as a justification for his emphasis on the citizen soldier.

War plans in the post-World War I era centered on the only two nations believed to posses the resources to threaten American interests: Great Britain (Red Plan) and Japan (Orange Plan). Although war with Britain was unlikely, both "color" plans depended heavily on naval rather than ground forces. Strategic planning did not officially change until the summer of 1939 when the General Staff began war plans for war against Germany, Italy, and Japan—either separately or together. These RAINBOW plans, as they were labeled, focused on hemispheric defense rather than on expeditionary forces to Europe or Asia.[26]

Mobilization planning during the 1920s and early 1930s was based on the concept of massed armies facing each other in a Great War scenario. Planners envisioned recreating the American Expeditionary Force (AEF) using the expandable army and existing stores of supplies, most of which were already obsolete. Not until General Douglas MacArthur's tenure as chief of staff did mobilization planning take into account the resources on hand and a realistic expectation of expansion. MacArthur proposed three stages of mobilization planning based on (1) current strength, (2) hoped for strength of 165,000 enlisted men, and (3) the authorized peacetime strength of 280,000. But the forces raised to form the so-called Initial Protective Force, even augmented by the Guard, could only defend the continental United States. With little or no support from Presidents Hoover or Roosevelt, the Congress, or the public, MacArthur's plan remained for years little more than a future goal. By 1938 his persistence and that of General Malin Craig eventually brought the manpower level of the Army to 170,000, realizing the second stage of MacArthur's plan. However, the Army's only large scale practice at mobilization during this time resulted from the operation of the Civilian Conservation Corps (CCC). In a few short weeks the Army mobilized and looked after nearly 300,000 young men. Evidence indicated that the Army's operation of the program hindered the training of Army personnel and that it depleted up part of the Army's stocks of supplies.[27]

However, ongoing events in Europe and their implications for the Western Hemisphere spurred a change in defense policy. During the 1930s, Germany initiated a well organized, if some times ill conceived, propaganda campaign in the Americas. At first designed to raise Germany's political and economic standing, the policy ultimately worked toward indoctrinating the ethnic Germans living in the Americas to the Nazi philosophy and the support of "native" right-wing elements.[28] The Third Reich also enthusiastically engaged in trade with Brazil, Argentina, and other South American states. These anti-United States propaganda and economic campaigns greatly alarmed the Roosevelt Administration. While the State Department formulated policy to counter Nazi political and economic infiltration, the Army attempted to lessen Germany's growing military influence. In April 1939, Roosevelt established the Standing Liaison Committee composed of the Undersecretary of State, the Army Chief of Staff, and the Chief of Naval Operations. Its purpose was to strengthen military missions in Latin America, establish U.S. or local control over commercial airlines, supply arms to friendly governments, and lay the foundation for future military cooperation.[29]

During the latter part of the decade Brazil purchased increasing amounts of arms and equipment from Germany. In mid-1939 the War Department countered by sending General Marshall, Craig's announced successor, on a good will mission to Brazil. In Washington, however, the General Staff drafted plans to counter an Axis thrust in the hemisphere. Because of its large German immigrant population, perhaps one million, and its proximity to European occupied West Africa, Brazil became a key focal point of hemisphere defense planning.[30] As a result, the Standing Liaison Committee "changed War Department planning from a passive to an active defense attitude." General Staff planners and their Navy counterparts began formulating plans to defend the Western Hemisphere rather than just the

United States. The plans that emerged from the deliberations of the Joint Planning Committee, named RAINBOW for the combination of "color" plans that structured defenses against several adversaries at once, called for "defending the Western Hemisphere against military attack from the Old World."[31]

Hitler's invasion of Poland heightened Administration concerns over defending both North and South America. Although Britain and France had substantial forces, the General Staff could not rule out the possibility of a German victory and its subsequent occupation of Allied colonies, which could serve as springboards for invading the Western Hemisphere. When Hitler invaded Poland, the United States Army lacked adequate resources to defend the nation, let alone the hemisphere.[32]

ADDING FLESH TO SKELETONS

Marshall's immediate concern in September 1939 was to increase the size, training, and resources of the Army and the National Guard. Although the Army could not immediately remedy all the adversities the two organizations had suffered over two decades, the Chief of Staff hoped to reach at least peacetime strength and to begin acquiring needed material. He also hoped to create a force capable of moving anywhere in the hemisphere to counter Axis aggression. Neither of his goals was easily obtainable. First, Marshall needed the President's approval to increase the Army and Guard's manpower to 280,000 and 425,000 men, respectively. This move required a presidential order and a request for additional funds from Congress. On September 4, Marshall went to the White House to seek the necessary executive order. He left the meeting believing that he had presidential approval for expanding the Army and the Guard and the next day Marshall told his staff that Roosevelt approved the requested increases. On September 6, he ordered the War Plans Division (WPD) to draft a letter from Secretary Woodring to the President "recommending the increase of the Regular Army to 280,000 and the National Guard to 435,000 and also to prepare the drafts of letters from the President to the Secretary of War directing such increases."[33]

On September 7, the Chief of Staff sent a memorandum to Secretary Woodring which dealt with the "question of *immediate increase* of the Regular Army and the National Guard."[34] In the first paragraph Marshall noted that the latest Congressional appropriation provided for an increase in forces from the current level of 165,000 to 202,000 men, with most of this increase going to the Air Corps. Marshall wanted to use the already approved increase to "complete the missing links of the ground forces."[35] But he warned that members of Congress would react adversely once they discovered the War Department's redirection of the increase.[36] The growing preparedness movement, even among some isolationists, placed emphasis on air and naval power rather than ground forces to provide the major bulwark against possible invasion, a philosophy Roosevelt strong endorsed. They believed that the limited range of military aircraft insured that they could not be used as an offensive weapons. However, General Marshall believed that "it [was] highly desirable from a military standpoint, and . . . from the public reaction standpoint" to increase the Army and the Guard to near their statutory peacetime strengths.[37] He proposed dividing the increase into three increments, which would end by February 1, 1940. General Staff planners believed this timetable would provide the Army and the Guard with the needed manpower at a rate they could absorb.

Although Congress had already appropriated money for an increase in the regular forces, albeit designated for the Air Corps, the Guard would have to bear some of the costs of additional men without the benefit of additional federal funds. The War Department would pay some of the Guard's costs for drills, rations, clothing, etc., but

Recruitment of the National Guard, under peace conditions is a matter for the respective Governors. The War Department merely *authorized* the States to increase the strength of units by certain numbers—meaning that clothing, equipment, weekly drill night pay, and summer two weeks' training pay and rations, will be provided by the Federal Government. The Governor will increase his military forces above the War Department authorization, but it would be entirely at the expense of the state, and no government equipment would be provided.[38]

The War Department would not aid in recruiting new Guardsmen nor would it provide money for new armories or camps to house new equipment.

Marshall's immediate plan, however, never saw the light of day. Roosevelt changed his mind even as Marshall drafted his note to Woodring. The President decided to limit the increase to the first increment of Marshall's plan; on September 8, he issued an executive order authorizing an increase in the Army and Guard to 227,000 and 235,000, respectively.[39] Historian Robert Dallek noted that

Roosevelt resisted pressure for substantial increases in national defense forces and rapid industrial mobilization. Fearful that these actions would agitate suspicions about his peaceful intentions and make Neutrality change appear as a step toward involvement, Roosevelt temporarily limited expansion of the regular Army and National Guard to less than 50 per cent of what defense chiefs asked and suspended economic and fiscal preparations for war.[40]

In a secret memorandum to Deputy Chief of Staff Brigadier General Lorenzo D. Gasser, Marshall stated that Roosevelt could not

consider at this time more than the first increment, as he thought that was all the public would be ready to accept without un-due excitement. He indicated that he would give us further increases up to the figures we proposed, but this prospect would have to be treated as highly confidential.[41]

Marshall closed the memo by informing Gasser that the General Staff could continue to make plans based on an Army of 250,000 and a Guard increased by 126,000 men. Yet the President's tone was clear, he wanted their moves to receive as little visibility as possible.[42]

The main basis for Roosevelt's caution was his desire to keep the United States out of the war and, undoubtedly, his concerns about isolationist political reaction. Public opinion worked in his favor. In the wake of Hitler's attack on Poland, the American public supported increasing America's armed forces. Polls conducted during the second week of September showed that 90 percent of respondents favored giving voluntary military training to the Civilian Conservation Corps. By the end of the month over 86 percent of respondents favored increasing the armed forces.[43] While Roosevelt initiated efforts to aid Britain and France, the General Staff accelerated the task of improving the Army.

STREAMLINING THE ARMY

Although Marshall did not gain the manpower increases he wanted, he did have the President's assurance that more men would be added to the Army and Guard as the political climate became favorable. With this in mind, Marshall started reforms designed to bring the Army, at least structurally, in line with modern military thought.

The first recommendation for restructuring the Army came the day after Roosevelt issued the executive order enlarging the Army and Guard. The War Plans Division of the General Staff, which had been working on the plan for some time, recommended reorganizing the Army's infantry divisions from their current "square" structure, a relic of General Pershing's World War I reorganization, to "triangular" formations. On paper, square divisions contained a peacetime strength of nearly 14,000 men in a division headquarters, two infantry brigades of two regiments each, an artillery brigade, and support troops. Yet, as already noted, none of the divisions was near peacetime strength. A triangular division had a peacetime strength of 9,000 men in three infantry and two artillery regiments plus support troops. Reorganization of existing units would provide enough men for five complete triangular divisions plus sufficient troops to man one corps, fill five antiaircraft regiments to peacetime strength, and establish cadres for four future divisions.[44]

The WPD plan did not, however, provide for streamlining Guard divisions. Marshall hesitated at reorganizing the Guard's divisions because of the plan's experimental nature and the potential for confusion caused by reorganization.

In a letter to Major General James K. Parson, Third Corps Area commander, Marshall stated that "a change in the guard at this time would be devastating."[45] Undoubtedly the Guard's poor performance at the First Army maneuvers in August 1939 influenced his decision, and thus the WPD report. The WPD recommended, and Marshall concurred, that additional training would aid the Guard better than reorganization.[46] The Chief of Staff therefore directed the Guard to increase its customary forty-eight, ninety minute drills to a total of sixty, plus seven days of field training near home station. The extra drills and field training were to be completed by the end of January 1940. Because of regulations preventing more than one drill per day, the Guard would have to make up the difference by holding at least two drills per week. In addition to armory drills, the Army announced that summer encampments were increased from fifteen to twenty-one days. Although the added training placed a hardship on Guardsmen, Marshall believed it was necessary to raise the Guard's proficiency.[47]

He also knew that both the increase in training and the number of troops were likely to cause friction with the Guard leadership.[48] The Guard had a tradition of close relations with the business community, but no law required businesses to release employees for drills or summer encampments, with the result that working Guardsmen might be forced to choose between a job and military service. Marshall understood the difficult position with employers that additional training created for Guardsmen, but he saw no alternative other than mobilization as a means to improve their abilities. As Marshall wrote his to old friend Charles H. Cole, former Adjutant General of Massachusetts, he wished "at all cost to avoid taking men away from their personal pursuits until an emergency develop[ed] of such a nature that drastic action [became] necessary."[49] Yet the Chief of Staff also indicated that even more training might be expected. He told Cole of the possibility of battalion, regimental, and perhaps even brigade assemblies for two or three days each and of his intent to call in Guard division commanders and their staffs for additional training in large unit maneuvering, a weak area in the Guard's training detected during the 1939 maneuvers.[50]

The second possible point of conflict concerned enlarging Guard units in excess of state needs. As at the federal level, during the 1920s and 1930s, state governments had been reluctant to expend money on the Guard. Their units seemed adequate to meet any emergency, whether the result of domestic trouble or natural disaster. Providing for additional men, though their numbers were not as large as Marshall would have liked, created an added burden on the state governments. The political repercussions from the states would undoubtedly reverberate through the Guard and eventually reach Congress. But once again Marshall believed that he had plotted the best course available.

On September 20, the General Staff officially notified the National Guard Bureau[51] of the September 8 manpower increases and the new training schedule. Within forty-eight hours the Bureau had informed each state of its share of the increase in men. The Guard reacted enthusiastically. The war in Europe boosted interest in the Guard. Units long under strength began vigorous recruitment drives that netted thousands of new troops. The *Army and Navy Journal* reported that it had "learned . . . unofficially that units in many communities [were] putting on special demonstrations in their drives for new recruits."[52] In the first week 6,700 men in thirty-nine states joined the Guard; by the end of the second week a total of 13,000 had signed up. In terms of raw numbers, the Guard added the equivalent of one square division at just under peacetime strength. [53]

FIGHTING FOR REPEAL

While Marshall and the General Staff laid plans for an increased Army and National Guard, Roosevelt prepared to renew the struggle for repeal of the embargo provision of the Neutrality Act. Germany's invasion of Poland sent shock waves through the nation, which reverberated in Congress. Although still influential, the isolationists were weakened by Hitler's aggression, with some moving closer to the President's position on neutrality. Defeated on the embargo before, Roosevelt decided the international crisis warranted another attempt to gain discretionary powers. Cautiously he laid the political groundwork to reintroduce a repeal of the mandatory embargo. By mid-September he was ready; on September 13, he issued a proclamation calling Congress into special session beginning September 21.

Isolationist reaction came swiftly. Senator Borah maintained that repealing the mandatory embargo was an act that would lead to aid for only one side, the Allies. Charles Lindbergh, hero of the 1927 solo crossing of the Atlantic, felt so strongly about the issue that on September 15 the normally shy aviator took to the radio to defend American neutrality laws. During the previous three and a half years, with the encouragement of the U.S. Army and State Department, Lindbergh was a guest of Reichmarshal Hermann Goering, who bestowed on the American aviator a medal that later became a source of controversy. Lindbergh's celebrity enabled him witness to the might of the *Luftwaffe* and even fly one of its most advanced fighters. Firsthand experience convinced Lindbergh of Germany's air superiority but also of its inability to strike at the United States. Although Lindbergh's statement received mixed public reaction, isolationists reveled at gaining such a popular spokesman. Internationalists cast him in the role of a Nazi sympathizer.[54]

Roosevelt expected the isolationists' reaction and took steps to undercut their support in Congress. On September 20, a day before Congress met, the President organized a bipartisan White House conference with leading politicians sympathetic to his position. In attendance were Alf Landon and Frank Knox, the 1936 Republican presidential and vice-presidential candidates, as well as non-isolationist Congressmen from the Northeast and South. The meeting provided the air of bipartisan commitment that the President needed. At the special joint session of Congress the next day Roosevelt continued to project a noninterventionist image by stating that the government "must lose no time or effort to keep [the] nation from being drawn into war."[55]

The issue of repealing the embargo and restoring the expired cash-and-carry provision of the 1937 Act also found support in the isolationist bloc. Isolationist Senator Robert A. Taft of Ohio viewed the proposal as in no "way calculated to increase the chances" of involving the nation in Europe's war.[56] While Senator Warren Barbour of New Jersey accepted the President's proposal because it would ultimately benefit large industry concerns in his state. George W. Norris, who had begun to fear the Axis menace, backed Roosevelt's latest attempt at eliminating the embargo as a way of keeping America out of the war and at the same time aiding the Allies.[57]

Roosevelt's skillful political maneuvers enabled the Administration to gain control of the issue in the House where Democratic representatives were nearly unanimous in support of the President. However, true opposition centered in the Senate. Isolationists such as Borah, Nye, and Johnson, along with twenty others, resisted the Administration's interpretation of events in Europe and maintained their opposition to a repeal of the embargo. Yet, at the same time most of the opposition to repeal of the embargo favored cash-and-carry. Roosevelt's linking of the two issues left the isolationists little room to maneuver. Unable to muster the votes to call for a separate vote, they were thus left with the prospect of voting against cash-and-carry.

Isolationist troubles increased when they tried to formulate a strategy to combat the Administration. Senator Robert La Follette, Jr., suggested those opposed to changing the neutrality law form a nationwide campaign to arouse public support. He hoped to put public pressure on undecided senators. Borah and Nye did not agree with La Follette and advised against forming a nation-wide campaign. Isolationists eventually adopted a strategy of prolonging the debate in hopes of arousing the public against Roosevelt. La Follette later claimed that this decision was a critical mistake.

In the past public opinion had aided the isolationists against the Administration in foreign affairs, as it had affected Roosevelt at the beginning of the New Deal. After Hitler violated the Munich Agreement, however, public opinion began to change. The Nazi invasion of Poland accelerated the shift of public opinion toward the Administration's point of view. Although mail to Roosevelt, and senators, greatly favored retaining the embargo, George A. Gallup's opinion polls revealed a different picture. Shortly after the invasion of Poland fifty-seven percent of the public favored repeal of the embargo. After Roosevelt's September 21 address to Congress, the percentage increased to sixty-seven for repeal. However, Roosevelt's gain in the public opinion polls did not signal a willingness of the people to support American entry into the war. Ninety-five percent of those polled in April opposed American involvement in a European war. As historian Michael Leigh stated: "In August and again in October majorities opposed American troop involvement in Europe even if it appeared that Britain and France faced defeat."[58] While the vast majority of Americans opposed entering a new world war, by September 1939 seventy-six percent of the public believed the nation would eventually be drawn into the conflict.[59]

Debate on the Administration bill, again sponsored by Senator Key Pittman, began on October 2. Supporters were instructed by the White House to characterize the bill as a way of retaining traditional rights of commerce while also preserving neutrality. The embargo, they asserted, had not worked in the recent past. Indeed, it aided one side against the other. At the same time, supporters carefully avoided any hint that removing the embargo would directly help the Allies.

Isolationists attacked the measure as a blatant attempt by the President and interventionists to aid Britain and France. Borah, Nye, and Johnson, followed by twenty-seven supporters, argued that repeal was unneutral, that it would lead the nation into war on the side of the Allies. The debate continued until October 27, by which time the isolationists recognized defeat. Their amendment to vote on cash-and-carry and repeal as separate issues failed, as did other amendments aimed at altering the bill. The Senate passed the repeal by a vote of sixty-three to thirty. A week later the House followed suit by approving the bill by a vote of 243 to 181. Roosevelt gladly signed the bill two days later.[60]

Passage of the Neutrality Act of 1939 marked a substantial Administration victory over the isolationists, but they were not completely defeated. Attempting to put the best face on the isolationist loss, Republican Senator Arthur H. Vandenberg viewed the public debate as a great moral victory for the still isolationist American public. More than before, the battle over the embargo became a struggle by opposing sides to win public opinion. Both the interventionists and the isolationists began campaigns to win public support. The interventionists began organizations in virtually every state while isolationists relied primarily on public speaking and mail campaigns. The battle continued through the winter and spring.[61]

AVOIDING A FIGHT

While Roosevelt struggled against the isolationists, General Marshall campaigned to avoid a political battle with the National Guard Association of the United States (NGA). He was well aware of its potential. The NGA's grass roots organization gave it easy access to Congress. In addition, most of its members belonged to other groups such as the American Legion and the

National Rifle Association. When the need arose, NGA leaders could exert pressure on Congress by using their ties to these organizations.

Historians have termed relations between the NGA and the Army as peaceful during the thirties; however, this tranquil period was not the norm. Martha Derthick, a student of the NGA's lobbying tactics, summarized the period as one of live and let live. With the Army and the Guard attempting to stay alive during a period of public apathy towards the military, neither possessed the desire nor the ability to wage a campaign against the other. Their shared instinct for survival resulted, therefore, in a diminution of exchanged hostilities. But it had not always been so.[62]

The NGA was born in politics. The militia system envisioned by the founding fathers never lived up to their ideal, and in the years following the end of the Civil War that system virtually collapsed. Although the idea of a universal male military obligation continued as a legal principle, it ceased as a reality. A voluntary system spawned before the outbreak of the Civil War eventually took its place. After the war, the former Confederate states formed new militias as a continuation of the antebellum slave patrols to maintain control over the freedmen.[63] In the North the militia became big business's bulwark against organized labor, creating an antagonism between labor unions and the Guard that lasted well into the 1960s. Officers in these units, North and South, generally came from the social elite and thus had strong ties to local political power. These bonds were further strengthened when the business community and the state governments realized that the militia could serve as a state constabulary. The Guard protected property rights against striking unions and in return received business's financial support.[64]

Local influence led inevitably to political connections at the state level. With state governors as commanders-in-chief, the militias, generally called National Guards, soon became political organizations. In most states the positions of adjutant general, the military head of the state Guard, quickly became a patronage position. But Guard politics did not stop at this leve; each company usually elected its own officers, resulting in a separate political structure, an "old boy" network similar to the courthouse's "rings."

For many local officers, the Guard's role as a state constabulary proved too small. They desired a national defense role for the Guard and in 1879 formed the National Guard Association to set and achieve nationally oriented goals. Their first aim was to secure Congressional appropriations for the state militias. Second, they wanted an established place for the Guard in the national defense structure.[65] Yet these officers also committed themselves to retaining strong ties to the states and autonomy from Army control. These goals led to a persistent dilemma for the Guard. Pursuit of federal money by the NGA risked increased control over the Guard by the federal government. The critical factor that held off, or at least slowed the pace of, increased federal control was the NGA's close relationship with members of Congress.[66]

Congressmen brought with them the sentiments or prejudices of their regions and their connections to state political machines. In the South, this natural connection was strengthened by a deep seated desire to preserve states' rights in the face of a growing federal government. Congressmen suspicious of a large standing Army viewed the Guard as a means of providing a defense while preserving the traditional ideal of civic responsibility and diminishing the threat of a federal tyranny presented by a large standing army. And so was born a natural though imperfect coalition between a politically active NGA and Congress.[67]

The NGA's agenda brought it into direct conflict with the Army. Although the Army lacked a constituency, it represented the profession of arms in America, a fact Congress could not ignore. Increased federal money for the Guard led to demands for the Guard's submission to federal controls. The Army was the only agency capable of exercising effective supervision; however, it had an agenda and prejudices of its own. Professional military men looked down upon the militia as undisciplined and uncooperative amateurs. Their conduct in the War of 1812 and the Mexican War seemed to prove the professionals right. In the early days of the Civil War, state troops did little better. Their behavior at Manassass Junction shaped the thought of one of the Army's future theorists, Emory Upton, who came out of the war with a strong distaste for the militia. He believed that the militia detracted from the national defense, consuming military resources better spent under centralized control. Upton envisioned an expandable army with a peacetime mission of training men brought to the colors by universal military training. However, he did not advocate the establishment of a federally controlled reserve, although such an organization seemed a logical outgrowth of a centralized military authority.[68]

Besides the prejudices gathered over the years, professional soldiers had legitimate concerns over the constitutionality of using militiamen in external wars. The Militia Clause of the Constitution gave only three circumstances for calling out the militia: "To provide for calling forth the Militia to execute the Laws of the Union, suppress Insurrections and repel Invasions."[69] The Army came to the conclusion that it could not use the militia, and thus the National Guard, outside the Union. This interpretation restricted the NGA in its quest for a national role for the Guard.

As America moved towards war with Spain in 1898, the logic of a federal reserve became a subject of debate in Congress. Congressman John A. T. Hull of Iowa,[70] with the support of President William McKinley, introduced a bill to create a national reserve with only loose state connections. The bill was the opening shot in a struggle that would occupy the NGA and the Army for decades to come. The NGA opposed Hull's plan for several reasons. First, it left the Guard out of the proposed organization. Second, any federally controlled reserve threatened the existence of the National Guard by eliminating the need for federally financed state units. Not surprisingly the NGA campaigned against the measure. In the first major test of the NGA's alliance with states righters and those opposed to a large standing army, the NGA came away victorious. The defeat of Hull's bill by Guard supporters forced McKinley to bow to the NGA's influence. With limited options available to form a fighting force quickly, the Army allowed Guard units that volunteered *in toto* for duty.

The second attempt at establishing a national reserve free of any significant state connections came in the wake of the Spanish-American War. Secretary of War Elihu Root hoped to revamp the Army by creating a general staff under a strong chief of staff. This new system would replace the old established bureau system with its independent chiefs. As part of this reform, Root's plan to create a federal reserve of 100,000 men came under immediate attack from the NGA and its supporters, who saw it as a way of keeping the Guard a state organization with no national role. Root's plan passed the House but ran into trouble in the Senate. Faced with strong opposition, Root withdrew the clause creating the reserve. With the offending passage removed, the bill, commonly referred to as the Dick Act of 1903[71] (for Congressman Charles Dick), sailed through the Senate. It was the first major revision of federal militia law in 111 years.[72]

Thus the Guard gained a measure of federal recognition and federal money. The NGA's victory, however, did not come without a price. To obtain federal aid for the Guard, governors had to submit a formal request to the federal government, which opened the door to Army inspections. Only after the Army certificated units as meeting set standards could state units receive federal funds. After the initial inspection, each Guard unit had to stand a yearly reinspection to keep its certification. The Army had gained its first measure of control over the Guard.

Secretary Root never considered the Guard a real fighting force, rather he viewed it as a training ground for individual soldiers who showed promise. He opened military schools to Guardsmen; those who did well, according to the Secretary's plan, would be taken into the Army at the outbreak of hostilities. As a 1907 General Order showed, the Army had no plans to use the Guard as organizations. Yet such planning did not mean the Army had abandoned hopes of establishing an independent reserve.

In 1908 the NGA sought and gained a revision to the Dick Act to strengthen its hold on its place as the first reserve. The 1903 Act had empowered the President to call the Guard before any other volunteer organizations and to set their term of service, up to nine months. This measure provided the Guard with a modicum of assurance that it had a national role. The 1908 change stated that all units of the Guard would be inducted before any other reserve component. It also enabled the federal government to send the Guard outside the country for as long as needed.

However, the changes of 1908 did not last. In 1912, Attorney General George W. Wickersham and Judge Advocate of General of the Army Enoch H. Crowder reached the conclusion that the 1908 Act was unconstitutional, reopening the issue of the value of the Guard as a federal reserve force. The War Department at once attempted to establish a reserve and succeeded in getting Congress to pass a weak measure. "When the 1912 reserve failed, Chief of Staff [Leonard] Wood put his weight behind the 'Plattsburgh Idea,' a project to create a trained reserve through Citizen's Military Training Camps."[73]

The issue of a national reserve came to the fore once again in 1915-16 when President Woodrow Wilson's Secretary of War Lindley Garrison presented a plan to create a "Continental Army" of 100,000 regulars and 400,000 reserves; however, the Guard was conspicuously absent from the plan.[74] Garrison's proposal met immediate hostility from the NGA and several prominent congressmen, particularly Virginia's states rights advocate Representative James Hay, Chairman of the House Committee on Military Affairs. He received advice from retired Major General Fred C. Ainsworth, the former Adjutant General of the Army who had opposed Root's reorganization of the War Department. With Ainsworth's assistance, Hay submitted a counter plan that won the support of the NGA. Although the final bill was a conglomeration of several proposals, Garrison's idea was defeated, prompting his resignation. The National Defense Act of 1916 established reserves for both officers and enlisted men and the Reserve Officer's Training Corps for college students.

The Act included a statement that the Guard "was an integral part of the Army of the United States when in federal service."[75] Although the wording was vague, the Guard had secured a place as a component of the Army. The NGA had also gained tangible results in the form of additional drill pay. But the number of training sessions doubled and summer training was extended to two weeks. In addition, the President could draft Guardsmen as individuals, thus stripping them of their state connection and any "guarantee" of remaining in their units. Guardsmen became painfully aware of this provision when Wilson drafted Guardsmen as individuals, not units, for service in World War I. The Army unceremoniously stripped units with long traditions and histories of their state affiliations, shifting officers and men from unit to unit. At the top, the Army removed 501 Guard officers as unfit for command, permitted 638 to resign, and reclassified 341 more. Guardsmen charged that the Army perpetrated many of these removals simply to provide promotions for the regular officers who took the place of Guard officers. Having taken in Guardsman as individuals, at the end of the war the Army released Guardsmen as individuals, returning Guard units to state control with no men.[76]

Because of this action the NGA seethed with anger toward the Army during the post-war period. When, in 1920, the Army presented yet another plan—the Baker-March Bill—to create a reserve based on universal military training (UMT) and enlarge the army, the NGA rose to the attack.[77] Association President Colonel Bennett C. Clark stated that "the Guard would smash the Regular Army,"[78] to wrest control over the Guard from the General Staff, which the NGA considered hostile, and place it under the Secretary of War. Perhaps more important, the NGA wanted a guarantee that in the next war the Army would use the Guard as indivisible units. Its pressure on Congress resulted in the National Defense Act of 1920, which granted many of these changes. A Guard officer would head the Militia Bureau and sit on the General Staff. Guardsmen would sit on boards that determined their fate. As political scientist Martha Derthick stated, "the Bureau became the Guard's source of information on events in the War Department—its eyes and ears—while the Association remained its spokesman. The Bureau supplemented rather than supplanted the Association."[79] The Act also reiterated that the Guard, when in the service of the nation, was an integral part of the Army of the United States. However, it did not guarantee the integrity of Guard units summoned into federal service, and the old question of constitutional restrictions remained unresolved. For its part the Army continued to doubt the Guard's legal ability to serve outside the United States. Congress, unwilling to test the long held idea that the Militia Clause restricted the Guard's usefulness, deferred to the Army.

For the next thirteen years, Guard leaders sought a way to remove constitutional restrictions on federal service, and after much study the NGA formulated a plan by which the Guard could circumvent the Militia Clause restrictions. In 1933, the NGA proposed a new National Defense Act which created a double existence for the Guard. In time of peace, the Guard belonged to the states, but once Congress declared a state of national emergency the National Guard of the United States was constituted as a Federally controlled component of the Army, becoming the first reserve component of the Army. The Officer Reserve Corps, the Organized Reserve, and the Enlisted Reserve Corps followed the Guard in priority. With the passage of the 1933 Act, the NGA had at last achieved its long sought goal of an assured national mission with limited Army control; however, it remained untested.

After the passage of the 1933 Act the NGA settled down to a quiet period, from time to time pressing for additional funds and winning an occasional victory. If aroused it could still present a formidable presence in the halls of Congress. But for the most part the organization faced no significant challenges.

Having served as an adivisor to the Illinois National Guard, Marshall understood the NGA's point of view and its power. He actively attempted to allay any misgivings it might have about a rapid expansion of the Army and the Guard's role. His first opportunity came at the October 13 Pennsylvania

National Guard Association meeting. Invited by Pennsylvania's politically active Adjutant General Edward Martin,[80] Marshall took the podium with full knowledge that the meeting was more than just a local affair and that his remarks were more than just an after-dinner speech. Also at the head table was Major General Milton A. Reckord, Maryland's adjutant general for almost two decades and the NGA's powerful lobbyist. "One Hundred Percent" Reckord, as he was some times called, usually got what he wanted from Congress.

Reckord had joined the Guard in 1901, quickly rose in the ranks, served on the Mexican border in 1916, and as a colonel commanded the 115th Infantry in World War I. While in Europe he became a close friend of Brigadier General John McAuley Palmer, a champion of the citizen soldier idea. Their wartime friendship continued after their return to the United States. In 1919 Reckord testified before the Wadsworth Committee, which was attempting to reorganize the Army, in support of Palmer and General John F. O'Ryan's proposal to turn the Guard into a national force. Reckord's persuasive manner and close proximity to the capital quickly drew him into the political life of the Guard. At first on an informal basis and later as head of the Association's Legislative Committee, Reckord pursued Guard causes in the halls of Congress and wrote most of the legislation involving the Guard. As Reckord himself put it: "I always went to Congress with a written bill or amendment."[81] He was generally successful in his lobbying efforts, as passage of the 1933 Act demonstrated. In addition, he served as Executive Vice President of the National Rifle Association, wielding considerable influence with its members.[82] With a phone call or a telegram Reckord could flood senators and representatives with letters and telegrams from Guard constituents.

Aware of his audience, Marshall aimed his opening remarks toward establishing a common bond between himself and them. The Chief of Staff told of his early experiences with the Pennsylvania Guard as a young Army officer both before and after the Great War. He then related his three year's service with the Illinois National Guard and noted that he understood the "various traditions, conditions, methods of the National Guard in various portions of the United States."[83]

Having established in his listeners' minds that he understood their concerns, Marshall launched into the major topic of his speech—the necessity of improving Guard training. He declared:

At this time . . . it is vital that the National Guard training be stimulated this winter to produce a greater degree of efficiency, and particularly to bring in these new men on a basis of quick development in order to make them familiar with the duties they will be called upon to perform.[84]

He explained that one of the "simpler" ways the War Department had of increasing proficiency was to increase the number of drills. He also mentioned the eventuality of seven days of field training to be conducted during the winter and an addition week added to the traditional two week summer camps. This additional winter training would be arranged on a local basis, or "decentralized" as Marshall put it, to allow for varying conditions across the country. For Guard officers, especially division staffs, he planned to coordinate Guard training sessions with regular units. During their stay with the regulars, Guard officers would be allowed to command regular troops for twenty-four hours. Marshall was putting his training ideas, as expressed to Cole, into action.

Turning from training to future hopes, Marshall told his audience that he expected the Guard and the Army to shortly reach their full peacetime strengths. Once the Army reached those levels, he noted, it could form nine corps of one regular and two Guard divisions each along with two corps of regular troops who could be "used in any sudden emergency . . . to do anything in this hemisphere on very short notice."[85]

By his remarks Marshall tried to inform Guardsmen not only of what was happening in the Army but also of their role in national defense. However, his speech was also notable for what it left out. Although he mentioned that the Army would provide additional rations for Guardsmen during the extra training sessions, Marshall made no reference to any other aid. By omission he laid upon the states the responsibility of providing funds for extra Guard pay and facilities. The issue of funding was to become one of the focal points of discussion two weeks later at the national convention of the NGA.

THE BALTIMORE CONVENTION

Two weeks after the Pennsylvania meeting, the National Guard Association of the United States held its annual convention in Baltimore, Maryland. As in past years, delegates from around the country gathered to hear reports from their outgoing president, Brigadier General James C. Dozier, and from Reckord, the chairman of the Legislative Committee. National figures such as Secretary of War Woodring, General Marshall, and Congressman J. Buell Snyder, chairman of the War Department Subcommittee of the House Appropriations Committee, were on hand to give the obligatory speeches on the worth of the Guard. This year, however, war in Europe and the changes it brought to the Guard increased the importance of the Association's deliberations.

By the time the convention started, the Guard was aware of the potential problems caused by federally ordered manpower and training increases. Delegates came ready to debate the issues on the floor of the convention. In characteristic style, General Reckord began the debate on the most sensitive of the issues facing the Guard and the NGA, men and equipment in excess of state needs. He referred to Marshall's statement at the Pennsylvania convention that the expansion ordered by Roosevelt might represent "the first bite" of more expansions to come. He continued:

I do say definitely that there are many very essential and important Corps and Army units needed to make this Army of the United States a real army, and it would not surprise me at all if we aren't asked after we finish this first task [completing the first increase] to take on some other responsibilities.[86]

Such responsibilities meant expanding the Guard's corps troops and support units. The states' lack of enthusiasm for maintaining units in excess of their needs, especially "support" as opposed to combat troops, promised to make recruiting extremely difficult. Additionally, state financial responsibility for more units caused strains on already tight budgets.

Reckord was aware of resistance the Army faced from state adjutants and governors; however, he recognized that if the Guard was to be the primary reserve of the Army it would have to add the needed support troops. However, the federal government's policy would have to change as well. Reckord told the convention that he had no qualms in accepting more equipment, and by implication men, in excess of state needs as long as the federal government paid for them. He stated to the Association:

I believe the time has come when we should call upon the Congress to assist us in housing a lot of this equipment; perhaps in assisting in the building of armories for some of these anti-aircraft and heavy artillery regiments; perhaps the building of hangars and assistance in building air fields, all of these items being of much more value to the nation than to the individual state.[87]

Other NGA members quickly followed Reckord's lead in calling for federal money to construct housing for more equipment. Brigadier General Herbert Johnson of Vermont stated:

There are a lot of states who do not want any more National Guard, who already have more than their proportion on a population basis and can not properly be asked to build more armories. I think I am safe in saying that every state in the Union now has all the National Guard which they need from a purely state's standpoint; therefore, this question must be considered from the standpoint of national need and the state's ability to maintain.[88]

Brigadier General Raymond H. Fleming of Louisiana added to Johnson's remarks that not only did the new equipment required more storage space it also demanded more administrative work. He suggested that the federal government cover that cost as well. Generals Gilson D. Light of Ohio and Ellard A. Walsh of Minnesota, a future Association president, added their voices to this chorus.[89]

The next morning, October 27, Brigadier General Samuel T. Lawton of Illinois addressed the Association, resuming the previous day's discussion. He reminded the Guardsmen of their added obligation as part of the nation's army. Lawton stated that he detected in the earlier discussion "signs of unwillingness to go along with the larger program of the National Guard Bureau [actually the War Department's plan]."[90] He believed that Johnson and others held the idea that "the strength of the National Guard, with respect to the states, which the Federal Government should call upon [to] maintain should be limited to . . . needs for local defense."[91] Lawton rejected the notion. "If there is any such theory in the minds of any of the officers of the Guard," he declared, "I think it is based upon a misunderstanding of the part the National Guard plays in the national defense."[92] The Illinois general reminded his audience of the struggle won in 1933:

We were all delighted when in '33 or '34, whenever the bill was passed, the Federal Government recognized the National Guard of the United States as a reserve component of the U.S. Army. That is what we must consider ourselves. Now, we are not down here, and we don't meet annually just for the sake of considering local defense. We are meeting here as representatives of a reserve component of the U.S. Army, and I think it should be within the spirit of that status that we should consider our ability and our willingness to go ahead with the program . . . laid down by Federal authorities.[93]

Assuring his audience that executing the plan would not be easy, Lawton concluded his remarks by saying: "On this program asked of us, and the bigger program that may be asked of us, I say, 'Let's agree to do it. Let's do it and go right down the line until it hurts.'"[94]

The applause Lawton received indicated that many of the more than four hundred delegates agreed with at least the sentiments of his appeal. Yet the convention continued to lean towards Reckord's proposal to approach Congress on the matter. While the convention debated, Reckord waited to hear from Woodring, Marshall, and Snyder. If he hoped for a statement of federal support, he came away disheartened.

Speaking later that same day, Marshall concentrated, as he had at the Pennsylvania meeting, on the issue of Guard training. However, before the national convention the Chief of Staff hit the subject with greater force. Although he had wished to leave training in the hands of the states, where it traditionally resided, the local units could not continue certain aspects of training. Marshall illustrated what he considered a bad situation:

Under the old scheme of training, which we have followed for years, new men taken into service at this time might go until next summer, and certainly as long as next May, without ever having fired a rifle. Think of it, 45,000 new men and possibly 126,000 new men, in uniform and being trained, but having to wait at least six months before having the experience of firing a weapon.[95]

He counseled making better use of the time available. Officers should use more imagination to improve the quality of training that even small doses provided.[96]

But Marshall issued no clear words of hope for more federal funds for the Guard. The best he could do was to offer the War Department's aid in obtaining badly needed transportation for the infantry. The Guard had already enjoyed a measure of success in funding transportation. At a time when the Army was forbidden by Congress to expend money on vehicles —even for repairs—the Association gained funds from Congress to outfit most of its artillery units with new vehicles.[97] "We are hopeful," Marshall stated, "to receive funds that will permit us to procure for the National Guard certain percentage of their peace strength requirement for transportation."[98] Again the Chief of Staff refrained from extending any hope of federal aid for housing the new vehicles. Nor did he mention any other form of financial aid to the Guard.

Presentations by Major General James K. Parsons, commander of the Third Corps Area, and Lieutenant General Hugh A. Drum, commander of the First Army and the Second Corps Area, added nothing to the Guard's knowledge of the federal government's intentions. Even an address by Representative J. Buell Snyder, chairman of the War Department Subcommittee of the House Appropriations Committee and long-time friend of the Guard, inspired little confidence in the Guard's receiving substantial federal aid. Snyder spent much of his time on past accomplishments in building up the Guard to its present level and none on the future.[99]

That night Roosevelt's noninterventionist Secretary of War Harry H. Woodring addressed the convention and the nation by way of a coast-to-coast radio broadcast. Reckord hoped that the Secretary would touch on the issue of more federal funding for the preparedness movement. However, with the House debating the Neutrality revision, Woodring took the opportunity to assure the nation that the administration's recent increase in the Army and the Guard was for self-defense only. He had come to the convention to console the isolationists, not the Guard.[100]

With no redress of grievances forthcoming from the Army or the Administration, the Association began entertaining resolutions designed to put pressure on Congress. Reckord was in his element when it came time to submit resolutions to the convention. As in the past, the Maryland general pointed the way by drafting resolutions and then shepherding them through Congress. The strategy was simple; on the surface the Guard pledged its support to the War Department plan while also pursuing its own course.

The Association began its divergent course by rejecting Marshall's decision not to reorganize the Guard's infantry divisions. The Association's leadership took offense at being left out of the Army's streamlining, believing that some confusion over reorganization during peacetime was preferable to a hasty modification during war. In response to Marshall, the Association resolved that

Tables of Organization [for Guard units] should be brought into conformity with the Regular Army's especially in the Infantry division. If the triangular division is to be used in time of war . . . troops should be converted to that organization in time of peace.[101]

Reckord introduced a second resolution that challenged the Army's method of handling Guard affairs. Soon after the Army increased the number of drills from forty-eight to sixty per year, Reckord became convinced that holding one three hour drill per week made more sense than two one and one half hour drills, as called for by the Army. The General Staff met Reckord's formal request to combine the two weekly drills with an unyielding "disapproved." Reckord was puzzled by the General Staff's rejection of what seemed a way to lighten Guardsmen's hardships. General Lawton informed the convention that he learned through hearsay that "the refusal to permit two drills on one evening [was] based upon an interpretation of the National Defense Act, some sections of which [seem] to prohibit the payment of more than one day's pay for one day's work."[102] Not to be denied in his efforts, Reckord immediately offered an amendment to his own resolution and he added a call to amend the National Defense Act to allow combined drills. General Birkhead of Texas seconded the motion, which carried without opposition.[103]

The last major resolution dealt with the issue most on the minds of the assembled Guardsmen, federal funding for the men and equipment in excess of state needs. Brigadier General Ellard A. Walsh, chairman of the Association's Resolution Committee, introduced a proposal strongly influenced, if not written, by Reckord. The resolution called for more camps, storage facilities, target ranges, and other construction projects to support the increase in the Guard. It also empowered the Association's Executive Committee "to secure from the Congress for the fiscal year 1941, the sum of $10,000,000."[104] Not surprisingly the resolution passed by acclamation. The Guard would pursue its own course with Congress, and Reckord would lead the fight.

From past experience with Congress, Reckord did not hold out great hopes that the Guard would get all it desired. Several months later he told the Adjutants General Association meeting: "I am a good trader. I will take $3,000,000 and be happy."[105] He knew that getting money out of Congress would not be easy, it never had been, but he could mobilize the citizen soldiers of the states in a political pressure campaign that the Army could never match.

The Baltimore Convention showed that the old animosities toward the Army lingered despite a decade of relative tranquility. The Association was still watchful of Army intentions and willing to go outside of military channels to obtain what it desired. For its part the Army had failed to win the Guard over. On the surface, both the Army and the Guard would cooperate; however, beneath lay troubled waters. Marshall and the General Staff would try again to forge a common front with the NGA.

NOTES

1. Secretary of War Harry H. Woodring to President Franklin D. Roosevelt, September 8, 1939, George C. Marshall Papers, Box 80, File Folder 28 (George C. Marshall Foundation Library, Lexington, VA, hereafter referred to as the Marshall Library).

2. Selig Adler defined the term isolationist as one determined "to stay out of foreign wars with an unwavering refusal to enter into alliances." See *The Isolationist Impulse: Its Twentieth Century Reaction* (New York, 1957), 32.

3. Robert A. Divine, *The Reluctant Belligerent* (New York, 1979), 9; Manfred Jonas, *Isolationism in America: 1935-1941* (Ithaca, NY, 1966), 26-31; William E. Leuchtenburg, *Franklin D. Roosevelt and the New Deal* (New York, 1963), 217-219.

4. Nye came to the Senate in November 1925 to fill the unexpired term of Edwin F. Ladd. A Wisconsin native and a newspaperman at heart, Nye moved to North Dakota in 1915 to become the editor and publisher of the *Billings County Pioneer*.

5. See Robert A. Divine, *Roosevelt and World War II* (Baltimore, MD, 1969) for an examination of Roosevelt as both isolationist and interventionist.

6. Divine, *Roosevelt and World War II*, 16-18; Stetson Conn and Byron Fairchild, *The Framework of Hemisphere Defense* (Washington, DC, 1960), 172-173.

7. Elliot Roosevelt and James Brough, *A Rendezvous with Destiny: The Roosevelts of the White House* (New York, 1975), 239.

8. Ibid., 240.

9. Ibid.

10. Cordell Hull, *Memoirs of Cordell Hull*, 2 vols. (New York, 1948), I, 675.

11. Wayne S. Cole provided an excellent portrait of the power and influence of the isolationists on Roosevelt in his book *Roosevelt and the Isolationists* (Lincoln, NE, 1983). Selig Adler's *The Isolationist Impulse* (London, 1957), studied the roots of American isolationism. Robert Divine broke with the traditional view of Roosevelt as an interventionist with his essay on him as a noninter-ventionist. See Divine, *Roosevelt and World War II* (Baltimore, MD, 1969). Manfred Jonas demonstrated in *Isolationism in America, 1935-1941* (Ithaca, NY, 1966) that the isolationism in the United States was not limited to the Mid-West but was pervasive in American society.

12. See Cole, *Roosevelt and the Isolationists*, pages 8 and 9 for a brief overview of isolationists support. For a more detailed treatment of American isolationists' support see Jonas, *Isolationism in American, 1935-1941* (Ithaca, NY, 1966). For information on Senator Nye and the Senate Munitions Investigation see John E. Wiltz, *In Search of Peace: The Senate Munitions Inquiry, 1934-1936* (Baton Rouge, LA, 1963) and Wayne

S. Cole, *Senator Gerald P. Nye and American Foreign Relations* (Minneapolis, MN, 1962).

13. Divine, *Roosevelt and World War II*, 7.

14. As John C. Donovan pointed out in *Causes and Consequences of World War II* (Chicago, IL, 1969), edited by Robert A. Divine, Congress had infringed on the President's power and ability to conduct foreign policy. See pages 84-86.

15. Robert A. Divine, *The Illusion of Neutrality* (Chicago, IL, 1968), 81-161.

16. Ibid., 162-199.

17. Dorothy Borg, "Notes on Roosevelt's 'Quarantine Speech,'" *Political Science Quarterly*, 72 (September 1957):405-407.

18. Divine, *Roosevelt and World War II*, 15-27.

19. Robert Dallek, *Franklin D. Roosevelt and American Foreign Policy, 1932-1945* (New York, 1979), 173.

20. Maurer Maurer, *Aviation in the U.S. Army, 1919-1939* (Washington, DC, 1987), 447.

21. Richard B. Crossland and James T. Currie, *Twice the Citizen: A History of the United States Army Reserve, 1908-1983* (Washington, DC, 1984), pp. 63-66, 296.

22. The Act also placed a Guard officer at the head of the National Guard Bureau, this person also sat on the General Staff.

23. War Department, *Annual Report of the Chief of the National Guard Bureau, 1941* (Washington, DC, 1941), 12.

24. Charles Wiltse, *John C. Calhoun: Nationalist, 1782-1828* (Indianapolis, IN, 1944), 223-224; For biographies of General Emory Upton and examinations of his theories of military organization see Richard C. Brown, "General Emory Upton—The Army's Mahon," *Military Affairs*, 17 (Fall 1953):125-131; Stephen E. Ambrose, *Upton and the Army* (Baton Rouge, LA, 1964). For a brief history of the evolution of the General Staff from 1900 to World War I see James E. Hewes, Jr., *From Root to McNamara: Army Organization and Administration, 1900-1963* (Washington, DC, 1975), 4-21; Russell F. Weigley, *The American Way of War* (New York, 1973), 54, 60, 221-222.

25. See John A. Logan, *The Volunteer Soldier of America* (Chicago, 1887). Palmer's views were presented in his book *America in Arms: The Experience of the United States with Military Organization* (Washington, DC, 1941). I. B. Holley, Jr.'s *General John M. Palmer, Citizen Soldiers, and the Army of a Democracy* (Westport, CT, 1982) further states Palmer's views on the need of a citizen army. See especially pages 56-57, 203, 386.

26. Kent Roberts Greenfield, ed., *Command Decisions* (Washington, DC, 1960), 11-27.

27. Kreidberg and Henry, *Mobilization*, 461-463.

28. In 1937 one such group, Brazil's fascist party, the *Integralistas*, attempted to overthrow the government of Getulio Vargas. Although no Nazi complicity was ever proven, the *Integralistas* received financial and propaganda support from the Third Reich.

29. Dallek, *Roosevelt and American Foreign Policy*, 176.

30. Alton Frye, *Nazi Germany and the American Hemisphere, 1933-1941* (New Haven, CT, 1967), 30-31, 65-79, 101-117; Frank D. McCann, Jr., *The Brazilian-American Alliance, 1937-1945* (Princeton, NJ, 1973), 11-105; Department of State, *Foreign Relations of the United States, 1937* (Washington, DC, 1954), 5:318-350; Department of State *Foreign Relations of the United States, 1938* (Washington, DC, 1956), 5:408-420; Bland, ed., Marshall Papers, I, 715-720; Stetson Conn and Byron Fairchild, *The*

Framework of Hemisphere Defense (Washington, DC, 1960), 141-142; Cordell Hull, *The Memoirs of Cordell Hull*, I, 601.

31. Conn and Fairchild, *The Framework of Hemisphere Defense*, 10; Maurice Matloff and Edwin M. Snell, *Strategic Planning for Coalition Warfare, 1941-1942* (Washington, DC, 1953), 5.

32. Kreidberg and Henry, *Mobilization*, 556-560.

33. Ibid., 554.

34. General George C. Marshall to Secretary of War Harry H. Woodring, September 7, 1939, Marshall Foundation Archives Microfilm Project, Reel 20, Item 763A (Marshall Library).

35. Ibid.

36. Congress had refused to purchase long range bombers because of their "offensive" nature as opposed to shorter ranged aircraft for defensive purposes. The General Staff agreed, in part because of Navy pressure stemming from the *Rex* incident of 1938. The Air Corps was limited to flights from 100 to 300 miles off the coast, depending on the mission. See Maurer, *Aviation in the U.S. Army*, 408-420.

37. General George C. Marshall to Secretary of War Harry H. Woodring, September 7, 1939, Marshall Foundation Archives Microfilm Project, Reel 20, Item 763A (Marshall Library).

38. Ibid.

39. Kreidberg and Henry, *Mobilization*, 563.

40. Dallek, *Roosevelt and Foreign Policy*, 203.

41. Memorandum from General Marshall to General L. D. Gasser, September 8, 1939, Bland, ed., *Marshall Papers*, II, 53.

42. Memorandum from General Marshall to General L. D. Gasser, September 8, 1939, Bland, ed., *Marshall Papers*, II, 53; Harry H. Woodring to Franklin D. Roosevelt, September 8, 1939, George C. Marshall Papers, Box 80, Folder 28 (Marshall Library); Langer and Gleason, *Challenge to Isolation*, 48.

43. Eighty-six percent favored expanding the Army while eighty-eight percent and ninety-one percent of respondents favored increasing the size of the Navy and Army Air Forces, respectively. See George Gallup, *The Gallup Poll: Public Opinion, 1935-1971*, 3 vols. (New York, 1972), I, 183, 189-190.

44. Kreidberg and Henry, *Mobilization*, 555.

45. General Marshall to Major General James K. Parsons, September 21, 1939, Bland, ed., *Marshall Papers*, II, 61.

46. Ironically, prior to World War I the National Guard had pioneered the triangular division arrangement. See Elbridge Colby, *The National Guard of the United States: A Half Century of Progress* (Manhattan, KS, 1977), VII-9.

47. Mark Skinner Watson, *Chief of Staff: Prewar Plans and Preparations* (Washington, DC, 1950), 158-159; General Marshall to General Malin Craig, September 19, 1939, Bland, ed., *Marshall Papers*, II, 59-60; Kreidberg and Henry, *Mobilization*, 555.

48. Responsibility for recruiting Guardsmen above the authorized limit rested with the individual state governors, but the War Department decided the distribution of these forces. The War Plans Division suggested allocating the added Guard strength as follows: 2,000 men for corps, army, and GHQ troops; 30,000 for the infantry divisions; 6,000 men for the thirteen antiaircraft regiments; and 5,000 for harbor defense units. See Kreidberg and Henry, *Mobilization*, 555.

49. General Marshall to Brigadier General Charles H. Cole, September 26, 1939, Bland, ed., *Marshall Papers*, II, 67.

50. Ibid., II, 67.

51. In 1933 the Militia Bureau was renamed the National Guard Bureau. The Chief of the Bureau, a Guardsman since 1920, sat on the General Staff, and acted as a conduit of funds and direction from the General Staff to the National Guard. He was also considered the eyes, ears, and, occasionally, mouth of the National Guard Association in the General Staff.

52. *Army and Navy Journal*, October 14, 1939, p. 151.

53. Ibid.

54. Cole, *Roosevelt and the Isolationists*, 328; Langer and Gleason, *Challenge to Isolation*, 218-221; Wayne S. Cole, *Charles A. Lindbergh and the Battle Against American Intervention in World War II* (New York, 1974), 73-74.

55. Burton K. Wheeler with Paul F. Healy, *Yankee from the West* (Garden City, NY, 1962), 387.

56. Cole, *Roosevelt and the Isolationists*, 325.

57. Ibid.; Robert E. Sherwood, *Roosevelt and Hopkins: An Intimate History* (New York, 1948), 125.

58. Michael Leigh, *Mobilizing Consent: Public Opinion and American Foreign Policy, 1937-1947* (Westport, CT, 1976), 41-46.

59. Ibid., 42-43; Allan Nevins, *The New Deal and World Affairs* (New York, 1950), 194-196; Langer and Gleason, *Challenge to Isolation*, 225.

60. Langer and Gleason, *Challenge to Isolation*, 226-231.

61. Ibid., 225; Cole, *Roosevelt and the Isolationists*, 326-327.

62. Martha Derthick, *The National Guard in Politics* (Cambridge, MA, 1965), 46-47.

63. Passage of the Posse Comitatus Law of 1878 was a direct result of Southern resistance to the use of federal troops to enforce Freedmen's voting rights during Reconstruction. See H. W. C. Furman, "Restriction on the Use of the Army Imposed by the Posse Comitatus Act," *Military Law Review*, 85 (Winter 1960):85-129.

64. Of the 481 calls for the Guard from 1865 to 1906, 156 were for labor troubles. See John K. Mahon, *History of the Militia and the National Guard* (New York, 1983), 108-124.

65. In the 1880s, the Army and to a lesser degree Congress saw the value of the emerging National Guards as a second line of defense. Many states responded eagerly to the Army's overtures. See C. Joseph Bernardo and Eugene H. Bacon, *American Military Policy: Its Development Since 1775* (Harrisburg, PA, 1955), 247-251.

66. One of the post-Civil War supporters of a citizen army was John A. Logan. His work, *The Volunteer Soldier of America* (Chicago, 1887), castigated the West Point system as harmful to the volunteer spirit.

67. Derthick, *The National Guard in Politics*, 15-22.

68. For Upton's views on the militia see his book, *The Military Policy of the United States* (Washington, DC, 1917).

69. U.S. *Constitution*, Art. I, sec. 7.

70. Hull had been a lieutenant and a captain in the Twenty-third Regiment, Iowa Volunteer Infantry. Forced to resign due to wounds, he entered state politics in 1872 and was elected to Congress in 1890.

71. Elbridge Colby called the Act of 1903 the true beginning of the National Guard. See Colby, *The National Guard of the United States*, I-1. Also see Colby and Lieutenant

Colonel James F. Glass, "The Legal Status of the National Guard," *Virginia Law Review*, 29 (May 1943):839-840.

72. Charles Dick of Ohio was chairman of the House Committee on the Militia, the commanding major general of the Ohio National Guard, and president of the NGA. He appointed a committee that presented a rival bill to Root's plans for an independent reserve. See Mahon, *Militia and the National Guard*, 138-139. For Root's reforms and his relations with the Guard see James E. Hewes, Jr., *From Root to McNamara: Army Organization and Administration, 1900-1963* (Washington, DC, 1975), 3-12; Elbridge Colby, "Elihu Root and the National Guard," *Military Affairs*, 23(Spring 1959):28-34; Louis Cantor, "Elihu Root and the National Guard: Friend or Foe?" *Military Affairs*, 33(December 1969):361-373.

73. Mahon, *Militia and the National Guard*, 143.

74. In 1941, Brigadier General John McAuley Palmer wrote that several in the Guard, General O'Ryan of New York for one, had hoped to adjust the Guard's constitutional status to make it a more useful national tool. "But that was not what the General Staff wanted. It was not trying to contrive a more effective constitutional harness. It wanted to kill the horse." See Palmer, *American in Arms*, 153.

75. Mahon, *Militia and the National Guard*, 148.

76. On the eve of the Meuse-Argonne offensive, Major General Clarence E. Edwards, commander of the Twenty-Sixth Division commander, and Brigadier General Charles I. Martin, commander of the Seventieth Infantry Brigade (Thirty-fifth Infantry Division), were replaced with Regular officers. See Mahon, *Militia and National Guard*, 162-163.

77. Colonel (later Brigadier General) John McAuley Palmer, an advocate of the citizen soldier concept (though not a strong supporter of the Guard) submitted his own plan for a national reserve based on Universal Military Training. For Palmer's ideas on American military policy and his participation in the reorganization of 1920 see *America in Arms*, 153-180.

78. Jim Dan Hill, *The Minute Man in Peace and War* (Harrisburg, PA, 1964), 305.

79. Derthick, *The National Guard in Politics*, 55.

80. Martin joined the National Guard in 1898 as a private. He served in the Spanish-American War, on the Mexican border, and in World War I. A lawyer by profession, Martin was actively involved in state politics, as his place as Adjutant General suggests, and in the affairs of the NGA. He later became a U.S. senator.

81. Derthick, *The National Guard in Politics*, 94-95.

82. The NRA started in the post-Civil War era to promote marksmanship in the militia. In 1903 it became allied with the Army by means of the National Board for the Promotion of Rifle Practice, with the government paying the bill. The Army supplied it with surplus weapons for $10 each, but only to NRA members. As a result, the NRA rapidly became a large organization capable of influencing legislation. As executive vice president, Reckord was able to muster enough support to "almost wipe out the earlier gun-control law, the National Firearms Act of 1934." See Robert Sherrill, *Saturday Night Special* (New York, 1973), 66, 218-221.

83. General Marshall's speech to the National Guard Association of Pennsylvania, October 13, 1939, p. 8, George C. Marshall Papers, Box 110, Folder 41 (Marshall Library).

84. Ibid., 9.

85. Ibid., 12.

86. Minutes of the National Guard of the United States Annual Convention, *Proceedings, 1939*, p. 34 (National Guard Association of the United States Library, Washington, DC, hereafter referred to as National Guard Association Library).

87. Ibid., 35.

88. Ibid., 53.

89. Ibid., 56-68.

90. Ibid., 65.

91. Ibid., 66.

92. Ibid.

93. Ibid., 67.

94. Ibid., 68.

95. General Marshall's speech to the National Guard Association of the United States, October 27, 1939, p. 2, George C. Marshall Papers, Box 110, Folder 43 (Marshall Library).

96. Ibid., 6.

97. In 1935, Major General George Leach, Chief of the National Guard Bureau, proposed a plan to Congress by which the Guard would equip its artillery units with motor transports, replacing animal teams. Leach had the support of Representative Ross Collins of Mississippi and the NGA. The Army, with no political power group for support, was ordered to restrict maintenance of its vehicles. See Elbridge Colby, *The National Guard of the United States: A Half Century of Progress* (Manhattan, KS, 1977), IX-18.

98. General Marshall's speech to the National Guard Association of the United States, October 27, 1939, p. 4, George C. Marshall Papers, Box 110, File Folder 43 (Marshall Library).

99. National Guard Association, *Proceedings, 1939*, pp. 99. 20-23, 87-92, 72-75 (National Guard Association Library).

100. Ibid., 34-35; *Army and Navy Journal*, October 28, 1939, pp. 180, 183; Keith D. McFarland, *Harry H. Woodring: A Political Biography of FDR's Controversial Secretary of War* (Lawrence, KS, 1975), 200.

101. *Army and Navy Journal*, October 28, 1939, p. 204.

102. National Guard Association, *Proceedings, 1939*, pp. 161-162 (National Guard Association Library).

103. Ibid., 162.

104. Ibid., 155.

105. Adjutants General Association conference notes, March 1940, p. 34 (National Guard Association Library).

3

Funding, Feuds,
and a Common Front

> While it is true . . . that the plan of the War Department possibly is
> a little hard, nevertheless we are ready, 100 percent to cooperate
> with the program.
> —Brigadier General Walter A. DeLamater[1]

THE CAMPAIGN FOR FEDERAL FUNDS

Reckord and the Association threw down the gauntlet at Baltimore. The
Guard sought additional funds for more men and material by lobbying
Congress. Marshall and the General Staff, however, were reluctant to press
for the full amount the NGA demanded, doubting their chances of gaining
the full appropriations. Roosevelt had consistently cut Army requests, fearing
adverse public reaction and Congress' increasingly conservative nature. When
the war in Poland ended without igniting major fighting on the Western
front, the nation's concern over a general war in Europe subsided. Calmed
by the lull after Poland's defeat, Congress turned its attention to trimming
the budget. Marshall had to present a strong case for even meager
appropriations.

The NGA's Baltimore stand added an unwelcome dimension to the Chief
of Staff's problems. Not only did Marshall have to contend with an economy-
minded Congress and a hesitant chief executive but with a renegade NGA as
well. By declaring the need for $10,000,000 the Guard, in effect, rejected the
Army's leadership on budget matters. The General Staff may have believed
that Congress would take the large outlays demanded by the NGA out of the
Army's pocket. Additionally, Reckord's insistence on combining drills and
other Guard leaders' grumbling over the War Department's training schedule

threatened trouble. However, the Guard would have to wait. Marshall's struggle over the supplemental request for Fiscal Year 1940 from an economy-minded Congress came first.

The increase in troops and training hesitantly ordered by Roosevelt in September caused a severe drain on the Army's resources. By October the Secretary of War estimated the Army needed $900,000,000 for the next fiscal year (1941). However, because of the increase in men and the planned concentration of divisions in the southern United States for maneuvers, the War Department needed $150,000,000 more to finish out Fiscal Year 1940. The War Department's Congressional liaison officer, Major James D. McIntyre, told Marshall shortly after the eruption of war in Europe that he

spoke to several Congressmen yesterday, including Mr. [Andrew J.] May and Mr. [Foster Waterman] Starnes. Everyone is for adequate National Defense. I firmly believe that now is the time to ask for *everything* the War Department needs. We will get it. Let us strike while the iron is hot.[2]

But Roosevelt decided to request no more than $120,000,000. As historian Mark S. Watson wrote: "Again the inception of a long-range, over-all program was delayed."[3] As a result of the shortfall of funds the Army delayed purchasing needed supplies and slowed its recruitment of men. Roosevelt, always aware of the shifting political winds, asked for what he thought Congress and the public would accept.

On November 27 Marshall traveled to Capitol Hill where he appeared before a subcommittee of the House Appropriations Committee to defend the Administration's program against isolationists and budget cutters. While Marshall presented a statement on the status of the Army, isolationist Congressman Louis Ludlow, author of a proposed constitutional amendment to allow a popular referendum on declaring war, interrupted to ask Marshall to explain the General Staff's plans for the National Guard. Marshall answered Ludlow by describing how the War Department distributed the September 8 increase:

In the first place, we distributed the increased personnel to those units in which we thought more men most urgently needed. Signal Corps units are being brought to full peace strength, antiaircraft and 155mm. gun units to 85 percent, and other artillery units to 80 percent peace strength.

That permits bringing the infantry, cavalry, engineer, and other active units to about 75 percent of their authorized peace strength.[4]

Marshall then summarized the increase in armory drills and the advance training proposed for staff officers.

Ludlow's questioning of Marshall suggested to Administration supporters that the isolationist from Indiana was attempting to characterize the Administration's program as preparing for a war. Democrat George W.

Johnson of West Virginia, responding to Ludlow's implications, joined the discussion and in a series of questions attempted to clarify the Guard's position in the national defense and the Administration's intent. "It is," Johnson asked, speaking of the Guard, "an auxiliary of the Army, is it?"[5] "It is a part of the Army of the United States," replied the Chief of Staff.[6] He stressed his point by telling the Congressmen that it "constitut[ed] 60 percent of the Army as contemplated by the National Defense Act."[7] From there Marshall and Johnson entered a discourse over the possibility of war.

Marshall:	We had in this country when we sent troops to Puerto Rico only 70,000 combatant troops of the Regular Army.
Johnson:	In respect to the time with which we are dealing—
Marshall:	It is not necessarily a matter of time. Those were the only combatant troops we had in this country outside of the National Guard.

Johnson then tried to allay concerns over the Administration's program.

Johnson:	The point I was trying to make is this: We do not contemplate going to war with anybody, do we?
Marshall:	I see no signs of it in this program.
Johnson:	You feel the appropriation requested here is necessary?
Marshall:	Absolutely; it is a very modest program.[8]

His experience before the subcommittee, along with White House meetings, left the Chief of Staff skeptical about winning the budget as introduced. The day after the committee meeting, November 28, Marshall dispatched a secret memorandum to General Gasser, in which the Chief of Staff related his experience with the Bureau of the Budget Director Harold D. Smith at a White House conference on November 20. "I gathered," Marshall wrote, "the idea from Mr. Smith that he was hopeful we would not press for further increase to 280,000."[9] Secretary Woodring told Marshall the same thing on the morning of November 28. The Secretary had "in mind . . . a compromise figure of about 20,000 men" which would have raised the Army to 245,000 or 250,000 men. It became clear to Marshall that he had no support for a large increase from either Congress or the Administration.[10]

On November 28 representatives from the National Guard Bureau fared little better before the committee. Major General Albert H. Blanding, retiring Chief of the National Guard Bureau, accompanied by Lieutenant Colonels S. G. Brown and W. D. Dabney, testified on the Guard's increases. They ran into a wall of skepticism from several on the committee. Fiscal conservatives Clifton A. Woodrum, Democrat from Virginia, Republican John Taber of New York, and Republican Richard B. Wigglesworth of Massachusetts, reviewed the budget line by line, questioning several items. They paid special attention to transportation costs. The Guard requested funds for 1,639 one and a half ton trucks. Taber asked: "if you had 800 of them [one and a half ton trucks], you would get by pretty well would you not?"[11] Caught in a corner, Colonel Brown responded that the Guard had gotten by with less, but he hastened to add, needed more.

Johnson of West Virginia asked: "You could get along with horses and mules, if you had to, could you not?"[12] The committee chairman saved the Bureau from embarrassment by asking: "Generally speaking, you look upon all of these appropriations as not only incidental but as necessary to this expansion for defense?" Brown replied simply, "Yes, sir."[13]

Marshall returned before the committee on November 30, intending to defend the Army's planned maneuvers. Marshall, however, quickly realized that the committee wanted to trim the requested appropriation. It recommended, and the House passed, a bill cutting over $7,000,000 from the already reduced $120,000,000 request. The Guard lost nearly $3,000,000 of the $17,000,000 it requested for transportation. The bill then went to the Senate for consideration, which deferred taking up the measure until the new year. The War Department and the Guard would have to wait.[14]

THE GUARD LEADERSHIP MEETS

A month after the conclusion of the Baltimore convention newly elected NGA President Brigadier General Walter A. DeLamater of New York scheduled a December 3-4 joint meeting of the Executive Council and the Legislative Committee for Washington. He also issued several comments to the press, which telegraphed the Association's agenda to Congress and the Administration. Stating that the men of the Guard realized the importance of the sacrifices the nation called upon them to make, he maintained that the Guard should "receive hearty and full cooperation of Congress and the War Department."[15] This statement, along with a call for Guard representation in General Staff conferences, made clear his intent to press for federal money for armories and camps and a greater voice in determining the Guard's role. DeLamater's statements served notice to the Army that the Guard would press its own agenda, even at the Army's expense. The latter statement highlighted the continuing feud between the NGA and the Army over control of the Guard. Although NGA leaders wanted a larger role in national defense they would not surrender to Army control.[16]

On December 3, NGA leaders met Secretary of War Woodring, General Marshall, and other General Staff officers at the Washington Hotel where they discussed the need for federal funding, armory construction, and changes contemplated by the War Department. The meeting marked the first time that NGA committees received addresses from such high-ranking officials.[17] Marshall anticipated trouble on the subject of the new, nontraditional (Corps support troops) Guard units the War Department was contemplating.[18] However, as the discussion progressed, Marshall realized that Guard leaders did not object to the new units per se. In compliance with Reckord's appeal at the Baltimore convention, NGA leaders called instead for a greater national role for the Guard, at federal expense. At the close of the conference, an unnamed participant commented that "though the States had borne and were willing to bear the cost of constructing and maintaining armories for the present Guard, it was felt that the new units [were] intended solely for national defense and that the Federal government...should bear all expense entailed by them."[19] Neither Secretary Woodring nor General Marshall made a public reply.

After the meeting General Marshall hosted a lunch at the Mayflower Hotel. There Guard generals and members of the Guard Staff continued discussions on reorganization, training, future expansion, and finances. During the off-the-record lunch, NGA and War Department representatives undoubtedly discussed the proposal to expand field training to twenty-one days with six days of optional attendance.[20] No clear consensus emerged on this subject, yet the Guard did publicly support War Department programs 100 percent. However, criticism of increased drills voiced at Baltimore indicated that some members were increasingly unhappy over the proposed training schedule. This criticism had increased after the fall of Poland and the onset of the "Phoney War." The lull in Europe seemingly negated the need for more training. However, the meeting did improve the Guard's public expression about the War Department. Woodring and Marshall's willingness to meet with Guard leaders suggested their sensitivity to Guard feelings. General DeLamater illustrated this point in a December 5 letter to Marshall. "General," DeLamater wrote, "we feel closer to the War Department than ever before and feel that you personally are interested in our problems, anxious to get our viewpoint and to cooperate in every possible way and I can assure you that you will find in us the same spirit and that we will loyally do our part."[21]

However genuine DeLamater's sentiment, by late December Marshall sensed a cooling in the Guard's ardor from its September-October high. The meeting with Guard officials and the decline in recruiting rates reflected diminished public anxieties about foreign aggression. The Guard had no immunity from these feelings. With the major European powers holding an uneasy standoff, the ranks of the Guard saw little reason to continue the extra drills. During that winter concern over jobs began to replace the anticipation of war. Marshall concluded that the time had come to "turn off the heat, as it were, at the same time not giving public indication of any intention to abandon . . . additional drills."[22] He thought that by allowing the Guard one more month to complete the twelve additional drills ordered in September, and originally scheduled to end January 31, 1940, some of the grumbling would end.[23] Extending the time limit to complete extra drills had little effect on the Guard's mood. Complaints continued among all ranks over the issue of combining drills, and War Department plans for the next fiscal year guaranteed increased dissent.

PLANNING FOR THE GUARD

On September 19, 1939, the Secretary of the General Staff, Lieutenant Colonel Orlando Ward, instructed the Assistant Chief of Staff, War Plans Division (WPD), Brigadier General George V. Strong, to begin preparing manpower objectives for the National Guard.[24] The next day General Strong presented the WPD's proposal for a National Guard reorganized for easy integration into the Regular Army. Strong wrote that the Army needed the National Guard to have harbor defense units and mobile forces to form, in conjunction with the larger regular Army, balanced tactical units such as corps and armies.[25] WPD envisioned a Guard consisting of Army troops for two field armies, some General Headquarters troops, and Corps troops for six corps raised on a thirty day mobilization schedule. The proposal also called for increasing the eighteen divisions to seventy-five percent of their peacetime strength.[26] In terms of raw numbers, WPD proposed reorganizing a portion of the 189,000 Guardsmen into 12,600 for Army and General Headquarters troops, and 6,000 for corps troops. The infantry, cavalry, antiaircraft, and harbor defense units would constitute the bulk of the remaining force of 171,400 men. Strong's proposal also projected various manning levels for each branch of the Guard from strengths of 235,000, and 320,000 to the full peace strength of 425,000 men.[27]

Planning continued during October and by November 14, WPD had completed its revisions.[28] It's new objectives were essentially the same as the September model with two exceptions. The November manpower objectives increased the number of antiaircraft regiments from twenty-eight to thirty and increased Guard supported corps from six to seven. Each change decreased the number of men for the Guard's infantry divisions. General Strong stated in his letter to Colonel Ward that the WPD based the proposal on retaining the Guard's square divisional structure, which he wished to change, believing that reorganizing the Guard into triangular divisions would "probably justify the maintenance of such a division at approximately full peace strength and [would] provide . . . 23,000 men for use as additional corps, Army and GHQ troops."[29]

Two weeks later, Strong submitted a formal report to General Marshall that detailed a plan for a Guard of 320,000 men. In the cover letter, Strong told the Chief of Staff that the attached tabulation proposes an allocation of 320,000 men, which is possible within the framework of our existing organization and which will accomplish the objective set with a minimum of wasted strength, coordinating National Guard and Regular Army augmentations toward a balanced force of two armies.[30]

To achieve this balanced force, WPD suggested 38,000 men for the seven corps, 16,000 for the army troops, and 19,000 men for antiaircraft units. However, meeting these needs required substantial increases in the number of existing support units in the Guard and the creation of additional support units beyond the strength traditionally required for the Guard's role as a combat arm. At the corps level WPD proposed additional signal battalions and combat engineer regiments. It also required antitank battalions, cavalry reconnaissance regiments in place of a cavalry division, observation groups, and field artillery. At the army troop level the Guard would be required to provide photographic companies, general service engineers, and medical regiments. Field artillery and engineering support units composed most of GHQ's reserve troops. As Table 3.1 illustrates, the Guard had only a few of the required units.

Table 3.1
Proposed New Guard Units

Units	Number Required	Units on Hand	New Units
Signal	11	1	10
Cavalry	7	2	5
Air (Obsn)	40	21	19
Coast Artillery	31	13	18
Field Artillery	54	6.33	47.66
Engineers	25	0	25
Medical	12	1	11
Ordnance	4	0	4

Source: Memorandum for the Chief of Staff from General Strong, December 1, 1939, National Archives, RG 165, 15W3, Box 143, WPD 3674-18.

On December 13, ten days after the Army-Guard conference, General Blanding, Chief of the National Guard Bureau (NGB), received a copy of the plan. The next day he submitted several responses to the WPD proposal. Although he concurred with the general principle of forming the National

Guard into a balanced force, two matters disturbed him. Blanding noted that the plan required ten general service regiments from the Guard (part of the engineers listed in Table 3.1). Blanding viewed these regiments as simple labor troops, not combat troops. The Guard's tradition of wanting only combat units or those that directly supported combat troops, compelled Blanding to write that "it is believed that it would be difficult to raise such regiments . . . in the National Guard."[31] However, he believed that WPD's proposed changes in the Guard would eventually occur. In a subtle way the NGB Chief suggested a way of accomplishing Strong's goal. "It is the understanding of the Chief, National Guard Bureau, that the [new] units listed would be activated over a period of years as the necessary equipment became available."[32] In essence Blanding cautioned a gradual approach to the subject of creating a National Guard easily integrated into the Army. Indeed, NGA leaders might not have given their approval of the Army plan had they known of the WPD proposal. His second objection came from Strong's idea of triangularizing the Guard's divisions and shifting the extra men (possibly 25,000) to corps, army, and GHQ units. Blanding noted that

It is not possible in dealing with figures of National Guard strength to say that a definite number of men left over after deducting certain units are available for specific purposes, as can be done in the Regular Army, for the reason that units in the National Guard have to be dealt with as such.[33]

Blanding reminded Strong that the National Guard was locally organized with strong state ties. Thus, any such plan to shift excess units or men from one division to another was impossible.

Marshall next sent WPD's proposal, with Blanding's comments, to Lieutenant Colonel Kenneth Buchanan of the General Staff College. Buchanan's comments on the plan illustrated a considerable understanding of both the Army's position and the Guard's sensitivities. As an example, he responded to one part of the plan, which called for converting two Guard cavalry divisions into cavalry reconnaissance regiments, by recommending retaining the divisions "for administrative purposes and to avoid causing the bad feeling in the Guard which would result if the Division were disbanded."[34] Buchanan's approach would carry out WPD's purpose, that is, reducing the size of the divisions, without offending the Guard.

Buchanan also reinforced Blanding's view that the WPD plan failed to recognize the special nature of the Guard as a peacetime implement of the states. "It is impossible," he wrote, "to deal with National Guard personnel in mere figures as is done in the Regular Army. National Guard personnel is in units that are geographically tied down."[35] He also agreed with Blanding that labor units, and the like, held little attraction for the Guard. However, he proposed "that the peace time nucleus for such regiments could be organized and maintained in the National Guard in time of peace by designating them as combat units and making them not larger than a battalion or squadron."[36] Buchanan's solution implied that once the Army federalized the Guard the General Staff need not have any worry about the Guard's feelings.

The Chief of Staff dispatched his comments to Strong on January 3, 1940. Marshall's critique echoed most of the comments made by both Blanding and Buchanan. However, concerning the creation of new support units for higher echelons, Marshall added his own analysis. He believed that an increase in the Guard to 320,000 men, including new units, would force "the War Department to a different viewpoint as to the primary mission and status of the National Guard."[37] Until that time the War Department treated the Officers' Reserve Corps (ORC) and the Guard in different ways, providing certain benefits for reserve officers but not for Guard officers. From the Army's perspective, the ORC belonged exclusively to the federal government while the Guard, in peacetime, belonged to their respective states. Changing that view threatened a conflict with the states over control of the Guard and with the NGA over the unequal treatment of officers. Knowing the Association's influence with Congress, Marshall understandably wished to avoid this conflict with the NGA.[38]

In closing, the Chief of Staff agreed with WPD that "from a military viewpoint, provision for the necessary corps, Army, and GHQ units is very desirable."[39] But he surmised that public opinion and Congress would "clamor for an increase in the number of aircraft and antiaircraft troops" to meet any threat of attack against American territory.[40] "The diversion," he continued, "of National Guard units to meet public demand would be less harmful than the diversion of Regular Army units."[41] In planning for an expanded Guard, Marshall advised WPD to consider "the possibility of this situation."[42] In spite of his comments, Marshall approved the WPD proposal, as he put it, for "training purposes." However, in the absence of any other proposal, WPD's plan became the guide for organizing an expanded Guard.

DISSENT WITHIN THE GUARD

As WPD's proposal made its way through the various offices of the War Department and the National Guard Bureau, the NGA's Executive Council and the Legislative Committee became aware of its existence and met to determine a course of action. General Staff officials sought ways to ease any tension the study might create, but two other items threatened even more controversy. Within the Fiscal Year 1941 budget lay a provision for a total of twenty-seven days of field training, rather than the traditional fifteen days. Regular field training would be expanded to twenty-one days, most of which would be taken up by large-scale maneuvers with the Army. Six additional days of local field training were added to the already burdensome amount.

Although the Association had given its approval to the schedule in October, by January the opinion of some of the NGA's members was that such expanded training was not as urgently needed.

The first public criticism of the enlarged field training schedule came from Major General William N. Haskell, commanding general of New York's Twenty-Seventh Infantry Division and the Adjutant General of the state. In an interview with the *New York Times*, Haskell stated that he objected to the Guard participation in the Army's maneuvers, the second consecutive year that New York's troops would participate, claiming that such large-scale exercises seriously threatened the efficiency of the Guard. He argued that (1) large unit maneuvers deprived Guardsmen of small unit training, which he believed they needed urgently; and (2) the field artillery would not receive live-fire practice during the maneuver. At best the artillery would fire only blank rounds, which made judging unit proficiency impossible.[43] Privately, Haskell was not completely against the maneuvers. In response to a Guard Bureau questionnaire he favored the maneuver, but only after "the entire New York National Guard [conducted] the normal 2 weeks [training] as a distinct priority, and, if money [was] available, then have the maneuver and let those go who [could]."[44]

Other Guard commanders shared Haskell's criticism of the proposed training schedule, but for different reasons. Brigadier General Edward Martin, commander of the Twenty-eighth Division and the National Guard Association's newly elected vice-president, favored both the additional armory drills and the twenty-seven days of field training. However, he qualified this support by stating that he would go along with the schedule as long as the Administration publicly announced that additional training was part of a program to meet the national emergency Roosevelt proclaimed in September. Martin believed that without publicity "a longer period than 15 days training will be injurious to the Guard."[45] Without the public statement, Guardsmen would be hard pressed if caught between supporting a family and country. Major General Gilson D. Light of Ohio echoed Martin's sentiment. He stated that compelling men to attend the twenty-one days of training meant "considerable [financial] loss to many officers and enlisted men. Especially enlisted men."[46]

General Reckord expressed the beliefs of many Guardsmen when he stated to the Adjutant General Association: "I don't mind saying very frankly that I feel the training program is too severe," adding, "but, at any rate, we are following the leader and we are going through one hundred percent in an attempt to secure all the money that is in the budget."[47] While giving public assurances of unqualified support, Reckord's statement implied that if the budget did not pass the NGA would work against the training schedule.

Haskell's remarks and Reckord's veiled hint of an adverse Guard reaction came at an awkward time for Marshall. The Chief of Staff faced a two stage funding battle with Congress. The Senate Appropriations Committee had scheduled mid-January hearings on the 1940 Emergency Appropriations bill already trimmed by the House. After that came Congressional consideration of the Fiscal Year 1941 Budget. Back-to-back budget presentations invited close scrutiny by a spending conscious Congress. But Marshall's troubles did not end here. At roughly the same time, an internal conflict threatened stability in the War Department. Secretary of War Woodring, a noninterventionist, objected to the sale of large amounts of war material, including army surplus, to the Allies. While Roosevelt viewed material aid to the Allies as vital to national security, Woodring believed such sales were detrimental to the national defense. Although many Army officers, including Marshall, sometimes agreed with Woodring, Assistant Secretary of War Louis Johnson favored the sales. Johnson, who thought he should have been secretary instead of Woodring, used the issue to badger the Secretary. Roosevelt also wanted to replace his recalcitrant Secretary of War, but feared stirring up Woodring's isolationist supporters in Congress.[48]

The effect of General Haskell's remarks to the press, and perhaps to New York's Congressional delegation, became clear when a subcommittee of the Senate Appropriations Committee examined the National Guard portion of the Emergency Appropriation Bill. On January 18, Senator Richard D. Russell of Georgia questioned Brigadier General Lorenzo D. Gasser, deputy chief of staff, on the worth of the additional armory drills and by inference the value of the proposed extended field training.[49] While discussing the increase in Guard training, Russell stated: "I had heard that it was rather doubtful as to the benefits of it [the additional training]."[50] Gasser responded that reports about the training seemed "uniformly enthusiastic."[51] Russell seemed unimpressed. "It sounds very much like the old time militia summer encampment," the Senator noted, "when they went off to the seashore for a couple of weeks."[52] Gasser was emphatic in disagreement:

It has been just the opposite, sir. It was held at a time of the year, in the fall and winter, when the weather conditions were a little bit more zippy. Due to the international situation, the training was taken seriously. There is one thing that I am quite certain that you recognize, and that is that the Guard is getting better and better every year.[53]

After concluding testimony the subcommittee reported in favor of the bill. As a result the Senate passed the Emergency Bill but eliminated $12,788,664 from the total Army-Navy package, "$3,000,000 from the appropriation for Army field exercise in the division and corps maneuvers," and $1,000,000 in funds for transportation.[54] On February 12, the bill emerged from Congress. The Army's original request of $120,000,000 had dwindled to $109,416,689.[55]

THE GUARD REQUESTS A MEETING

Reckord's anxiety over the next round of budget debates compelled Maryland's Adjutant General to request a conference between members of the Guard's leadership and General Marshall, who suggested a luncheon on February 26. Reckord agreed.[56] On February 16, as a preliminary to both the meeting with Reckord and the House Appropriations committee, Marshall met with Generals Gasser (Personnel Section, or G-1), Frank Andrews (Operations Section, or G-3), and Major General John F. Williams, the new Chief of the National Guard Bureau, to discuss the Guard situation.[57] Marshall stated that he believed Reckord might oppose the extended training schedule. General Williams assured the Chief of Staff that by taking such a position Reckord would place himself "in a ridiculous attitude if he [undertook] to speak on this subject for the entire National Guard."[58] Marshall reiterated his commitment to increase the Guard's training. He told the generals that under the old fifteen day schedule, establishing and breaking camp, Governor's Day, and other interruptions cost the Guard six days of valuable time. The Chief of Staff explained that by adding the six days to summer camp he hoped portions of the Guard could travel to camp sites early so that "when the full complement arrived at camp they would step into a going concern."[59] This would allow two uninterrupted weeks of training.

Williams pointed out to Marshall that the issue divided the Guard. State Adjutants General, who were gubernatorial appointees, resisted the increased schedule simply because it would extend training beyond state borders, and thus out of their control. "They wish," the Bureau chief stated, "to put state guards in little self-contained camps; it is difficult to get them to think across state lines."[60] To that end he warned: "It is the state officials who object to the new program and their attitude is penetrating Congress."[61] Division commanders represented the other side of the coin, viewing training and the Guard's place in national defense in a broader way. "They want," said Williams, "to put into effect the bigger Army picture."[62]

Burdensome as the twenty-seven day of aggregate training were on the Guard, Marshall would have liked to further expand the summer session from the already expanded twenty-one to twenty-eight days. Increasing summer training to nearly one month would enable the Guard to participate in all the planned Army maneuvers. However, he realized that Congress might cut funds requested for the twenty-seven day package. Assuming that there would be a budget cut, Marshall estimated the cost of twenty-eight days of training ($19,500,000) and the savings from a twenty-one day schedule ($5,000,000). A further reduction to the usual fifteen days meant another $5,000,000 saved. Marshall, however, planned to press for the full amount, even though he expected Congress would fund less. With these facts and opinions in mind, Marshall prepared to meet with Reckord and NGA leaders.

But first he faced the subcommittee on the War Department of the House Appropriation committee.[63]

On February 23, when Marshall testified in support of the Fiscal Year 1941 Army budget, his opening remarks touched on such subjects as the enlisted strength of the Regular Army, material program, mechanization, and training but most importantly he tried to impart to the listening Congressmen, and the nation, a sense of urgency, to convince those who did not perceive a real danger to American security. Seated before the subcommittee, the Chief of Staff uttered the now famous words:

As to the existing crisis ahead, we must face the facts. Any major developments there should be parallel by added precautions in this country. If the situation grows more desperate, we should add to the numbers of seasoned troops in the Regular Army and to the strength of the National Guard. If Europe blazes in the late spring or summer, we must put our house in order before the sparks reach the Western Hemisphere.[64]

As for the Guard, Marshall informed the subcommittee that he sought equipment for 235,000 Guardsmen and funds to support twenty-one days of field training plus another six days. Between February 16 and his testimony before the committee, he had dropped the idea of holding the Guard for twenty-eight days of summer training. He anticipated trouble; Guard grumbling over the extra drills and Haskell's criticism of the maneuvers combined to give some Congressmen strong doubts about the efficacy of the program.[65]

To some extent, Marshall's statements before the subcommittee represented a shift in the General's posture. From September to the early part of the new year, Marshall pushed training as the first priority. However, his testimony on February 23 revealed that the quest for material held first priority. He would follow the same line with Guard leaders three days later.

THE TWO SIDES MEET

On February 26, Generals Reckord, DeLamater, Martin, and Williams called on the Chief of Staff. Reckord stated later that he intended to discuss the Guard's budget and, if Congress decided to reduce the Administration's request, to reach some agreement on the least harmful cuts. He was convinced that the cuts should come out of training funds, but suspected that Marshall would object. Marshall expected this attitude from Reckord and planned to give him exactly what he wanted but not at once. Reckord began by stating that he thought the training program was too severe. It presented hardships for individuals and entire communities. Marshall understood this point, but he did not quite expect Reckord's next move. Despite his personal feelings on the matter, Reckord declared that he would back the Army's plan one hundred percent.[66]

Although pleased, Marshall did not fully reveal his new position until he knew the substance of the Guard's demands, and exactly what cuts were acceptable to the NGA. According to Reckord, the conversation bounced back and forth until the Guardsmen told Marshall that they believed cuts in training were preferable to less material. Although this opinion was not new, it represented the first authoritative statement Marshall had received from the NGA on the subject. Reckord and his fellow Guardsmen were reluctant to be totally candid with the General Marshall for fear of alienating him. From the time of Marshall's address before the Pennsylvania Association through that day Guard leaders believed he wanted training above all else. Marshall's response surprised Reckord and, he thought, the others as well. The Chief of Staff simply told them: "You will have no fight with me on that. I think you are right."[67] He continued to astound his listeners by revealing that if cuts came, he would first eliminate the additional six days of training, leaving twenty-one, including the maneuvers and the sixty armory drills. He told the generals that he would use all his influence to keep those programs.[68]

By the end of the meeting both sides agreed to support the entire budget. If cuts came, they would come from training. Marshall's agreement with the Guard position meant that he could expect full public support from most of the Guard leadership. He gained much but gave up nothing. Guard support strengthened his cause before Congress and removed a potential obstacle. Having already anticipated cuts at the hands of Congress, the Chief of Staff could afford to reach an understanding with the Guard.

Guard leaders entered the meeting not knowing how Marshall would react to their stand and expecting considerable friction. They left the meeting with greater regard for the Chief of Staff. Having gained his understanding, they could now meet with members of the NGA and the Adjutants General Association (AGA) in March and announce their full support for the Army's plan. Guard leaders had what they wanted; now they had to convince the rest of the Guard.

THE AGA AND NGA HOLD COUNCIL

On March 18, the AGA assembled at the Hall of Nations in the Washington Hotel. Unlike previous years, the AGA held a special session with key NGA members and division commanders. Battle lines that developed at the meeting followed the pattern Williams had predicted to Marshall a month before. Reckord, DeLamater, and Martin, the three most influential men in the NGA, came out in unquestioned support for the War Department program. The majority of the twenty-two division commanders fell quickly into line behind them. However, many Adjutants General with deep-seated reservations planned to thoroughly discuss the program at a meeting before Guard representatives testified before the House committee.

General Williams addressed the conference first. Attempting to win over those who feared the Army's plan, Williams' speech ranged between sermon and pep talk. He warned those present of the seriousness of the world crisis and of the danger that America faced. However, he informed the generals that the Guard stood at a level of preparedness never before reached in peacetime. "Equipment," he told them, "steadily flowing into our hands through the timely and generous appropriations of Congress, and the cooperation of the War Department General Staff, is the best that can be had."[69] In some cases the Guard received modern equipment before the Regular Army. As for men: "Generally speaking, our volunteer citizen force is steadily recruiting a better type. More of our men . . . are receiving the advantage of the courses at the general and special service schools."[70] A portion of this success Williams attributed to an increasingly cordial relationship between the Guard and the Army. The source for this cordiality, William asserted, was General Marshall. "He thinks in terms of the Army of the United States," the Chief of the Bureau assured the gathering.[71]

Williams closed his brief and sweeping remarks by emphasizing that the Guard's status resulted from a team effort. "It has been an attainment reached by all agencies working together," he told them, "though the greater part of the credit belongs to the personnel of the Guard itself and especially to the State Adjutants General and the commanders of the Guard divisions."[72] By such friendly backslapping Williams hoped to win over any adjutants general or division commanders who felt threatened by the Army's moves to control training. Many of those who harbored suspicion of the Army remembered the treatment Guard officers and units received in the last war. Some believed that Army control of training meant the severance of state ties. The Army's training plan seemed one method of pulling the Guard toward complete federal control.

Colonel B. M. Bailey of the Bureau took the rostrum next to present his opinions, and presumably those of the Bureau, on three major topics: the twenty-one days of field training with six days optional attendance, six days of field training at home stations, and sixty armory drills per year. He disapproved of the idea of allowing some men to arrive at summer training late or leave early to meet personal needs. Units, as a whole, should go and return together even if it meant training for only the customary fifteen days. As for having six more days of training at home stations, Bailey found the idea desirable and practical "If limited to those units that [could] practice."[73] But Bailey echoed Haskell's concerns when he stated that no unit should be required to follow the plan if it could not "practice with the basic weapons."[74]

Bailey could not find a justification for sixty separate one and one-half hour drills a year. They required "radical readjustments in both family and business life . . . [and] interfer[ed] with officers and non-commissioned officers' schools and proper administrative work."[75] However, neither could he support the idea of combining two drills in a single day. This would "be asking for two days' pay for three hours' work."[76] He believed that such a request would result in severe criticism of the entire training program.

Seeking views from across the nation, Bailey called upon several individuals to express their opinions. Brigadier General Edgar C. Erickson, Adjutant General of Massachusetts; Major General Roy D. Keehn, commander of the Thirty-third Infantry Division; and Major General Henry D. Russell, commander of the Thirtieth Infantry Division, favored the training schedule as proposed. However, they saw a need for a nationwide public education campaign on the issue of extended training. Erickson noted the business community's deep concern over the prospect of losing workers. He told the meeting:

Now, there are calls from manufacturers in my office practically every day who are anxious to know whether or not this extra training period is to be held, and in our state these manufacturers have for the first time in many years considerable business and they have big contracts, and many of their key men are members of the National Guard.[77]

Erickson stressed that publicity from Washington would make their job of winning public and business support easier. "But unless you have created in the minds of the public generally that we ought to have three weeks," the General warned, "it places a hard responsibility on those of us who have to educate our people at home."[78]

General Russell objected to the idea of allowing units to determine their length of training, whether fifteen or twenty-one days. "I think we are trifling with the question when we start talking about part of the National Guard training fifteen days and part . . . training twenty-one or thirty days," stated Russell. "I think we should have a uniform plan of training throughout the country for all of the guard units."[79]

In his capacity as chairman of the NGA Legislative Committee, Reckord took the floor during the afternoon session to explain the Guard's budgetary victories and future prospects. He reminded the assembled Guard leaders that Congress had passed the Emergency Appropriations bill, thus repaying the states for funds spent on increased training. Congress had also added $3,846,600 for motorized equipment. Looking ahead, Reckord explained that the 1941 budget would combine the regular budget formulated in 1939 and a supplement to cover emergency items for a total of $96,000,000. It also included amounts for four Army maneuvers ($800,000), twelve additional drills ($4,500,000), and new motorized equipment ($17,568,880). Though he expected the budget to pass the Congress he did not suppose that it would pass intact. The Bureau of the Budget had already trimmed the original request of $101,000,000 by $5,000,000; Congress was likely to reduce it even further. Backed by Marshall's assurance, Reckord suggested that when cuts came they should come from training funds and not money to buy additional equipment. Reckord gladly told his listeners that the Chief of Staff understood this point and agreed. News of Marshall's flexibility undoubtedly eased some of the tensions felt by both associations.[80]

However, the issue of combining drills remained unresolved. The War Department, especially G-1, opposed combining drills, as Bailey mentioned, because it constituted two days' pay for only three hours' work. Unable to win support from the General Staff, the Association took its case directly to Congress. There Reckord successfully inserted a provision in the pending revision of the National Defense Act, changing Section 92 by adding: "Provided further that a single drill shall be of one and one-half hours' duration and that two such drills might be held on a single calendar day."[81]

Although Reckord looked to Congress to solve this problem he did not stop negotiating with the War Department on a way to settle the dispute. Standing before the meeting, he told the NGA members that talks between the two parties were close to yielding a compromise. Reckord proposed combining twenty-five percent of the sixty drills into two sessions per day. It would not completely solve the problem as Reckord saw it, but would reduce the burden on Guardsmen. Proof of increased training efficiency, he told them, would justify the change and thus remove any objections voiced by G-1. Yet Reckord did not mention that the Army would violate its own regulations if it accepted the compromise.[82]

Reckord's proposals met with the general approval of the assembled members from both associations. All that remained undone was to present their united front to Congress. Therefore, the assembled associations selected a group of forty-four general and field grade officers to meet with the House and Senate appropriations committees.

BEFORE THE COMMITTEE

On Tuesday, March 19, representatives from the joint AGA-NGA conference traveled to Capitol Hill to present their case to members of the House Appropriations Committee. DeLamater, as NGA President, led the delegation and told the listening Congressmen that the conference had:

studied very carefully the proposed budget for the National Guard and also the plan of the War Department. While it is true, perhaps, that the plan of the War Department possibly is a little hard, nevertheless we are ready, 100 percent to cooperate with the program of the War Department and the Chief of Staff.[83]

DeLamater's expression of thinly veiled dissatisfaction with the Army's training schedule suggested to the Committee that the NGA and the AGA wanted it cut. Next he turned to the budget. He told them that the special joint meeting of Adjutants General, NGA officials, and division commanders had examined the budget closely and had determined that "every item in the Budget [was] satisfactory . . . with the possible exception of the item dealing with camp construction."[84] The Guard leadership had found this single item "quite considerably out of line" with the Guard's thinking.[85] DeLamater then read into the record the NGA resolution which called for more federal money to cover the cost of maintaining the new equipment. It read in part:

Whereas the several States have cooperated with the Federal Government to the limit of their respective financial abilities in the maintenance of the National Guard and providing necessary housing and training facilities far beyond normal State requirements:

Now, therefore, be it *Resolved*, That it is incumbent upon the Federal Government to assume the additional financial cost for the housing, equipping, and maintenance of such additional units and equipment as are essential to a well-organized initial protective force, which units are provided primarily for the *National rather than State security* [emphasis added].[86]

Having clearly set the tone and objective, of Guard testimony, DeLamater presented several of his fellow Guardsmen to the committee.

Brigadier General Ellard A. Walsh of Minnesota spoke on the issue of camp construction. The War Department's budget allowed only $200,000 for purely Guard construction, a figure that Walsh and the others rejected as "utterly inadequate" to the Guard's needs in light of the personnel increases. Walsh suggested that "the committee . . . give serious consideration to the figure submitted by the chief of the National Guard Bureau, namely, $2,964,000 for camp construction."[87] He believed that this amount, large as it seemed, represented "the completion of installations . . . essential and vital for existing organizations based on" the Guard at that time, not for housing equipment called for under the Fiscal Year 1941 budget.[88] Although his statement hinted at the need for future capital outlays, Walsh presented a way for the economy-minded Congress to stretch its money. He suggested that many states could take advantage of the Works Progress Administration's funds already set aside to build the needed facilities. The money spent could thus provide employment and serve the interest of national defense. The result, Walsh concluded, would be four and one half million dollars worth of badly needed work spread among all the states. Undoubtedly his argument presented a tempting idea for Congressmen interested in saving money and in providing employment in their states.

The Minnesota general ended his remarks by echoing DeLamater's opening statement that troops called for by the Army's plan exceeded reasonable state needs.

But when we enter the field of artillery, antiaircraft, aviation, tanks, corps, and army troops, and a general headquarters reserve we have entered the realm of national security and national defense, and conceivably the States must have some help if they are to maintain that force and provide the installations which are so essential.[89]

While questioning General Blanding, who had resumed command of the Thirty-first Division (Florida, Alabama, Mississippi, and Louisiana), on the need for purchasing certain types of vehicles, Democrat David D. Terry of Arkansas raised the issue of training within the context of the budget. Terry believed that the increased number of drills from forty-eight to sixty created troubles for Guardsmen. Taking up the issue from Blanding, General Thomas E. Rilea of Oregon answered Terry by saying that "perhaps in many sections of the United States the training program as advocated . . . [would] work a hardship," but he believed that Guardsmen recognized the seriousness of the situation and the need for the training.[90]

D. Lane Powers of New Jersey continued the questioning on the need for the added drills: "Does the Guard really want these 60 drills, or are you just agreeing with the War Department policy?" Without waiting for a response Powers questioned the rationale for the extra training: "the reason [for the increase] was to give the new recruits their initial training. That has more or less been done . . . do you actually feel that the 60 drills are necessary?"[91] Rilea responded that the world situation warranted the extra drills. Powers then asked that if material and construction were so badly needed "would it not be better to cut down the number of drills to 48 and apply that money to things that are more essential to the moment?"[92] Perhaps sensing where Powers was leading, Terry interrupted the New Jersey Congressman by asking Rilea what the Guard really wanted. Without hesitation Rilea, responded by saying: "I believe that under the conditions we now face we [the Guard] probably would have suggested the additional training even if the War Department had not asked for it."[93]

General Walsh interjected that the main trouble rested not in the amount of training, although the increase would be hard to absorb, but with the public reaction to the plan. As he had done at the Guard meeting of the previous day, Walsh pointed to the business community as a source of concern. An adverse reaction from employers or a misunderstanding over the need for Guardsmen to leave their jobs for training might force many citizen soldiers to choose between job or country. He warned that "unless Congress and the President [presented] this in a favorable light to business the Guard would have trouble."[94]

The attitude of the Committee became apparent from the thrust of the questions. Without a threat to the nation, Congress was reluctant to provide all the funds requested. Marshall and Reckord now had to wait for the budget ax to fall.

CONGRESSIONAL CUTS

On March 27, Reckord wrote to Marshall with news both men expected. Apparently from a source on the House Appropriations Committee (perhaps longtime Guard supporter Ross A. Collins of Mississippi) Reckord learned of cuts in the Guard appropriations. He also learned that the Committee intended to cut the six days of field training and the twelve additional drills, but the appropriations for material seemed safe.[95]

Marshall replied to Reckord's letter the following day, telling the Maryland General:

I get about the same reaction that you give me in regard to the possible cuts. Apparently there is nothing that can be done at the moment to change matters. But quite apparently we are going to have a tremendous fight in the Senate, unless Europe development re-focus attention on the dangers of the situation.[96]

In the first week of April the House Appropriations Committee reported the budget to the whole House. As expected, it recommended cutting $67,000,000 from the Army's request, reducing the Guard's share by a total of $8,333,273. Cuts came primarily from eliminating the six field training days and the twelve extra drills, as Reckord had expected. Inadvertently, the Committee removed one of the major source of irritation between the Guard and the Army. For without the additional drills the Guard had no reason to press for combining the extra training. In submitting its report the Committee claimed that the extended training schedule would interfere with Guardsmen's regular civilian pursuits, but endorsed a last minute compromise suggested by Reckord, that the federal government provide rations for weekend drills not already paid for with federal funds. Reckord's solution provided some additional training while reducing the states' burden.[97]

The Committee cut the NGA's request for construction funds from $10,000,000 to $5,753,447; this did not sadden Reckord, who had told the AGA that he would have been satisfied with much less. Even though the House whittled down the NGA's enormous figure, the expenditure was still nearly double what Reckord had expected.

The last major item of the Guard's budget cut by the House Committee was the request for additional motor vehicles. The Committee's questioning of the proposed expenditure indicated that it was vulnerable to reduction. But the Committee's cut of $3,000,000 from the requested amount did not hurt Reckord as much as Congress might have supposed. He could cheerfully report to the Chief of Staff on April 4 that the Guard would "make out very satisfactorily."[98]

However, serious trouble loomed on the horizon for the four maneuvers planned for later in the year. In the same letter Reckord told Marshall that Representative Walter G. Andrews of New York proposed to offer an amendment to the budget bill that would eliminate the maneuvers. Reckord learned of Andrews' plan late on April 4, and immediately mounted a campaign to thwart the New York lawmaker. Reckord telephoned several NGA leaders urging them to telegraph their own Congressmen to support the bill as written. Reckord then sent his own wire to Congressman James W. Wadsworth of New York, with copies going to Maryland's House delegation. The telegram read:

Understand Congressman Andrews will offer amendment today to strike out Army maneuvers. This is not in accord with desires of the National Guard we have agreed to participate in Army maneuvers this year and respectfully request that you support all items in the bill as reported by the Committee.[99]

Reckord suspected General Haskell's involvement in the attempt to ruin the maneuvers. All concerned knew of his opposition to the field exercises. "Congressman Andrews' actions," Reckord wrote Marshall, "indicates to me as though our mutual friend, General Haskell, is trying to throw a monkey wrench in your army maneuver program."[100]

Reckord's efforts paid off later that day. Congressman Francis D. Culkin of New York gained the floor of the House and at once attacked Andrews' proposal. Culkin, a twelve year Guard veteran, stated that the Guard wanted the maneuvers and that any obstacle regarding Guardsmen's employment could be handled. In rebuttal to the argument advanced by Andrews, and by Haskell, that the training would hurt Guard efficiency rather than help, Culkin told the House:

It is the judgement of the Chief of Staff and the almost unanimous opinion of the National Guard that these maneuvers will do no violence to the future enlistments of the guard, but on the contrary, will make the citizen soldier self-reliant and able to take care of himself under combat conditions if that time comes.[101]

Culkin concluded by saying: "I feel confident that the House will leave this appropriation as reported by the committee."[102]

Andrews made no reply to Culkin. When the House passed the bill, minus the Andrews amendment, Andrews cast no vote. Once again the power of the NGA, led by Reckord, was manifest in the halls of Congress. The battle over the budget, however, was not over. The Senate would not take up the measure until the end of the month. Marshall expected more trouble for the bill there, but events in Europe aided its passage.

On April 9 Hitler invaded the neutral nations of Denmark and Norway. Denmark fell with virtually no bloodshed while German forces encountered resistance from the Norwegians. Although the invasions came as no surprise to the Roosevelt Administration, Congress once again reversed its attitude toward defense spending. Marshall took advantage of the crisis by sending a memorandum to Woodring for presentation to the President. In the memo,

Marshall stated that even though the President reserved $37,000,000 for critical equipment and that the House had added $14,250,000, the Army still needed $25,000,000 "for the modern equipment necessary to outfit the existing units of the Regular establishment and the National Guard."[103] The President reviewed the document and Woodring's cover letter, also drafted by Marshall, and simply penciled in "Seems necessary. F.D.R."[104] However, two weeks passed before Roosevelt cautiously added $18,000,000 to the 1941 budget. And even then the funds were requested for only support equipment—nothing to arouse the isolationists.[105]

On April 30 Marshall appeared before the Senate Appropriations Committee seeking to restore the funds cut by the House. In his opening remarks the Chief of Staff reminded senators of his warning delivered to the House committee some months before. "If Europe blazes . . . we must put our house in order before the sparks reach the Western Hemisphere." He then added: "Since that time Europe has blazed."[106] He called for increased defense spending along the lines approved by the President and detailed how the War Department planned to use the money. Marshall told the senators that the funds would go for more equipment, flight pay for the Air Corps, more airplanes, bases in Alaska, and additional funds for Guard transportation. Suspecting that even an alarmed Congress might not vote all he requested, Marshall told the Committee:

I hope you will agree with me when I say that further reductions in this bill will seriously endanger the national defense . . . . However, the War Department appreciates the situation facing the Congress and is prepared to accept many of the reductions made by the House.[107]

Marshall's fears proved unfounded. The invasions of Denmark and Norway profoundly shook Congress. The focus of the Senate committee turned from cutting the Army's budget to virtually issuing a blank check. As Senator Carl Hayden stated: "'Anyone who reads the hearings will note that the principal discussion is not what was in the bill, but what ought to be in the bill in order properly to meet the situation which confronts us.'"[108] Even Republican Henry Cabot Lodge, Jr., told Marshall that all the Army had to do to get money for national defense was to ask for it.[109] However, before the Administration could revise its request upward Europe plunged into full-scale war.

NOTES

1. U.S. Congress, House, Appropriations Committee, *Military Establishment Appropriation Bill for 1941, hearing before a sub-committee of the House Committee on Appropriations H.R. 9209,* 76th Cong., 3rd sess., 1940, p. 858.

2. Watson, *Chief of Staff,* 161.

3. Ibid., 162.

4. U.S. Congress, House, Appropriations Committee, *Emergency Supplemental Appropriation Bill for 1940, hearings before a subcommittee of the House Committee on Appropriations on H.R. 7805*, 76th Cong., 3rd sess., 1939, p. 10.

5. Ibid., 11.

6. Ibid.

7. Ibid.

8. Ibid.

9. General George C. Marshall to General L.D. Gasser, November 28, 1939, Bland, ed., *Marshall Papers*, II, 112-113.

10. Ibid., II, 113.

11. U.S. Congress, House, Appropriations Committee, *Emergency Supplemental Appropriation Bill for 1940, hearing before a subcommittee of the House Committee on Appropriation on H.R. 7805*, 76th Cong., 3rd sess., 1939, p. 126.

12. Ibid.

13. Ibid.

14. *Army and Navy Journal*, January 27, 1940, p. 487.

15. Ibid., November 25, 1939, p. 271.

16. Ibid.

17. General Walter A. DeLamater to General George C. Marshall, December 5, 1939, George C. Marshall, Box 20, File Folder ff 16 (Marshall Library).

18. Memorandum from Marshall to A.C. of S., WPD, January 3, 1940, National Archives, RG 165, 15W3, Box 143, WPD 3674-18.

19. *Army and Navy Journal*, December 9, 1939, p. 313.

20. Ibid., 319.

21. DeLamater to Marshall, December 5, 1939, George C. Marshall Papers, Box 20, File Folder 16 (Marshall Library).

22. General George C. Marshall to General Blanding, Bland, ed., *Marshall Papers*, II, 121.

23. Ibid.

24. Memorandum from Lt. Col. Orlando Ward to General George V. Strong, September 19, 1939, National Archives, RG 165, 15W3, WPD 3674-18.

25. Memorandum for the Chief of Staff, September 20, 1939, National Archives, RG 165, 15W3, Box 143, WPD 3674-18.

26. Ibid.

27. Ibid.

28. Planning the Guard's allocation was delayed in October by a lack of approval for corps organizational charts by the Operations and Training Division (G-3) of the General Staff under Major General Frank Andrews. See Memorandum for the Assistant Chief of Staff, WPD from General Andrews, November 8, 1939, National Archives, RG 165, 15W3, Box 143, WPD 3674-18.

29. Memorandum for the Secretary of the General Staff from General Strong, November 14, 1939, National Archives, RG 165, 15W3, Box 143, WPD 3674-18.

30. Memorandum for the Chief of Staff from General Strong, December 1, 1939, National Archives, RG 165, 15W3, Box 143, WPD 3674-18.

31. Memorandum to the Assistant Chief of Staff, War Plans Division from General Blanding, December 14, 1939, National Archives, RG 165, 15W3, Box 143, WPD 3674-18.

32. Ibid.

33. Ibid.

34. Memorandum for the Chief of Staff from Lieutenant Colonel Buchanan, December 20, 1939, National Archives, RG 165, 15W3, Box 143, WPD 3674-18.

35. Ibid.

36. Ibid.

37. Memorandum for the Assistant Chief of Staff, War Plans Division from the Chief of Staff, January 3, 1940, National Archives, RG 165, 15W3, Box 143, WPD 3674-18.

38. Ibid.

39. Ibid.

40. Ibid.

41. Ibid.

42. Ibid.

43. *New York Times*, January 14, 1940, p. 35.

44. Memorandum for the Chief of Staff from General John F. Williams, February 26, 1940, National Archives, RG 165, Box 883, Chief of Staff Emergency Planning File.

45. Ibid.

46. *Ibid.* Of the twenty Guard division commanders queried, only three objected to the additional training. Eleven generals made specific qualifications to their support for the schedule. Only six commanders gave their unqualified concurrence.

47. Minutes of the Adjutants General Association Annual Conference, March 1940, p. 32 (National Guard Association Library).

48. For more information on the Roosevelt's attitude on sales of material to the Allies and the Woodring-Johnson dispute see Langer and Gleason, *Challenge to Isolation*, 290-291; and McFarland, *Harry H. Woodring*, 157-159.

49. Marshall departed for California earlier in the day to observe joint Army-Navy exercise. General Gasser took Marshall's place before the subcommittee.

50. U.S. Congress, Senate, Appropriations Committee, *Emergency Supplemental Appropriation Bill for 1940, hearing before a subcommittee of the Senate Committee on Appropriations*, 76th Cong., 3rd sess., 1940, p. 52.

51. Ibid.

52. Ibid.

53. Ibid.

54. *Army and Navy Journal*, January 27, 1940, p. 487.

55. See editor's note, *Marshall Papers*, II, 112.

56. General Milton A. Reckord to General George C. Marshall, February 13, 1940; General George C. Marshall to Major General Milton A. Reckord, February 15, 1940; Reckord to Marshall, February 20, 1940, George C. Marshall Papers, Box 82, File Folder 26 (Marshall Library).

57. General Blanding left the National Guard Bureau on January 31, 1940. Marshall selected Colonel John F. Williams as the new chief. Williams, who received the rank of major general as part of the assignment, was well versed in the operation of the Bureau having served Blanding as a staff officer from 1936 onward.

58. Report of Conference held in the Chief of Staff's office, February 16, 1940, p. 22 (document dated February 19, 1940), Marshall Foundation National Archives Project, Verifax 100, Item 762 (Marshall Library).

59. Ibid.

60. Ibid.

61. Ibid.

62. Ibid.

63. Ibid., 21.

64. U.S. Congress, House, Appropriations Committee, *Military Establishment Appropriation Bill for 1941, hearing before a subcommittee of the House Committee on Appropriations on H.R. 9209*, 76th Cong., 3 sess., 1940, p. 3.

65. Ibid., 12-13, 18-19.

66. Adjutants General Association notes, March 1940, p. 32 (National Guard Association Library).

67. Ibid., 33.

68. Ibid.

69. Ibid., 6.

70. Ibid.

71. Ibid.

72. Ibid., 7.

73. Ibid., 9.

74. Ibid., 7.

75. Ibid., 10.

76. Ibid.

77. Ibid., 11.

78. Ibid., 12.

79. Ibid., 13.

80. Ibid., 31-33.

81. Ibid., 37. The Senate began its deliberations on combining drills on the very day that the two associations considered the subject. See *Army and Navy Journal*, March 23, 1940, p. 670.

82. Adjutants General Association notes, March 1940, p. 37-38 (National Guard Association Library).

83. U.S. Congress, House, Appropriations Committee, *Military Establishment Appropriation Bill for 1941, hearing before a subcommittee of the House Committee on Appropriations H.R. 9209*, 76th Cong., 3rd sess., 1940, p. 858.

84. Ibid.

85. Ibid.

86. Ibid., 859.

87. Ibid., 861.

88. Ibid., 861.

89. Ibid.

90. Ibid., 867.

91. Ibid.

92. Ibid., 868.

93. Ibid.

94. Ibid.

95. Major General Milton A. Reckord to General Marshall, March 27, 1940, George C. Marshall Papers, Box 82, File Folder 26 (Marshall Library).

96. General Marshall to General Reckord, March 28, 1940, George C. Marshall Papers, Box 82, File Folder 26 (Marshall Library).

97. General Marshall to Mr. Bernard M. Baruch, April 3, 1940, Bland, ed., *Marshall Papers*, II, 188-189; *Army and Navy Journal*, March 6, 1940, p. 748; Adjutants General

Association notes, March 1940, p. 34 (National Guard Association Library).

98. General Reckord to General Marshall, April 4, 1940, George C. Marshall Papers, Box 82, File Folder 26 (Marshall Library).

99. Ibid.

100. Ibid.

101. U.S. Congress, House, *Congressional Record*, 76th Cong., 3rd sess., 1940, 86:4040-4041.

102. Ibid., 86:4041.

103. Draft memorandum for the Secretary of War, April 15, 1940, Bland, ed., *Marshall Papers*, II, 198.

104. Ibid.

105. See editor's notes, Bland, ed., *Marshall Papers*, II, 206.

106. U.S. Congress, Senate, *Appropriations Committee, Military Establishment Appropriation Bill for 1941, hearings before a subcommittee of the Senate Committee on Appropriations on H.R. 9209*, 76th Cong., 3 sess., 1940, p. 16.

107. Ibid.

108. Watson, *Chief of Staff*, 166.

109. Ibid.

4

Europe Blazes,
Washington Debates

There should be no delay . . . . My relief of mind would be
tremendous if we just had too much of something besides patriotism
and spirit.

—General George C. Marshall[1]

WAR IN THE WEST

In the early morning hours of May 10, 1940 Hitler unleashed the German
army against the Allies. Combining armor, infantry, and air assaults in a
ferocious blitzkrieg, they roared through the Low Countries. Three days later
the Germans smashed through the French Seventh Army, advancing even
more rapidly toward the coast. Pounded by relentless attacks, the Belgians
retreated. The Netherlands surrendered after four days, its lands flooded by
the populace in a vain attempt to slow the Nazi rampage. To the east
Colonel-General Gerd von Rundstedt and his army emerged from the
confines of the seemingly impenetrable Ardennes forest to fall upon the
Allies' left rear. Moving rapidly, the Germans crossed the Meuse River and
shattered the French Ninth Army in a separate drive to the sea. Once
German forces reached the English Channel, they could spring the trap on
the Allies, catching British and French forces between two pincers.

In Washington the eruption of war on the western front came as no
surprise. Just days before, the Minister to the Netherlands cabled Secretary
of State Hull that Queen Wilhelmina's government expected an invasion
within twenty-four hours. When Hitler struck, Roosevelt's only action was
to freeze "the credits of Belgium, Holland, and Luxembourg in the United
States so that the Nazis could not get possession of them."[2] When pressed

by King Leopold of Belgium for support in his nation's hour of crisis Roosevelt replied:

The people of the United States hope, as do I, that policies which seek to dominate peaceful and independent peoples through force and military aggression may be arrested, and that the Government and people of Belgium may preserve their integrity and their freedom.[3]

But beyond freezing Belgium's assets and arranging the evacuation of American citizens, the Administration could do little. The outbreak of war would inevitably lead to a renewal of isolationist pressure to remain neutral. The long prophesied European war had come and the isolationists were not about to let the nation be dragged into it.

The General Staff's view of the crisis had been shaped by long months of examining the question of general war in Europe. Planners concluded that although the danger of a German invasion of the hemisphere was in reality small, they might stir up trouble in Latin America. As a result Marshall traveled to the White House during the first morning of the German offensive to meet with Roosevelt, Treasury Secretary Henry Morgenthau and others. The Chief of Staff requested a two-step increase in manpower levels to bring the Army to its full peacetime strength of 280,000 men by the fall. Characteristically, Roosevelt made no decision on the request but ordered a complete summary of the plan for a Monday, May 13, meeting. After the meeting Morgenthau advised Marshall to prepare an overall picture for the President, not a detailed analysis. Marshall estimated the bill for his plan at $640,000,000 for fiscal year 1941. "The secretary [Morgenthau] declared that he was not frightened by the numbers, but Marshall said, 'It makes me dizzy.' 'It makes me dizzy if we don't get it,' Morgenthau responded." Taking Morgenthau's advice to heart Marshall drafted a brief proposal for the President to expand the Army by 38,000 men and to acquire needed equipment.

When Marshall arrived for the Monday meeting he found Roosevelt unwilling to discuss military preparedness. Morgenthau, who was becoming an outspoken ally of Marshall within the Administration, attempted to get Roosevelt to listen to the Chief of Staff's ideas but was curtly rebuffed. "I know exactly what he would say," stated the President. "There is no necessity for my hearing him at all."[4] Unperturbed, Marshall waited until the end of the meeting and then approached Roosevelt. In a determined manner the Chief of Staff strongly requested a few moments with the President. Roosevelt cheerfully agreed. During his few moments Marshall touched upon several subjects, but on the issues of more men and equipment he said: "I don't know quite how to express myself about this to the president of the United States, but I will say this, *you have got to do something and you've got to do it today* [emphasis his]."[5]

The General's stand impressed Morgenthau. That evening he told Marshall: "You did a swell job and I think you are going to get about 75% of what you want."[6] Roosevelt must have shared Morgenthau's feeling, for the next day he made up his mind. After a larger staff meeting, Roosevelt delayed Marshall and informed him that he would increase the Army, but not as much as Marshall had proposed. Roosevelt decided to cut some seacoast defenses and to reduce the manpower request to 15,000 men. These cuts reduced the required funds by $24,000,000. "But he added $80,000,000 for two hundred B-17 bombers and $106,000,000 for pilot training. The president was thus prepared to request $732,000,000 in added funds for fiscal year 1941 for the army."[7] Later that day Marshall wrote Bernard M. Baruch concerning the increases: "At the moment he declined to go further than 15,000; but . . . he stated that he would give me the remaining 38,000 in July by Executive Order, creating a deficiency."[8]

Roosevelt's decision was politically risky but well within the bounds of the possible. Many isolationists and their supporters, Lindbergh among them, viewed the Air Corps as a bulwark against possible invasion. The Army's planes could patrol the sea lanes near the coast, but because of their limited range they could not violate the nation's neutrality. Nevertheless, Marshall took the results of the meeting as a sign to proceed, using caution, with plans for further increases. As a result, Marshall directed Lieutenant Colonel Ward to order the Personnel Section (G-1) to prepare arguments for deficiency appropriations for increasing the Guard as well as the Army, a summary of the plan for Marshall's presentation to Roosevelt, and a draft executive order.[9]

That same day Morgenthau's respect for the Chief of Staff manifest itself in a brief letter to the President. It read:

My dear Mr. President:
In view of my experience with the Army during the last couple of days, I am taking the liberty of making a suggestion.

Let General Marshall, and only General Marshall, do all the testifying in connection with the Bill which you are about to send up for additional appropriations for the Army.

Yours sincerely,
H. Morgenthau, Jr.[10]

When Morgenthau informed Marshall of this letter several days later he told the General to let him know if trouble arose with Woodring or Johnson, for in essence the President was about to bypass the two civilian heads of the War Department. Woodring, a strong supporter of noninterventionism, had been gradually cut out of policy making and only survived in office because Roosevelt did not wish to antagonize the Secretary's isolationist supporters. Johnson, an outspoken interventionist, was therefore unlikely to receive a warm welcome on Capital Hill. Marshall became the logical choice as a spokesman for the Administration on defense preparedness. Marshall attributed this trust not so much to ability as to the high regard that many members of Congress held for him. "In the first place," Marshall told Forrest C. Pogue during a 1956 oral history interview, "they were certain I had no ulterior motive."[11] Voting large sums at the behest of a respected general undoubtedly seemed more acceptable to Congressmen than appearing to follow the President's lead.[12]

On May 16 Roosevelt took full advantage of the war raging in Europe to pressure Congress for additional funds for the military. As William E. Leuchtenburg wrote: "President Roosevelt, after explaining how enemy bombers could leave West Africa and emerge in the skies of Omaha, requested vast sums to mechanize and motorize the Army . . . and funds for 50,000 planes a year."[13] Using the War Department's concern over a possible invasion of Brazil from occupied French West Africa, should France fall, Roosevelt presented a request for $1,184,000,000 to improve national defense. Of that amount the Administration earmarked $732,000,000 for the Army with the intent of providing 28,000 more men and equipment "necessary to field a Protective Mobilization force of 750,000 plus replacements."[14]

MOBILIZING THE GUARD?

The crisis in Europe prompted at least one old Guardsman to call for an immediate mobilization of the National Guard. In a telegram to Congressman James W. Wadsworth of New York, author of the 1917 draft bill, retired Major General John F. O'Ryan, World War I commander of New York's Twenty-seventh Division, called for more decisive action on the part of the government. He stated, in part:

People now seem leagues ahead of government in understanding of aggression menace. Wilson mobilized Guard divisions on border as War without hostile public reaction though with presidential campaign pending. This of great value to later war efficiency. Our man power urgently requires mobilization and training as defense measure for eventualities.[15]

O'Ryan's association with Wadsworth went back as early as 1920, when the General supported Wadsworth's proposal to turn the Guard "into a predominantly federal force."[16] His 1920 stand, endorsed by Reckord, on closer ties between Guard and the Army placed him in good stead in the War Department. However, his 1940 call for an early Guard mobilization placed him too far ahead of either the Army or the Guard.

Marshall received a copy of the telegram from Congressman Walter G. Andrews of New York, ranking Republican on the House Military Affairs

Committee, who sought the Chief of Staff's reaction. Marshall did not agree with O'Ryan's contention that the time had come to mobilize the Guard. He defended Roosevelt's course by saying "that he [Roosevelt] had moved in each instance almost as rapidly as public opinion would permit."[17] Marshall viewed mobilization of the Guard at that time as adding complications for the Army, the Guard, and the nation. Federalization meant diverting scarce resources from training and equipping the Army—Marshall's first priority—to supplying the Guard. He suggested increasing the Army by using young reserve officers and the Civilian Conservation Corps before causing the disruption of families and of the economy that federalizing the Guard entailed.[18]

O'Ryan's proposal did not set well with some members of the Guard leadership. General Haskell of New York sent Marshall a letter on May 28 clearly stating his, and presumably others', views on the subject. He wrote:

I just thought I would drop you this note to let you know that everyone up here doesn't agree with General O'Ryan's telegram. At least they don't agree with it unless and until you are able to foresee the continued use of the Guard in Federal service and the imminence involvement of the United States in war.[19]

But evidently the old New York General's telegram focused a number of legislators' attention on the idea. On the surface mobilizing the Guard would virtually double the size of the Army at little additional cost in equipment. But as early as May 17, Marshall began working to dispel any such idea even though the defeats the Allies suffered in Europe increased the danger to national security.

SEARCHING FOR ALTERNATIVES

On May 21, just eleven days after the offensive began, German forces reached the English Channel, effectively splitting the Allied forces in two. Squeezed from the south and east the Allies began a retreat to the sea. On May 27, Belgium surrendered, exposing the British and French forces trapped in the pocket. Winston S. Churchill, the newly installed British Prime Minister, ordered the evacuation of the British Expeditionary Force from the Continent.

The success of the German offensive rekindled concerns in Washington that a victory by Germany over France would lead to the German occupation of French colonial possessions. In particular, the General Staff feared that the Nazis might take over Dakar, French West Africa as a springboard for aggression in South America. In a secret memorandum to Marshall, Major Matthew B. Ridgway crystallized these concerns, plus the possibility of Japanese action in the Far East. Paragraph one briefly sketched the danger.

1. Further imminently probable complications of today's situation are:

a. Nazi-inspired revolution in Brazil.

b. Widespread disorders with attacks on U.S. citizens in Mexico and raids along our southern border.

c. Japanese hostilities against the United States in the Far East.

d. Decisive Allied defeat, followed by German aggression in the Western Hemisphere.

e. All combined.[20]

Ridgway stated that the lack of resources precluded any hope of defending American interests in Europe or the Far East. He concluded that the United States could mount only limited operations in the Western Hemisphere, including the occupation of European possessions to keep them out of German hands. Ridgway's final paragraph, echoing the thoughts of many in the War Department, called for planning and an early decision on what to do and what must be done.[21]

Marshall presented the memorandum to Roosevelt, Sumner Welles, and the Chief of Naval Operations, Admiral Harold R. Stark, that same afternoon. They agreed with the analysis of the situation, believing that United States involvement should stay within the boundary of the Western Hemisphere. Marshall suggested dispatching cruisers, with Marines aboard, to South American east coast ports "to be available to support the existing governments in the event of an attempted Nazi overthrow."[22]

Roosevelt's positive reaction at the meeting encouraged Marshall, as undoubtedly did the sudden change of mood in the public and in Congress. The public and Congress became increasingly concerned over military preparedness in the wake of the disaster in Flanders. More interventionist-minded public figures began looking for means to improve preparedness. Republican Frank Knox, whom Roosevelt had privately selected as the next Secretary of the Navy, founded a private organization to create volunteer pilot training camps in each of the nine corps areas. Grenville Clark's Military Training Camps Association (MTCA) endorsed this idea, an off-shoot of their own, while at the same time pressed for the immediate introduction of compulsory military training act. When approached by members of the MTCA for Army support of a conscription, Marshall gave his permission for a private meeting between the MTCA committee, retired General John McAuley Palmer and active duty Major Lewis B. Hershey, the General Staff's expert and planner on the draft. However, the Chief of Staff was careful not to give any public indication that he, or the Administration, endorsed a draft for fear of an isolationist reaction.[23]

As British troops evacuated Flanders, Marshall decided to press for more money for men and equipment; in all the Chief of Staff requested $709,000,000. The General's wife, Katherine Marshall, recorded the President's reaction as follows:

At first the President was outraged at Mr. Morgenthau and George bringing up a proposal for a second message after so short a time, but he was quickly convinced that he really had no choice in the matter, it clearly must be done, and George worked on the draft of a second message.[24]

The draft Marshall produced pinpointed Army needs for planes and mechanized equipment. Germany's lightning victories vividly illustrated the value of coordinated aviation and mechanized assaults. Therefore, he requested $90,000,000 for tanks and mechanized equipment and $300,000,000 "for 2,850 combat airplanes completely equipped, to speed up existing production facilities and to provide for the further increase of the GHQ Air Force."[25]

The issue of filling the gap between the Regular Army and a national Army raised after hostilities commenced also concerned Marshall. The General Staff believed that, if trouble came to the hemisphere, deploying the small numbers of Regular troops available would leave the nation virtually defenseless. Although considered only partially trained and equipped, the National Guard represented the only available force that could fill the void caused by a sudden departure of Regular Army soldiers. Under the laws that governed the Guard, the President could either "call" or "order" the Guard to active federal service, but under limited circumstances. By "calling" the Guard, the President requested its use from state governors, as set forth under the Militia Clause of the Constitution and the Militia Act. However, governors could ignore a "call," especially those opposed to Roosevelt or who felt the political pressure from isolationists. A "call" had other flaws. The law limited the called militia (National Guard of the Several States) to repelling an invasion or suppressing an insurrection, not relieving Regular troops for duty elsewhere. The Army therefore had limited control over the Guard. As a result, neither the War Department nor the president seriously considered a calling of the Guard.

The ability to "order" the National Guard to active duty stemmed from an untested provision of the NGA sponsored National Defense Act of 1933. As written, Roosevelt could order members of the National Guard of the Several States to federal service as part of the National Guard of the United States, a federally controlled reserve force of the Army. Here too the President and his advisors ran into a snag. The law stipulated that the Guard could be ordered to duty only after Congress declared a state of national emergency. The timing of a Guard mobilization greatly concerned Marshall because the Guard would have to fill the gap between the Army and a larger national army. The danger to the United Stated increased if Congress recessed prior to an emergency. Roosevelt foresaw the possibility that even if Congress could be summoned in a few days isolationists could filibuster a bill in the Senate ordering the Guard to active service. In an "eleventh hour" decision urged by Marshall, Roosevelt's defense message of May 31 included a request for authority to order the Guard to duty if Congress was in recess.[26] The section of Roosevelt's May 31 address read:

There is a specific recommendation I would make in concluding this message, that before adjournment this Congress grant me the authority to call into active service such portion of the National Guard as may be deemed necessary to maintain our position of neutrality and to safeguard the National Defense, this to include authority to call into active service the necessary Reserve personnel.[27]

CONGRESSIONAL REACTION

Although the President found support for his measure, several members of Congress, including Democrats, reacted negatively to his request. Senator Warren R. Austin of Vermont, a conservative Republican who had long opposed granting Roosevelt additional powers, stated: "I think we will be here all Summer before we grant that power. There will have to be some justification that doesn't appear now before Congress will be willing to do it, in my opinion."[28] Democratic Senator Walter F. George of Georgia, a political opponent of Roosevelt who had survived the 1938 purge, told reporters: "If the President seriously insists on this request, I think Congress will say: 'Mr. President, if there is an emergency of this nature in the offing, of which the country now knows nothing, we will stay here to meet it.'"[29] Senator Arthur H. Vandenberg of Michigan, a Republican presidential hopeful, called the proposal "shocking."[30]

On the evening of June 1, Republican Senator Robert A. Taft of Ohio, who was also running for the Republican presidential nomination, addressed the nation by radio. He lashed out first against the Administration's handling of the nation's defense and then against the request for increased authority over the Guard. On the first point Taft told the nation:

We are unprepared for attack by any foreign nation, or the possibility of a German victory, although the President has been talking about [it] for several years. . . .

The announcements and activities so far consist primarily in a demand for more power for the executive, without any detailed explanation as to why that power is necessary.[31]

As for the Guard, the Ohio senator challenged the need:

The Constitution authorizes the Congress to provide for calling out the National Guard first, to enforce the laws of the United States; second, to suppress insurrection; third, to repel invasion. We certainly don't need it to enforce the laws or suppress insurrection. Certainly no invasion is threatened today, and as soon as any such threat comes Congress should be called in session.

The demand for authority to call out the National Guard to repel invasion suggests a lack of sound judgement in the whole preparedness excitement.[32]

Faced with strident, although not numerous, objections, the President called a meeting at the White House for June 3. Although no meeting notes exist, those present were apparently Roosevelt, General Marshall, Representative Andrew J. May (chairman of the House Military Affairs Committee), Senate Majority Leader Alben Barkley, perhaps Secretary Morgenthau, and a few others. It seems likely that from what transpired later in the day this secret group discussed the situation and how best to handle critics. Representative May composed the language of the administration proposal ordering the Guard to active duty during a Congressional recess, authority to expire once the new Congress convened. The meeting also reached apparent agreement on strategy. The White House would pull back from the measure with only key Congressmen and Marshall acting as advocates. Within hours of the meeting, May introduced House Joint Resolution 555, which encapsulated Roosevelt's request and the agreed changes.[33]

PLANNING A MOBILIZATION

The issue of mobilization emerged in War Department discussions well before Roosevelt requested such authority. Marshall personally and professionally wished to delay calling the Guard into federal service and so advised Roosevelt in a June 4 memo.[34] He favored filling the Army's needs by the Civilian Volunteer Effort, "a high pressure civilian recruiting plan which had been drawn up under G-1 supervision."[35] Marshall believed early mobilization would strain the Army's personnel and material, and no doubt the political consequences of such an act also influenced him. Early federalization of the Guard, the General Staff feared, would cause adverse Congressional and public reaction.[36]

Despite his reluctance to push for mobilization of the Guard, Marshall recognized the need to plan for that eventuality. On May 29, 1940, two days before Roosevelt's message to Congress, Marshall held a special mobilization planning conference with Generals Williams (National Guard Bureau), Frank M. Andrews (Operations Section, or G-3), William E. Shedd (G-1), and Strong (WPD) attending. Several officers from the General Staff and NGB outlined a plan that mobilized units of the National Guard of the United States in successive increments. This made them more "digestible," that is, allowing the Army to absorb federalized units with the least harm to its structure and material. Planners feared that too great an influx of men would necessitate dispersing Regulars to train newly inducted units. The conferees also considered the national economic impact of a large-scale induction. Calling men from vital industries would delay production of needed war materials and disrupt local economies.[37]

As a result, the conference set priorities for mobilizing the Guard. Those present decided that the first priority would consist of "four infantry divisions, seven antiaircraft regiments, and certain harbor-defense units."[38] These units would come from "geographical locations which would least disturb industry."[39] They would enter service at maintenance strength with the infantry divisions stripped of their tank and aviation units. Even trimmed these units added a minimum of 40,000 men to the Army's ranks.[40]

The conference did not detail plans for second and third priorities but agreed that the second priority would be the induction of General Headquarters units, antiaircraft and medical regiments, and the Texas cavalry.[41] The third priority simply called for "all other units, balance of cavalry," including remaining infantry units and the Guard's twenty-one observation squadrons.[42]

As a result of the May 29 meeting, work began on an induction plan. On June 4, the War Plans Division gave to Marshall a preliminary plan titled "Plan for Partial Induction of the Nation Guard," breaking the original four priorities into six and redistributing the types of units required.[43] In the first priority, two brigades and five regiments of infantry along with artillery, antiaircraft, medical, engineering, signal, and quartermaster regiments would be ordered out. Second came four infantry divisions and fixed harbor defense units; and third were signal, artillery, medical, cavalry, and twenty-one observation squadrons. Under the plan, the remaining fourteen infantry divisions joined federal service under the fourth (nine divisions) and fifth priorities (five divisions). The balance of the National Guard entered federal service as the sixth priority.[44]

On the same day that the mobilization plan reached his desk, Marshall appeared before the House Committee on Military Affairs in support of House Joint Resolution 555, the interim Guard mobilization bill. His strategy, probably set at the June 3 meeting with Roosevelt, was to portray the measure as merely a contingency plan to be used in national defense.[45] Such a strategy left isolationists who strongly supported national defense, but opposed Roosevelt, little ground for opposing the measure. The resolution read:

To provide for the observance, safeguarding, and enforcement of neutrality, and the strengthening of the national defense, and the promotion of peace.

Resolved by the Senate and House of Representatives of the United States of America in Congress assembled. That if, at any time prior to the convening of the Seventy-seventh Congress, the present Congress is not in session and, in the opinion of the President, a national emergency arises requiring the use of troops in excess of those of the Regular Army, the President be, and is thereby, authorized to use any or all reserve components of the Army of the United States and returned personnel of the Regular Army to such extent and in such manner as he may deem necessary for the proper observance, safeguarding, and enforcement of the neutrality of the United States, and for the strengthening of the National defense.[46]

In his testimony, Marshall described to the committee, as he had earlier to the President, the constraints the established laws placed on use of the Guard. However, the Chief of Staff stressed that he in no way wished to mobilize the Guard. "We are adverse," he told the committee, "to mobilizing it at all if we can possibly get away from it."[47] Yet he acknowledged the possibility:

We visualize a partial mobilization of certain phases as we get them so they do not involve too much hardship to the men in civil activities and generally dragging in the National Guard unless it is clearly apparent that we have to have them for this present critical situation, whatever that may be.[48]

Marshall stated his desire to build-up Regular forces first, then to mobilize the reserves as needed. Making the Guard ready came third on his list.[49]

During the open hearing, the issue of when the proposed act had force aroused some concern. Texas Democrat R. Ewing Thomason, a supporter of the Administration's efforts, aware that isolationists already objected to the issue, asked Marshall: "What is the situation if something might develop when Congress is in session? What is the effect and force of this resolution if enacted into law?" The Chief of Staff deferred to Major General Allen W. Gullion, the Judge Advocate General, as a legal expert on the matter. Gullion informed Thomason that "If the present Congress is in session then the resolution will have no effect," and Roosevelt's power would dissolve when Congress reconvened.[50]

However, the truly divisive issue surfaced in the closed session as a result of Marshall's statement made in the public session on the scope of possible Guard deployments. At least three times, Marshall implied the possibility of sending Guard units outside the continental United States but within the Western Hemisphere. Congressman Thomason had asked a direct question on this point: "General Marshall, if Congress does adjourn and this House Joint Resolution is passed and the National Guard is called out, would this resolution give you the right and power to send Guardsmen out of the United Stated?" "Yes, sir, it would," responded Marshall. But he added, "We could not send the National Guard until they had long training."[51]

In closed session, after hearing Marshall's testimony, a split developed in the committee. Neither side denied the need for such a stop-gap measure; however, there was disagreement on what limitations to place on Roosevelt's power to send the Guard outside U.S. territory. The majority report quoted General Marshall's warnings and assurances virtually word for word, but stopped short of granting the President authority to send Guardsmen outside of American territory. While they believed the President could "call" the Guard into service under "existing law it would be impossible to send any part or units of the Guard to assist a Regular Army division in any one of the possible situations which might arise in this hemisphere."[52] As a result they amended the bill by inserting: "but shall not order same beyond the limits of continental United stated except to its territories and possessions, including the Panama Canal Zone."[53] The majority held "that the regular forces [could] be increased to a number sufficient to provide a suitable force for such eventualities."[54]

Eight members of the committee, including chairman Andrew J. May of Kentucky, differed with the majority. They maintained that the Regular Army did not possess enough men and could not acquire men fast enough to meet an external threat to the hemisphere. As an example, the author of the supplemental report recalled the image of General Pershing's 1916 Mexican expedition against Pancho Villa. Had the Guard been used in the pursuit, he believed, "the results would have been much more satisfactory."[55] Under the law at that time, the Guard could not venture beyond the border. While Pershing's too few Regular troops ineffectively pursued Villa, the Guard patrolled the border.[56] The minority committee members, fearing a recurrence of just such a situation where American troops would be stretched thinly throughout the hemisphere, concluded that the President needed greater authority.[57]

THE JUNE 17 MEETING

The fortunes of the French Army declined rapidly in the two weeks following Marshall's testimony on House Joint Resolution 555. By June 14 the Germans occupied Paris and had cornered French forces behind their own Maginot Line. Three days later the French government decided to sue for terms.

At 8:30 A.M. on June 17, General Marshall met with Generals George V. Strong (WPD), Frank M. Andrews (G-3) and Richard C. Moore (G-4). The European situation cast a pall over each man present. Marshall and the others already knew of Petain's ascent to power in France and his plan to capitulate. This development, plus Italian entry into the war on June 10, intensified concerns that Germany would soon control the French fleet and that combined Axis naval power would pose a dire threat to Great Britain. As General Strong wrote on December 15, 1945: "We believed at that time that German control of the French fleet would create a very serious situation in the South Atlantic. Should Great Britain fail, a hostile move toward South America was far from unlikely."[58] As a result of the collapse of the French army, the possibility of German control of the French fleet, the fighting between Russia and Japan, and Japan's war in China, Generals Strong and Andrews advised Marshall to federalize the National Guard.[59]

The June 17 meeting set the stage for a change in the Army's direction. Events in Europe and growing pressure at home for preparedness forced the General Staff to make a two-step decision. Staff planners began working towards the mobilization of the National Guard, either in whole or in part, to bolster the Army's ranks. At the same time the General Staff joined a growing civilian movement and pressured the White House for the nation's first peacetime draft. While the War Department had resisted conscription, the pressure of recent events made the two-phase plan the only alternative.[60]

That same day, Secretary of State Hull invited the foreign ministers of the American republics to meet in Havana, Cuba to discuss hemispheric defense. Hull was reluctant to take such a step but decided to call the meeting because of German pressure against the republics and because of the danger of Germany occupying French American colonies as spoils of war.[61]

GRENVILLE CLARK AND A PEACETIME DRAFT

The Army was not alone in its concern for an adequate supply of men to fill the ranks. In fact, its concern fell behind that of a private interventionist group that had long called for Universal Military Training of the nation's young men. One of the prominent leaders of this group was Grenville Clark, a former law partner of Elihu Root, Jr., and a long time friend of Roosevelt. On May 22, 1915, in the wake of the sinking of the British passenger liner *Lusitania*, Clark and Root decided to "do something to demonstrate a firm national policy against Germany."[62] Taking the Plattsburg, New York, civilian training camps as a model, they, along with Theodore Roosevelt, Jr., formed what would become the Military Training Camps Association, an organization to train young men as reserve officers. Although civilian in nature, the Association had the blessing and cooperation of the Army and even gained legal stature in 1920 as the Citizens' Military Training Camps (CMTC). Between 1925 and 1928 the CMTC trained nearly 20,000 young men.[63] On May 22, 1940, at the height of the battle for France, Grenville Clark and the members of the Military Training Camps Association met to commemorate their organization's twenty-fifth anniversary. Face with a situation similar to the one in 1915, Clark used the dinner to stimulate the old movement toward a new Selective Service law to improve the nation's defense. Two guests would become deeply involved in the drive for the first peacetime draft in American history. One was Former Secretary of State Henry L. Stimson;[64] soon to join the Roosevelt administration as Secretary of War, he vigorously campaigned for the establishment of a Selective Service. The other, retired Brigadier General John M. Palmer, champion of the citizen-soldier concept of national defense, used his connections with the War Department to gain Marshall's permission to meet with representatives of the joint Army and Navy Selective Service Committee, which was established during World War I and maintained selective service planning in case of war. However, no one in the Administration gave official backing to the Training Camps Association's proposal. Open support of a peacetime draft would have set the Administration on a collision course with the isolationists before the public was ready to accept the idea.[65]

Undaunted, Clark and his associates took their proposal to Capitol Hill, enlisting the aid of Senator Edward R. Burke, an anti-New Deal Democrat from Nebraska, and conservative Republican Congressman James W. Wadsworth, Jr., of New York. Wadsworth was a natural source of support for Clark because he had written the 1917 Draft Act and proposed a federally controlled reserve force in 1920. Neither man maintained close ties with Roosevelt. Indeed, both men supported Wendell L. Willkie for the presidency. On June 20, 1940, the day before France capitulated, Burke and Wadsworth introduced similar selective service bills in their respective houses of Congress.[66]

THE WAR DEPARTMENT MOVES TOWARD A DRAFT

Marshall's June 17 meeting ended voluntary recruitment as a formal policy. Although he had previously opposed a draft, Marshall now saw no alternative means to raise the needed manpower. Having reached that decision, his next task was to convince the President to back a conscription plan in peacetime, a difficult task in a year when a predominately isolationist American would be electing a president.

Marshall's staff consulted with their Navy counterparts and by June 22 had prepared a draft memorandum titled "Basis for Immediate Decisions Concerning the National Defense." Marshall and Chief of Naval Operations Admiral Harold R. Stark planned to present the document to Roosevelt to convey their concerns over national defense and to offer courses of action on such subjects as: the distribution of naval forces if Germany gained control of the French fleet; arms to Britain; defense of the Western Hemisphere; increased defense production; and increased manpower by means of a draft "along the lines of existing plans . . . followed at once by complete military and naval mobilization."[67] Both men knew that Roosevelt would hesitate on any form of military conscription, yet they believed it was the only way to adequately bring in men. True to form, Roosevelt declined to decide on conscription.

In their historical work, *The First Peacetime Draft*, J. Garry Clifford and Samuel R. Spencer speculated on reasons why Roosevelt delayed supporting either Clark's or the War Department's selective service measure. They offered two main reasons. First, the President did not believe a draft was vital to American security despite obvious shortcomings in the military establishment. Acquiring more war material took precedence on the President's agenda. Additionally, providing war material to Britain, including forty or fifty World War I vintage destroyers that Churchill requested on May 15, seemed a better defense at that time than did a draft.[68]

The second, and more complex, reason was the political ramifications of the President's actions, either planned or executed, in an election year. Roosevelt, who was about to make an unprecedented third term bid, considered timing all important. By June he was already contemplating several actions that would surely arouse the ire of isolationists, the Republicans, and anti-Roosevelt Democrats. Churchill's request was one such decision upon which, like the draft, Roosevelt could not bring himself to take immediate action, so placed it on a back burner. Another was the removal of his noninterventionist Secretary of War Harry Woodring, who had considerable support in Congress. Roosevelt had long considered replacing the Secretary but did not judge the moment right until after France signed the armistice with Germany on June 21. The international situation was now critical enough to allow Roosevelt to name Republican Henry L. Stimson as Woodring's replacement. At the same time he named another Republican, Frank Knox, as Secretary of the Navy. Including two Republicans in the Cabinet who were not always in favor of Roosevelt's New Deal, was, to be sure, a political ploy to undercut Republican criticism. However, Woodring's resignation and the nomination of two prominent Republican internationalists, coming just days before the Republicans convention, was a decided turn toward the interventionists.[69]

By the time of the introduction of the Burke-Wadsworth bill, Roosevelt was actively considering a third term, which in itself would involve criticism from several political quarters. To publicly support the draft before a national consensus developed risked alienating even more voters. He also had to consider the Republican's choice for president as part of his strategy. If the GOP nominated an isolationist, supporting a draft measure might give the Republicans powerful political ammunition. Therefore he waited to see their nominee. New York Governor Thomas Dewey had made an impressive showing in the primaries, especially for one so young and with limited political experience. However, public concern over national defence after the German victories in Western Europe rapidly cut into his popularity. Historian William E. Luechtenburg stated that "the deeper the Panzer divisions drove toward Paris, the less did young Dewey seem the man for the job."[70] Two conservative isolationists also threw their hats into the presidential ring—Senators Arthur H. Vandenberg of Michigan and Robert A. Taft. However, internationalists Alf Landon and soon-to-be Secretary of the Navy Frank Knox fought against their respective candidacies, indirectly aiding the dark-horse nomination of Wendell Willkie, a one time Democrat and president of Commonwealth and Southern Corporation who fought unsuccessfully against Roosevelt's Tennessee Valley Authority (TVA). Although he lost the TVA fight, his persuasive style and country manner won increasing support among anti-New Dealers.

Willkie's nomination posed a dilemma for Roosevelt. The selection of a candidate not firmly in the isolationist camp relieved the President. Roosevelt "considered this nomination a 'Godsend to the country,' for it tended to remove the isolationist-interventionist issue from the campaign . . . and thereby prevented the splitting of the people into two embittered factions."[71] Yet as a challenger, Roosevelt "considered Willkie the most formidable opponent for himself that the Republicans could have named."[72] In public opinion polls taken during the last week of July, fifty-one percent of the respondence favored the President while Willkie garnered forty-nine percent,[73] indicating that Roosevelt might not win a third term by a landslide, as he had in 1932 and 1936.[74]

Although Willkie privately favored a draft, publicly he remained silent on the issue, thus courting both sides of his party as well as wayward Democrats and forcing Roosevelt into a waiting game over the issue.[75]

Despite the political ramifications of their proposal, on June 24 the Army and Navy chiefs presented their memorandum to Roosevelt. He gave his opinion on each point, adding to some, subtracting from others. As for mobilization, he struck the word "complete" replacing it with "progressive". Roosevelt then expressed "his dislike for the [Burke-Wadsworth] draft plan itself, outlining 'at considerable length' his own views."[76] Roosevelt wanted more than just young men conscripted to fill the ranks of the Army and Navy. He wanted a year of service to the government in such other places as "arsenals and factories, or in mechanical training, others in the Civilian Conservation Corps or an equivalent."[77] Marshall and Stark made the required changes and returned to the White House three days later. If Marshall expected the President to quickly throw his political weight behind a draft plan or mobilization, he was disappointed. Roosevelt would take no immediate action. The political atmosphere was too unsettled for such a drastic move and the President was personally unwilling to take such a step.

THE GUARD'S REACTION TO THE DRAFT BILL

As with Roosevelt, the National Guard Association through its chief lobbyist, General Reckord, hesitated in fully backing the Selective Training and Service bill. Shortly after the bill's introduction, Reckord obtained two copies of it and returned to his Baltimore headquarters. The next morning, he gave a copy to members of his staff for close examination and took the other copy for his own critique. Halfway through his reading of the bill, Reckord received a call from an unnamed member of the Training Camps Association Committee, who requested that the Guard send a representative to the next day's hearing. Reckord himself agreed to go but told the caller that the Guard opposed the bill as written. Reckord's friend was concerned over possible NGA opposition.[78] Years later Reckord recalled the ensuing conversation:

Then I heard him talk to some other gentleman who afterwards proved to be Mr. [Grenville] Clark, and finally he introduced Mr. Clark to me over the telephone, and Mr. Clark asked me to withhold my fire until they could see me the next day, which I agreed to do.[79]

Reckord had ample reason to suspect Clark's intentions. In 1912, Clark had pushed the Plattsburg Movement of civilian summer camps to train reserve officers, writing one of his friends that "everyone interested in getting a sound system is preparing to knife the National Guard at the first opportunity."[80] But Reckord remained true to his word and attended the next day's hearing. Afterward, he met with members of the Military Training Camps Association and informed Clark and others that the bill, as presented, would destroy the National Guard. In Reckord's opinion, the bill ignored the Guard's role in national defense as expressed in the amended National Defense Act of 1916. As proposed, Burke-Wadsworth forced draftees into the Army Reserve once they completed a year's training. Undoubtedly Reckord pointed to this proposed bypassing of the Guard as the major source of friction between the NGA and MTCA. Amending the bill to allow men to complete their obligation in the Guard, after basic training, would greatly ease any objection. Although Clark's opinion of the Guard may not have changed since 1912, he recognized the political reality of the NGA's strength. On July 5, he told the press that a "carefully worded amendment would be offered early [that] next week to solve the one question raised . . . by National Guard officers."[81]

On July 9, 10, and 11, members of the NGA's Executive Council and the Legislative Committee met in Washington to consider the draft bill and other legislation pending in Congress. Major Lewis B. Hershey, the General Staff's expert on selective service planning, briefed them on the contents of the draft bill. After hearing Major Hershey, Association President DeLamater and Generals Reckord, Birkhead, Martin, Walsh and Grahl met to study the bill. That evening the special committee returned with a package of amendments designed to protect Guard interests.

Pressing first and foremost for an amendment written by Reckord to reaffirm the Guard's place in national defense, they also called for the Guard to "be at all times maintained and assured," thus ensuring its continued existence.[82] The committee also stated that when Congress required troops in excess of the Regular Army, it would order the Guard to "active Federal Service and [continue] therein so long as such necessity exist[ed]."[83] Additionally, committee members proposed an amendment to exempt Guardsmen from selective service registration, because they were already in military service under the terms of the National Defense Act of 1933. The generals also formalized Reckord's recommendation to Clark that men could serve out their last two years of military obligation in the Guard.[84]

These amendments offered the Guard a greater opportunity to use the draft to its advantage. If selective service became permanent, as Reckord expected, then the Guard's recruiting troubles would be gone forever.[85]

ROOSEVELT'S RELUCTANT MOVES

By the second week of July, Roosevelt began to respond to Marshall's pressure and the growing popularity of the Burke-Wadsworth bill, but he continued to move cautiously. On July 11, the day after being sworn in as Secretary of War, Stimson transmitted to Roosevelt a proposed joint resolution drafted by the War Department at the president's earlier request. It asked Congress for authority to order the National Guard of the United States into active service. The next day Roosevelt tested the political waters by announcing that he might federalize four Guard divisions if Congress passed appropriate legislation. However, Roosevelt did not send the War Department's draft resolution to Congress.[86]

In early July the British were in serious trouble. The Germans were consolidating their victory over France and threatened to invade Britain. On July 4, America's concern deepened with the news that a portion of the French fleet had surrendered to German control. While the War and Navy Departments viewed this development with dread, the President made no forthright statement of support for the Burke-Wadsworth bill or any other action to increase military manpower.

When confronted with questions concerning a draft in general and more pointedly Burke-Wadsworth, Roosevelt brushed the matter aside, remarking that due consideration would be given the bill. He then told reporters, as he had Marshall and Stark, that he favored the idea of compulsory government training "as differentiated from military training," but he did not elaborate.[87] Roosevelt's July 9 remarks indicated his uncertainty over public acceptance of a draft. Still testing the political waters, he allowed Marshall and others to begin addressing the issue of a draft but only in a general way.

On July 12, Marshall appeared before the Senate Military Affairs Committee on the subject of a draft, informing senators that although June witnessed the largest influx of volunteers until that time (15,000 men) it was still not enough.[88] Marshall stated he supported a draft but conspicuously omitted direct mention of Burke-Wadsworth. He did warn the committee that if they chose to draft men, one of two things must take place:

Either we must mobilize the National Guard for the purpose of training these men in its ranks, and also in the ranks of the Regular Army units, where we must have more men as quickly as possible, or we will have to emasculate the Regular Army and emasculate the National Guard, at this time, in order to provide the necessary training cadres to handle the new men in the manner that it would be desirable.[89]

He stressed to the committee that the Army simply could not handle training large groups of raw recruits. "Therefore," he informed then, "we would have to make the first step within the ranks of the Regular establishment, and within the ranks of the National Guard."[90] Marshall wanted the Guard for only one year but no longer.

The next day, Marshall reinforced these views in a statement to *Life* magazine, only a portion of which the magazine published. In the short piece, Marshall cast favorable light on Burke-Wadsworth but again insisted first on Guard mobilization. In conclusion he wrote: "The immediate adoption of some such method for increasing the strength of our armed forces is vital to our security."[91] But Marshall shared Secretary Stimson's view that the Congress would not move immediately.[92]

Nor did Roosevelt quicken his pace toward on endorsement of a draft. Willkie had remained silent on the issue, giving the President little room to maneuver. An early endorsement by Roosevelt left Willkie the opportunity to oppose the proposed draft law and thus gain the support of those opposed to Burke-Wadsworth. Although most politicians expected Roosevelt to run, many, including Burton K. Wheeler, thought a third term bid would be a mistake. As Wheeler told the President in early 1940, a third term bid would provide more ammunition for opponents and a defeat would wreck the New Deal. Although Roosevelt agreed with Wheeler that a third term was out of the question, events in Europe changed his mind. Yet Roosevelt told no one of his intentions.[93]

With Roosevelt's candidacy uncertain, a political vacuum developed in the Democratic Party, which Vice-President John Garner, Secretary of State Cordell Hull, and Postmaster General Jim Farley sought to fill. Wheeler, too, was considered by some as a likely candidate, although he later discounted any notion of a serious candidacy. The President neither encouraged nor discouraged their campaigns. Historian William E. Leuchtenburg speculated that Roosevelt decided to seek an unprecedented third term in late May due largely to the European crisis, but he would only run if it appeared as a draft.[94] Roosevelt allowed the Chicago convention to commence on July 15 with all its political battles. Then, on July 16, Roosevelt had Senate Majority Leader Alben Barkley, a loyal supporter, read a statement to the convention freeing delegates to vote for whomever they wished. The announcement prompted a demonstration organized by Chicago's Mayor Edward J. Kelly, who may have been prompted by Harry Hopkins, to draft Roosevelt. Roosevelt won the "forced" nomination on the first ballot.[95]

During his acceptance speech on July 19, Roosevelt touched briefly on the subject of a draft, telling the convention that "most right thinking persons are agreed that some form of selection by draft is as necessary and fair today as it was in 1917 and 1918."[96] This public endorsement of a draft measure undoubtedly encouraged Stimson, Marshall, and Clark. Later, on the same day, Secretary of War Stimson presented yet another draft of a joint resolution calling the Guard to active service, now changing it from permanent to temporary legislation in hopes of making it more palatable to Congress. But Roosevelt, apparently waiting to gauge the public's reaction to his speech and candidacy, made no move on the issue.[97]

By July 27, Marshall felt that Roosevelt had once again abandoned the idea of seeking authority to federalize the Guard as part of the selective service measure. On that day an exasperated Marshall wrote Secretary Stimson concerning Roosevelt's remarks at the previous day's press conference. His memo read in part:

The president was asked if he had any further program to submit to Congress that might hold them in session but he answered that as far as he knew now the Selective Service bill was holding their attention and that he had no other measure contemplated at this time that would be of sufficient importance to hold them in session.[98]

That Saturday morning Marshall called the White House concerning the Guard resolution. On July 29 he again wrote Stimson concerning the matter: "While we were not able to obtain definite information, it appears that he has not sent that Resolution to Congress."[99]

Marshall's frustration became apparent as he directed an appeal to the Secretary of War:

These delays are daily growing more serious from several points of view: the lack of adequate number of trained troops, in the present international situation; and now the dilemma in which the War Department is rapidly being thrown by reason of our inability to start construction in the camps necessary for the National Guard, and for the compulsory trainees, in time to have them ready in the event that the necessary legislative authority is given us . . . the longer this matter is delayed the less time we have to make preparations against the cold weather of early fall.[100]

The Chief of Staff proposed a memorandum to Roosevelt in the hope that some camp construction could begin. However, that day Roosevelt sent identical letters of transmittal to the President of the Senate and the Speaker of the House with the Army's proposed joint resolution empowering Roosevelt to federalize the Guard. Characterizing the international situation as increasingly serious, he told lawmakers that only "seasoned and highly trained troops [could] hope for success in combat."[101] Some Guardsmen had already obtained a high level of preparedness, but they needed more training. He proposed ordering "the guard to duty in successive increments to permit the effective use of training facilities and equipment immediately available," with each increment to "be released when it attains the desired state of efficiency."[102]

Roosevelt's decision to request authority to mobilize the Guard left him two possible courses of action. If he gained authority from Congress, he could federalize the Guard for training and to bolster the national defense without a draft. While some isolationists and the Republican party might grumble, they would not seriously object to federalization, each group having taken public stands for a prepared national defense.[103] However, Roosevelt could also follow Marshall's proposal and summon the Guard as part of a two step plan to bolster the national defense by ordering out the Guard and calling for a draft law. Federalization of the Guard did not automatically mean accepting a draft, but it did give Roosevelt an option.

Roosevelt's hesitation on the draft abruptly ended on August 2. During a morning press conference, in response to a question from Fred Essary of the *Baltimore Sun*, Roosevelt stated that he favored an immediate draft. Secretaries Stimson and Knox, unaware of the President's statement, met with Roosevelt that afternoon to press for decisions on the draft and "naval assistance to England."[104] Both were surprised when, after weeks of delay, Roosevelt announced that he had publicly endorsed a draft plan, the Burke-Wadsworth bill by inference if not by name. Roosevelt told Stimson and Knox that he would "'call some of the leaders in and make it clear to them that they must get busy on that bill,' which he regarded as 'one of the two great fundamental pillars of national defense,' along with aid to England."[105]

NOTES

1. Bland, ed., *Marshall Papers*, II, 264.
2. Hull, *Memoirs of Cordell Hull*, I, 763.
3. Ibid., I, 764.
4. Leonard Mosley, *Marshall: Hero for Our Times* (New York, 1982), 137-138.
5. Forest C. Pogue, *George C. Marshall: Ordeal and Hope, 1939-1942* (New York, 1966), p. 31; Blanding, ed., *Marshall Papers*, II, 211.
6. Bland, ed., *Marshall Papers*, II, 211.
7. Ibid., II, 213.
8. Letter from General Marshall to Bernard M. Baruch, May 14, 1940, Bland, ed., *Marshall Papers*, II, 212.
9. Memorandum for the A. C. of S., G-1, from the Secretary, General Staff, May 15, 1940, National Archives, RG 165, OCS 16810-105.
10. Letter from H. Morgenthau, Jr., to Franklin D. Roosevelt, May 15, 1940, Bland, ed., *Marshall Papers*, II, 214.
11. See editor's notes on Pogue interview with Marshall, Bland, ed., *Marshall Papers*, II, 214.
12. Ibid., II, 214-215.
13. Leuchtenburg, *Roosevelt and the New Deal*, 299.
14. See editor's notes, Bland, ed., *Marshall Papers*, II, 217. Roosevelt's speech prompted Rear Admiral Stanford C. Hooper, chairman of the Naval Research Committee and the director of the Naval Operations' Technical Division, to visit Senator Burton Wheeler later in the month. The Admiral told Wheeler that he believed Roosevelt would lead the nation to war and that the idea of Germany invading the

Hemisphere, let alone the United States, was preposterous.   Wheeler used the information to attack the Administration's position that the Hemisphere was in peril, a theme later used in Senate debates. See Wheeler, *Yankee from the West*, 18-20.

15. Telegram from Major General John F. O'Ryan to Congressman James W. Wadsworth, May 20, 1940, Bland, ed., *Marshall Papers*, II, 217.

16. Derthick, *The National Guard in Politics*, 54.

17. Letter from General Marshall to Congressman Walter G. Andrews, May 26, 1940, Bland, ed., *Marshall Papers*, II, 215.

18. Ibid., II, 216-217.

19. Letter from Major General William N. Haskell to General Marshall, May 28, 1940, George C. Marshall Papers, Box 70, File Folder 16 (Marshall Library).

20. Memorandum, Subject: National Strategic Decisions, May 22, 1940, National Archives, RG 165, WPD 4175-7.

21. Ibid.

22. Memorandum for the War Plans Division from General Marshall, May 23, 1940, National Archives, RG 165, WPD 4175-10.

23. Palmer, *America in Arms*, 188.

24. Katherine Tupper Marshall, *Together: Annual of an Army Wife* (New York, 1946), 70.

25. Memorandum for the President, May 29, 1940, Bland, ed., *Marshall Papers*, II, 229-230.

26. *Complete Presidential Press Conferences of Franklin D. Roosevelt, Vol. 15-16* (25 Vols. in 12, New York, 1972), 442-445; Memorandum for General Edwin M. Watson from Major General Allen W. Gullion, June 1, 1940, Edwin M. Watson Papers (#9786) Manuscript Division, Special Collections Department, University of Virginia Library, Charlottesville, Virginia; Samuel Rosenman, ed., *The Public Papers and Addresses of Franklin D. Roosevelt* (13 vols., New York, 1938-50), IX, 252; "Statement by Chief of Staff on use of National Guard, "June 1, 1940, Bland, ed., *Marshall Papers*, II, 234-235.

27. Rosenman, ed., *The Public Papers and Addresses of Franklin D. Roosevelt*, IX, 252.

28. *New York Times*, June 2, 1940, p. 6.

29. Ibid.

30. Ibid., June 1, 1940, p. 1.

31. Ibid., June 2, 1940, p. 12.

32. Ibid.

33. Ibid., June 4, 1940, pp. 10, 14.

34. Memorandum for the Secretary of War, June 4, 1940, National Archives, Record Group 165, Chief of Staff Emergency File, Binder No. 2.

35. Kreidberg and Henry, *Mobilization*, 575.

36. Memorandum for the Chief of Staff, June 14, 1940, National Archives, Record group 165, WPD 4310-1.

37. War Department, *Annual Report of the Chief of the National Guard Bureau, 1941*, p. 19.

38. Ibid., 19.

39. Ibid.

40. The conference selected the Forty-fourt Division (NY, NJ), the Thirtieth Division (NC, SC, TN, GA), the Forty-fifth Division (OK, AZ, NM, CO), and the Forty-first

Division (ID, MI, OR, WY, WA). See War Department, *Annual Report of the Chief of the National Guard Bureau, 1941*, p. 19.

41. Ibid.

42. Ibid.

43. Ibid., 19-20.

44. Memorandum for the Chief of Staff from the War Plans Division, June 4, 1940, Marshall Foundation National Archives Project, Reel 296 Item 4402 (Marshall Library).

45. General Staff planner Major General Stanley D. Embick emphasized a strong defensive plan, consistent with planning over the previous decade. This outlook anticipated McCormick and the isolationist America First Committee. See Mark Stoler, "From Continentalism to Globalism: General Stanley D. Embick, the Joint Strategic Survey Committee, and the Military View of National Policy during the Second World War," *Diplomatic History*, 6 (Summer 1983):303-321.

46. General George C. Marshall's testimony before the House Committee on Military Affairs on HJR 555, June 4, 1940, p. 387, George C. Marshall Papers, Xerox Item 3020 (Marshall Library).

47. Ibid., 392-393.

48. Ibid.

49. Ibid., 394.

50. Ibid., 396.

51. Ibid., 397.

52. House of Representatives Report No. 2493, pt. 1, p. 2, 76th Cong., 3rd sess., 1940.

53. Ibid., 1.

54. House of Representatives Report No. 2493, pt. 2, p. 1, 76th Cong., 3rd sess., 1940.

55. Ibid., 2.

56. The National Defense Act of 1916 enabled the President to "order," that is draft, Guardsmen as individuals for federal service. President Woodrow Wilson used this legal device to bring Guardsmen into World War I, circumventing the Constitutional restriction on the militia.

57. House of Representatives Report No. 2493, pt. 2, p. 3, 76th Cong., 3rd sess., 1940.

58. U.S. Congress, *Hearing before the Joint Committee on the Investigation of the Pearl Harbor Attack*, 79th Cong., 1st sess., Part 15 (Washington, DC, 1946), p. 1908.

59. On December 15, 1945 General Strong reflected on the June 17, 1940 meeting. He believed at the time of the meeting that the Soviet Union was working with the Axis Powers. He pointed to Stalin's actions in the Baltic states and the June 10 treaty with Japan, which settled the Manchuko-Outer Mongolia border. As a result of relaxed relations in the wake of the treaty, Japan's military could move against other targets, namely the United States. See U.S. Congress, "Memorandum for General Marshall," dated 15 December 1945, *Pearl Harbor Attack*, Part 15, pp. 1907-1910.

60. Ibid., 1907-1910.

61. Langer and Gleason, *Challenge to Isolation*. 688-702; Conn and Fairchild, *The Framework of Hemisphere Defense*, 44-51.

62. Crossland, *Twice the Citizen*, 26-27.

63. Ibid., 39-40.

64. Born in 1867, Stimson was a Harvard trained lawyer who had served as President Taft's Secretary of War. During the First World War he served in the American Expeditionary Forces as an artillery colonel. Although he served under three Republican presidents as governor of the Philippines and as Herbert Hoover's Secretary of State, Stimson agreed with many of Roosevelt's foreign policies.

65. Watson, *Chief of Staff*, 191; Henry L. Stimson and McGeorge Bundy, *On Active Service in Peace and War* (New York, 1948), 345-346; Palmer, *America in Arms*, 188.

66. J. Gary Clifford and Samuel R. Spencer, Jr., *The First Peacetime Draft* (Lawrence, KS, 1986), 83-88.

67. Watson, *Chief of Staff*, 111-112.

68. Clifford and Spencer, *The First Peacetime Draft*, 52-56.

69. Stimson was confirmed as Secretary of War on July 9 after a two hour, not unfriendly, hearing. Clifford and Spencer, *The First Peacetime Draft*, 52-56, 88-92; Stimson and Bundy, *On Active Service*, 323-331; McFarland, *Harry H. Woodring*, 157-159.

70. Luechtenburg, *Roosevelt and the New Deal*, 313.

71. Sherwood, *Roosevelt and Hopkins*, 174.

72. Ibid.

73. Gallup, *Gallup Poll*, I, 235.

74. Roosevelt defeated Hoover by a vote of 22,800,000 (59%) to 15,750,000 (41%). In 1936 Roosevelt won by a vote of to 27,751,612 (61%) over Alf Landon's 16,681,913 (37%) votes.

75. Donald Bruce Johnson, *The Republican Party and Wendell Willkie* (Westport, CN, 1981),

76. Watson, *Chief of Staff*, 112.

77. Ibid.

78. National Guard Association of the United States, *Proceedings, 1940*, p. 59 (National Guard Association Library).

79. Derthick, *The National Guard in Politics*, 96.

80. Mahon, *History of the Militia and the National Guard*, 143.

81. *New York Times*, July 6, 1940, p. 1; National Guard Association, *Proceedings, 1940*, pp. 59-61 (National Guard Association Library).

82. National Guard Association, *Proceedings, 1940*, p. 60 (National Guard Association Library).

83. Ibid.

84. Ibid., 60-61.

85. Ibid., 62-63.

86. Letter from Secretary of War Henry L. Stimson to President Roosevelt, July 11, 1940, Franklin D. Roosevelt Papers, National Guard File (Franklin D. Roosevelt Library, Hyde Park, NY. Hereafter referred to as the Roosevelt Library.); *New York Times*, July 13, 1940, p. 1.

87. *New York Times*, July 10, 1940, p. 8.

88. Watson, *Chief of Staff*, 195-196.

89. U.S. Congress, Senate, Committee on Military Affairs, *Compulsory Military Training and Service, hearings before the Committee on Military Affairs on S 4164*, 76th Cong., 3rd sess., 1940, p. 328.

90. Ibid., 331.

91. Statement for *Life* Magazine, July 13, 1940, Bland, ed., *Marshall Papers*, II, 264-265.

92. Letter from General George C. Marshall to Major General Ray D. Keehn, July 15, 1940, Bland, ed., *Marshall Papers*, II, 266-267.

93. Sherwood, *Roosevelt and Hopkins*, 169; Wheeler, *Yankee from the West*, 352-359.

94. Leuchtenburg, *Roosevelt and the New Deal*, 315.

95. Wheeler, *Yankee from the West*, 363-365; Sherwood, *Roosevelt and Hopkins*, 173, 177.

96. Cole, *Roosevelt and the Isolationists*, 377.

97. Letter from Secretary of War Stimson to President Roosevelt, July 19, 1940, Franklin D. Roosevelt Papers, National Guard File (Roosevelt Library).

98. Memorandum for the Secretary of War, July 29, 1940, Bland, ed., *Marshall Papers*, II, 278.

99. Ibid.

100. Ibid.

101. Letter from President Roosevelt to the President of the Senate and the Speaker of the House of Representatives; and a memorandum for the Secretary of War, July 27, 1940, Franklin D. Roosevelt Papers, National Guard File (Roosevelt Library).

102. Ibid.

103. Steven Neal, *Dark Horse: A Biography of Wendell Willkie* (Garden City, NY, 1984), 84-85; Cole, *Roosevelt and the Isolationists*, 266-273.

104. Clifford and Spencer, *Peacetime Draft*, 170.

105. Ibid.

5

Setting the Terms

It is absurd and ridiculous to stand on this floor and imply that perhaps by calling out the National Guard we are doing something that nobody had previously contemplated.

—Lister Hill[1]

SENATE JOINT RESOLUTION 286

As a result of Roosevelt's decision to mobilize the Guard, on July 30 Senator Morris Sheppard, an Administration supporter and chairman of the Senate Military Affairs Committee, introduced the War Department's bill, labeled Senate Joint Resolution 286 (SJR 286). It proposed granting the President power to order reserve components to active service for not more than one year of training, with active service to last no later than June 30, 1942. This device, engineered by Stimson, made the bill more palatable to the majority in Congress.[2] A second limitation was added to the bill, perhaps for that same reason:

Provided, That the members and units of the reserve components of the Army . . . shall not be employed beyond the limits of the Western Hemisphere except in the territories and possessions of the United States, including the Philippine Islands.[3]

Far from quelling controversy, the second limitation sparked heated debate over the powers any president possessed in deploying the armed forces of the United States.

By 2 P.M. July 30, Sheppard had arranged a hearing on the bill, with General Marshall appearing as the first of three spokesmen. The rapidity with which the hearing took place, and the small number of witnesses testifying, indicated the desire of the Administration to rush the bill through Congress. Marshall opened his testimony with an earnest plea for passage of the SJR 286, telling the Committee that world affairs made mobilizing the reserves and retirees an absolute necessity. He closed by saying:

I might put it this way: I don't think we can afford in any degree at the present time to speculate with the security of this country. And that is my opinion as a professional soldier, as chief of staff, that is the opinion of the War Department, that we feel is our duty to make clear to the Congress.[4]

But the Chief of Staff was speaking to a committee already willing to order the Guard and reserves to active duty. All that remained was to make technical changes in the bill to ease its passage.

A main concern of many on the Committee was the hardship that the bill would impose on Guardsmen and reservists. Senator Elbert D. Thomas of Utah touched upon the issue of protecting Guardsmen from unnecessary hardships when he asked Marshall if "the spirit of . . . selective service would be adhered to in building up . . . Guard units."[5] The Chief of Staff replied that men with dependents, businesses, or other domestic hardships would be released from the Guard. He went on to say that in conferences with NGA leaders, he had stressed the transfer of these men to inactive status1xo avoid the delays in releasing them. However, the Committee sought even more ways to safeguard inducted men's livelihoods. When asked if he favored protecting Guardsmen's jobs while they served their country, Marshall replied that he thought the idea was splendid, if such protection could be given.

While committee members fretted over securing Guardsmen's jobs and insuring the release from duty of those with dependents or businesses vital to the nation's economy, Marshall hammered on the need to induct the Guard as soon as possible. The Guard's role was vital to national security because it would provide the resources to train expected selectees. Without the Guard, the Army would have to strip its formations to train a larger army, the result being no army for a long time.[6]

General Williams, Chief of the National Guard Bureau, followed the Chief of Staff bridging the War Department and the Association. Not surprisingly, one of the first questions asked of him concerned the feelings of the Guard towards induction. "The guard," he told the committee, "has been on its toes for some time, and is anxious that something be done about it."[7] He estimated that ninety-eight percent of the Guard wanted induction.

On the subject of deferments, Williams stated that in test mobilizations conducted in 1938, only eight percent of the enlisted men claimed dependents as a means of disqualification. Officers were not screened in this way because as older men they were presumed to have dependents and the ability to care for them. Since that time the Bureau urged states to replace men eligible for deferment with "men who could be counted on to stay in the service."[8] But, Williams related that each state handled such matters differently.[9]

Disqualifying officers due to physical debility proved a harder question. Physical examinations conducted on Guardsmen during mobilization exercises showed that "standards either were not clearly stated in regulations or the boards that did the examining hadn't made a complete study of them."[10] As a result, two nearly identical regiments experienced disqualification rates of four and twenty-eight percent, respectively. Although the Bureau estimated a loss rate of twenty percent, Williams estimated it would be only five percent. He concluded by stating that even though many men faced hardship because of induction the majority would "stay with it at a personal sacrifice."[11]

General Reckord came before the committee ready to support the bill, but with amendments. He told the committee that the Guard "as an institution . . . [had] gone on record officially in favor of some such legislation . . . with one slight modification." He wanted to change the Army's language: "for a period not in excess of a year," to "not less than a year."[12] During his testimony, it became clear that Reckord felt one year provided enough training and permitted the men to arrange their affairs. Reckord may have believed that with out this change in language, the Army could use the Guard to train draftees until it had a strong training cadre built up. At that point the Guard could be stripped of its equipment and sent home. General Williams agreed with Reckord that the language should be changed, but saw little difficulty, believing that if an emergency existed at the end of the year Congress could amend the law.[13]

Reckord sensed the time was ripe for placing the Guard on an equal, if not better, footing with draftees and to ensure a place for the Guard at the head of the reserves. The Burke-Wadsworth bill asserted that each male citizen owed three years' service to the nation. Draftees under the bill would receive a year's credit after training, but Guardsmen received none. He suggested amending another Guard bill, S 4164, to allow such credit. While this put Guardsmen and draftees on an equal bases, Reckord wished to go further by placing the Guard ahead of draftees in the expanded Army.[14] As an emergency measure, he favored the draft, but as a permanent institution he saw its dangerous potential. Senator Edwin C. Johnson of Colorado, who opposed conscription as a peacetime measure but supported SJR 286, raised the issue by stating: "if it [the draft] should be made a permanent piece of legislation, there would be no reason for having a National Guard."[15] Reckord maintained before the committee that as long as states existed as sovereign powers there would be a Guard. Privately, Reckord feared a permanent draft as the first step toward a new "Continental Army." Faced with this possibility he decided to protect the Guard by placing it ahead of draftees rather than by fighting the draft. Reckord recommended a slight change in section III of the National Defense Act of 1933. Section III stated in part: "that when the Congress shall have declared a national emergency and shall have authorized the use of troops in excess of the Regular Army, we may use the National Guard."[16] Reckord wanted to change the "may" to "the National Guard should be used," implying that Congress would federalize the Guard before calling upon the other reserves or draftees.[17] When asked by Senator Josh Lee of Oklahoma about the War Department's feeling on the subject, Reckord stated that Major General William E. Shedd (G-1) had told him "it was entirely satisfactory."[18]

After hearing Reckord, the committee retired into executive session. Shortly thereafter the committee reported SJR 286 to the Senate with several modifications. The first change concerned the length of service. Instead of ordering the Guard out for "a period not to exceed one year" the committee, following Senator Johnson, decided on the neutral "twelve consecutive months."[19] In section 3(A) the Committee acceded to Reckord's request and provided credit to Guardsmen completing a year's training. Their final change gave Guardsmen job protection as far as the National Labor Relations Act permitted.[20]

The Committee urged swift adoption of the bill but remained silent on Reckord's suggestion of a change in the National Defense Act. As a result, they left open an issue that Reckord and the NGA leadership believed vital to the Guard's future. The Senate took up the bill on August 4.

PUBLIC OPINION

Public opinion, as reflected in random sample polls, strongly favored federalizing the Guard. In December 1940, *Public Opinion Quarterly* reported the results of a survey taken at mid-year, which asked what respondents thought of federalizing the National Guard for one year of training. Eighty-five percent favored ordering out the Guard while only fifteen percent did not. However, only sixty-seven percent of those asked in another poll favored conscription. The wide gap between the two figures, nearly twenty percent, indicated a public view of two separate issues. A still largely isolationist public saw selective service as a prelude to armed intervention in the war. Although aiding the Allied cause was gaining popularity, keeping out of the conflict remained a higher priority. Federalizing the Guard, the figures indicated, seemed a way to bolster the defense of the United States (and perhaps the Western Hemisphere) without going to war.[21]

State governors began expressing their support soon after the President's first letter to Congress on the subject. Governor Burnet R. Maybank of South Carolina "wired the President that he [could] count on him to do anything he [could] to aid in calling out the National Guard and assisting in every way possible the President's desire to have the necessary authority to send them from without the State."[22] Governor Herbert H. Lehman of New

York sent telegrams to New York's senators and to Governor Lloyd C. Stark of Missouri, president of the Governors' conference then meeting in Duluth, urging Congress to grant Roosevelt authority to call the Guard.[23] Earl E. Bailey, governor of Arkansas, offered the use of his troops and further stated:

it would be fatal folly to place in the hands of undisciplined and untrained boys the advanced, equipment, and arms which the nation is now preparing to manufacture for use. . . . Adequate training of troops now means preservation of human lives in the future.[24]

If federal law proved inadequate to allow Roosevelt to call the Guard, Bailey pledged his own authority as a supplement.[25] Other governors manifested support by public proclamations, perhaps the boldest move came from Frank J. Dixon of Alabama, who called upon employers to allow men leave without risk to job or seniority. The NGA had obviously been at work convincing governors of the need for public support.[26]

However not everyone favored granting Roosevelt authority, and numerous citizens wrote Roosevelt in protest. One from Syracuse, New York wrote the President on June 3: "As a citizen . . . I protest against the calling out of the National Guard. I see no emergency that calls for such action."[27] Another wrote: "Until we examine our defense needs calmly and carefully let us avoid whipping up dogs of war by calling out National Guard."[28] Other writers from around the nation contended that the world situation did not justify mobilization, and that such action would only increase war hysteria in the nation.

THE PRESS AND GUARD REACT

Newspapers across the nation generally applauded Guardsmen as patriotic individuals. The *Salem (Mass) Evening News* declared: "they are all patriotic, and want to do their part in protecting this country."[29] But that same paper warned that "the country [would] be sorry to call these men away from their regular employments."[30] Other newspapers suggested alleviating the manpower shortage in other ways. The *Chicago Daily Tribune* wrote: "If the Guard is wanted merely to increase the Army as rapidly as possible with the least disturbance to business, the President should invite enlistments from among those who are already being supported by the taxpayers."[31] *The Macon (Georgia) Telegraph*, a Democratic paper, held that others should go before the Guard, namely draftees. It stated: "there is no good reason why members of the National Guard should be the only ones drawn from civil life who should make sacrifices."[32]

The National Guard, too, suffered from a split in opinion. The testimony of Generals Reckord and Williams along with resolutions passed by the NGA

Executive Council and the Adjutants General Association tended to present on image of solid support for mobilization.[33] However, not everyone in the Guard wished to leave private life for a year of training.

On July 12, Major General Roy D. Keehn, the one-armed commander of the Guard's Thirty-third Division and Marshall's friend from his tour with the Illinois Guard, wrote the Chief of Staff:

Everybody is calling up about the headlines in the newspapers, concerning what you say about calling out the National Guard *Immediately.* . . . Just between you and me, don't you let anybody kid you that the National Guard officers here want to be called for training. Everybody is up in the air today. . . . Of course, everybody is excited about the war and want to kill Hitler, but in my opinion the situation will have to be more imminent to justify an immediate call of the Guard with their scant equipment, etc. Besides, many of them are just getting jobs.[34]

Individual Guardsmen began requesting discharges as soon as the possibility of mobilization appeared. One concerned citizen sent the President a clipping from the *Columbus (Ohio) Citizen*, which told how twenty-one percent of the Ohio National Guard's medical staff resigned during June and July, while its air arm lost twelve and one half percent. Its remaining combat arms lost six percent. Most of these men, the newspaper reported, had ten or more years experience and earned over $700 a year from the Guard. The writer of the letter enclosed a list of the discharged men, with a note of outrage.[35]

By July 23, 1940, the Guard had discharged nearly 96,000 men, or just under half of its usual strength. As Table 5.1 illustrates, dependency of others on Guardsmen was the most cited reason for discharges, with nonresidence and release of under-aged Guardsmen a very distant second and third. The mass departure of so many trained men was masked, to a large degree, by the influx of new recruits, but it could not go unnoticed.

Rumors that the Guard was unwilling to serve for one year alarmed NGA leaders. Not only did loose talk threaten morale, Congressional support would suffer as well if these stories were not silenced. As early as July 9, a committee of General Raymond H. Fleming of Louisiana, General Blanding, and Colonel Herndon sent a letter to Secretary of War Stimson under DeLamater and AGA President Charles H. Grahl's signatures citing "unfounded, false, and malicious reports," which the authors characterized as "savoring of Fifth Column activities" and misrepresenting the attitude "of the National Guard toward emergency plans for the defense of this country."[36] To clear up any misunderstanding or misrepresentation, they informed Stimson that the Guard:

in [the] most emphatic manner possible . . . stands ready and willing to enter into the Service of the United States, as provided in the National Defense Act, TODAY,

TOMORROW, or at any time the President of the United States sees fit to use the National Guard in the defense of this country.[37]

Table 5.1
National Guard Discharges

Reasons	Officers	Warrant Officers	Enlisted
Dependency	359	13	51,216
Physical	233	8	3,386
Educational	1	-	1,163
Business	429	8	3,708
Key Workers	19	1	296
Minority	-	-	4,906
Nonresidence	6	1	5,336
Federal Enlistment	1	-	1,932
Other Reasons	725	12	22,284
Total	1,773	43	94,227

Source: War Department, *Annual Report of the Chief of the National Guard Bureau, 1941*, pp. 40-41.

Copies of the letter went to the Assistant Secretary of War, the Chief of Staff, the Chief of the National Guard Bureau, the Chairman of the Military Affairs Committees of both houses of Congress, to all members of Congress, all Adjutants General, and all major generals of the Guard. Despite the NGA's massive publicity campaign, however, doubts about the Guard's commitment continued.

THE SENATE DEBATES

Senate consideration of SJR 286 began on August 5, 1940. Roosevelt and Senate leaders expected the bill to pass with ease. Indeed, neither the Administration and its supporters nor those who opposed portions of the bill doubted it would pass because as a whole, it enjoyed bipartisan support. Only a minority in the Senate opposed the bill, generally because they feared Roosevelt was attempting to grab more power over the military by means of a manufactured crisis with the goal of dragging the nation into Europe's war.

With defeat of the bill not an option, opponents chose a strategy very similar to that taken during the embargo fight of October 1939, attempting to talk down the bill while diluting it with amendments. By such tactics, the isolationists, anti-Roosevelt Democrats, and a small number of Republicans hoped to curb some of the powers Roosevelt requested.

Republican opponents had their own strategy of dealing with such a widely supported bill. They distanced themselves from the fight, allowing the anti-Roosevelt Democrats to take the lead. By doing so they hoped to limit the President's powers without encountering the stigma of being against preparedness.

Supporters of SJR 286 formulated a strategy of mild defense, explaining the bill and defending it as vital to the defense of the nation and the Western Hemisphere. This stand fit well with the Democratic party platform, in part fostered by Wheeler, which stated:

The American people are determined that war, raging in Europe, Asia and Africa, shall not come to America. We will not participate in foreign wars, and we will not send our army, naval or air forces to fight in foreign lands outside the Americas, except in case of attack.[38]

The Republican party had taken a similar stand at their June convention.[39]

Senator Sheppard, the chairman of the Military Affairs Committee, took the floor of the Senate that August day to begin consideration of SJR 286, outlining the purpose, its temporary nature, and the limit on sending reserve components beyond the bounds of the Western Hemisphere, or the Philippines. He carefully explained section 3, which guaranteed Guardsmen job protection while in federal service. He closed by mentioning Marshall's support for the measure (although he did not mention that Marshall and his staff wrote the bill) and the Chief of Staff's belief that an adequate defense demanded federalizing the Guard.[40]

Progressive Democrat Burton K. Wheeler of Montana, one of the first to speak against the bill, had long been an outspoken critic of Roosevelt's policy concerning the war in Europe. Following the President's May 16 speech, Wheeler received a visit from Rear Admiral Stanford C. Hooper, who, concerned that the President was leading the nation to war, urged Wheeler to lead a public campaign against the President's policy (as he had against the Supreme Court packing scheme in 1937). On June 7 Wheeler used information supplied by Admiral Hooper to attack the notion of a German invasion as "mad hysteria" and "bogey stories." The next day, an unnamed Army Air Corps captain visited Wheeler to tell him that Germany did not possess the capability to bomb the United States, convincing Wheeler beyond any doubt that the nation was in no direct danger. Despite the growing German bomber offensive against Britain, on the Senate floor that opening day of debate Wheeler again attacked the Administration's premise that a direct threat to the hemisphere existed from Germany. Therefore, the troops asked for were unnecessary. Using the information gained from Hooper and the unnamed captain, Wheeler once again told his colleagues that he did not believe Germany could invade or bomb the Americas by sea or air, and he questioned the existence of an emergency great enough to warrant mobilizing the Guard and reserves.[41] If such an emergency existed, he asked, why didn't the Administration plan on ordering out all of the Guard at once? Sheppard responded: "If the Senator cannot see an emergency in the present world situation, I am certain I could not persuade him that here is one."[42] To which Wheeler, referring to Roosevelt's unprecedented third term bid, quipped: "I can see an emergency, but the only emergency I see is that an election is coming on."[43]

In light of the Army's seemingly successful recruiting drive, Wheeler questioned the need for such measures as the bill before them and the waiting Selective Training and Service bill. By using Army recruiting figures, he attempted to demonstrate that volunteers alone met the June and July quotas. Civilian Conservation Corps camps suffered no shortages of volunteers, and the Montana Senator believed that the Army would experience no trouble in the future with its goals. To support his statement, Wheeler quoted Major General James K. Parsons, commander of the Third Corps: "America can be defended by an Army and Navy of moderate size. There are alarmists who think we are wide open to attack. . . . We need calm intelligence now as perhaps we have needed it never before."[44] Yet, in spite of his attacks on the Administration, the Senator from Montana suddenly announced he would vote for the bill. Wheeler's reason was simple, he favored preparation for war to ensure peace and saw the Guard as the vehicle to attain that end. However, he made it very clear that while he supported SJR 286 he would vote against the upcoming Burke-Wadsworth bill.

Conservative isolationist Robert A. Taft of Ohio, recently thwarted Republican presidential hopeful, took the floor to object to certain portions of the bill, but like Wheeler he supported the bill as a whole. As James T. Patterson noted, Taft had voted for Roosevelt's early 1939 military appropriations requests because "defense spending seemed urgent, and it was popular. Because it involved no commitments to foreign nations and might even frighten the aggressors."[45] The pending resolution offered the same rationale, but with one provision Taft could not support. He strongly objected to granting Roosevelt the authority to send Guardsmen and reservists outside the country. Such power, he may have thought, would lead to commitments to other nations and eventual involvement in the war. In raising his objection, Taft asked Sheppard if the provision indicated "an intention or a possibility of using them [the Federalized troops] throughout South America?"[46] Sheppard, after some hesitation, indicated that it would. Taft continued: "So that, even though Congress has not declared war . . . an army could still be sent, without further reference to Congress, to Brazil or Argentina or any other friendly country."[47] Sheppard responded that it could, but he believed that the President would not use that power without Congressional approval. However, Taft's point had been made. The expansion of executive power would be a recurring theme in the debate.

Although Taft raised a serious point, the first significant challenge to the bill came from Democrat Alva Adams of Colorado, who since 1935 had turned increasingly against Roosevelt, largely due to the New Deal. Because of the Senator's opposition to domestic policies, the President had wanted to throw his political weight against Adams in the 1938 election, but political advisors had persuaded him that Adams could not be removed.[48] As a result, the President had to face more of Adams' challenges. Senate Joint Resolution 286 would be yet another point of conflict, although Adams' opposition may have stemmed more from ideology than from dislike for Rossevelt's policies. Adams, personally friendly towards General Marshall, had serious reservations about military preparations.[49] Whatever his motives, Adams introduced an amendment to SJR 286 to severely limit the President's freedom of action, proposing that federalized individuals and units be limited to service in the "Continental United States and Territories and Possessions of the United States," negating the Army's ability to rapidly dispatch forces to meet any Nazi aggression in the Western Hemisphere.[50]

Yet Adams' attack was not the only avenue open to Roosevelt's opponents that day. Democrat Guy M. Gillette of Iowa, next to assail the President's reasons for federalizing the Guard, first came into conflict with Roosevelt in 1937 over the packing of the Supreme Court. This earned him Roosevelt's enmity and an Administration attempt to unseat him in the 1938 elections. Gillette retained his seat in the Senate and emerged a fervent anti-Roosevelt Democrat. Less than two years later Gillette, considered a moderate on foreign policy, cast a deciding vote against neutrality revision. Distrusting Roosevelt and attacking any measure that granted the President additional powers, Gillette took the floor on August 5, pointing out that the President already possessed all the power he needed under the 1933 Act to order the Guard out, to whatever location, but only after Congress declared a national emergency.[51] In questions aimed at one of the Administration's strongest supporters, Republican Warren R. Austin of Vermont, Gillette argued against granting Roosevelt increased powers over the Guard. Gillette asked:

Is it then the purpose of those urging the joint resolution to add to our present statutory law a provision to permit the President in his own discretion, as he wills, and in the manner and at the time he wills, to call any units of the National Guard into service anywhere in the Western Hemisphere? Could the President . . . order the National Guard of New Hampshire to Rio de Janeiro for 12 months and permit the National Guard of Iowa to remain in this country?[52]

Austin attempted to deflect the point of Gillette's questions by stating that the President would have no authority over the New Hampshire National Guard. However, because Guardsmen in the New Hampshire National Guard also belonged to the National Guard of the United States they could be sent out of the country if the bill passed.

Although Gillette had attempted to portray the pending measure as another ploy by Roosevelt to increase his power, he had raised the issue of constitutional control over the Guard. Senator Wallace H. White of Maine touched on perhaps the greatest source of confusion when he referred to the Militia Clause of the Constitution as the governing law of the National Guard. The clause provided only three instances when the Congress could use the militia: to execute the laws of the Union, suppress insurrection, and to repel an invasion. White asked Austin: "Now because they have become Federalized, may the National Guard . . . be used for some other purpose than those three?"[53] Austin expertly explained that the National Defense Act of 1933 gave the Guard a dual status, as state troops when not in federal service and a component of the Army of the United States when federalized. Despite Austin's explanation clearly stating the Guard's role in national defense, as established by the 1933 Act, a minority of Senators remained confused over the Guard's dual nature.

Senator Norris took the floor after the Senate considered several minor committee amendments to SJR 286. The old progressive senator had turned toward Roosevelt's view of international affairs but was not an internationalist. He had supported Roosevelt's naval building program and although he did not think an enlarged army was necessary, Norris believed, as did a growing number of Americans, that the Regular Army was too small to adequately protect American interests. Therefore, he supported the President's request to order the Guard and reserve into service, believing it would add 200,000 to 400,000 to the Army. Yet that was as far as he would go. Norris parted company with the President when it came to granting the power to send troops anywhere in the Western Hemisphere. Nor could he support a peacetime draft or universal military training, foreseeing no need for such measures. He found the main trouble in the Senate itself:

The Senate is a hotbed of hysteria. The Senate is where the country will obtain its ammunition to become worked up and hysterical if it becomes hysterical. To my mind, there is no danger that we shall be confronted with an invading army in the next 30 days. If there is such danger, God help us! The law which we propose to pass would not do any good.[54]

Norris would vote for the bill as a prudent defense measure, that would, he believed, obviate the need for a peacetime draft.[55]

Norris' oration was the last major address of the day. After considering several other minor committee changes in the bill's language, the Senate suspended its deliberations. As the first day of debate drew to a close it became evident that the Administration's confidence in passing the measure was justified; the Senate would grant the President the power to federalize the Guard. The Adams amendment, however, represented a serious challenge to one of the major provisions of the bill, the President's ability to send the Guard and reserve outside the United States.

On August 6, a heated exchange over the Burke-Wadsworth bill by supporter Sherman Minton of Indiana against draft opponent Rush Holt of West Virginia delayed debate on SJR 286. The volley of personal insults foreshadowed the coming national debate over conscription. Although polls indicated that at least 64 percent of the population supported some form of conscription, a vocal opposition minority began to organize. Such groups as the Keep America Out of the War Congress and the forming, though not yet public, America First Committee organized to counter William Allen White's Committee to Defend America by Aiding the Allies. As the summer continued, more tempers would boil over as the nation debated whether to conscript some of its young men.[56]

Foreshadowing the coming choice over conscription, opponents to sections of SJR 286 continued their previous day's attack on its legality and offered reservists their own choice in the matter. Senator Austin began that day's debate by defending the constitutionality of the Guard bill. He maintained that since the most important responsibility of Congress was national defense, it possessed the power to declare war and to raise and support armies, and therefore, its constitutional powers, under the Army clause, encompassed the measure. If enacted, Austin told the Senate, the act changed only one portion of existing law: the requirement of a congressional declaration of emergency before ordering out the Guard.[57]

Gillette, a former Guardsmen, disagreed with Austin. He felt that the pending legislation drastically clashed with previous legislation. Guardsmen, he stated, entered service with the idea of serving their states and nation only in time of danger, and had not enlisted with the expectation of one year's peacetime training or being sent anywhere in the Western Hemisphere.

Republican John A. Danaher of Connecticut, who had opposed discretionary powers for Roosevelt in neutrality legislation, agreed with Gillette's stand and offered an amendment as a solution stating that "Any person now subject to the provisions of section I may resign his status within 20 days after the approval of this joint resolution."[58] Marking the second threat to the integrity of the measure, the amendment proposed that any Guardsman (officer or enlisted) could resign as soon as the bill became law. The wording of the amendment, in theory, allowed the entire National Guard, the Officer Reserve Corps, and the enlisted reserve to reject mobilization. This left the President, state governors, and the War Department powerless to decide who should, or should not, be released from service.

Not surprisingly, Danaher's amendment became the focal point of the August 7 debate. Danaher took the floor at the opening of the time allotted to the measure, stating his main objection to the bill came from its unequal protection of those called. He maintained that the bill contained no real protection for men taken from their jobs. In his opinion, the language inserted by the committee possessed no legal force because Congress did not have the power to enforce it, thus misleading those called to believe that the Congress would protect their jobs. Danaher wanted, in essence, to give those who volunteered for service in the reserves a chance to either re-volunteer under prevailing circumstances or to resign.[59]

Senator Alben W. Barkley of Kentucky and Lister Hill of Alabama, two of Roosevelt's strongest supporters in the Senate, quickly came to the bill's defense. Barkley had actively supported Roosevelt for re-election in 1938 and gave the 1940 Democratic convention the signal that Roosevelt would accept a draft for nomination. Hill also had the President's support. As an ardent New Dealer, Hill won the Alabama senatorial election of 1938, much to the delight of the Administration.[60] Barkley argued that all Guardsmen retained their state status and privileges until ordered to active service by the President. Under those privileges, any member could tender his resignation to his state governor. Barkley did not object to allowing men to resign, but only for good reason. If an individual's induction caused undue hardship on dependents or harm to the nation's industry, then deferment was justified. He objected to the amendment's language. It seemed to him that any inducted man could claim release as a right. Barkley wanted the review of each case to remain in the hands of state or federal officials.

Lister Hill rejected the amendment as unnecessary. Hill cited Marshall, Reckord, and Williams' testimony before the committee as evidence that the military intended to follow the spirit of selective service. Guardsmen with just cause would receive deferments from service. He also rejected Danaher's argument that Guardsmen had not volunteered for such a situation as confronted the nation. "It is absurd and ridiculous," said Hill, "to stand on this floor and imply that perhaps by calling out the National Guard we are doing something that nobody had previously contemplated."[61]

Senator Elbert D. Thomas of Utah supported Danaher's objective of protecting the jobs of those called to active service, but unlike Danaher, he believed that Congress had the right to force private employers to reinstate men ordered to duty. He cited several Supreme Court decisions, of which *United States v. Gettysburg Electric R. Co.* (160 U.S. 668) proved the most enlightening. The Court stated that under Article I of the Constitution, Congress possessed the stated powers to declare war, raise armies, and certain implied powers. The Court considered any act of Congress proper and necessary which enhanced the love of the citizen to defend the nation. Thus, any action that raised morale of fighting men could be construed as proper and necessary. Thomas maintained that guaranteeing the return of civilian jobs after demobilization clearly increased morale, thus making such an act constitutional.[62]

As time ran short for the day's debate, the Senate voted on the Danaher Amendment, rejecting it by eleven votes. The President, through the War Department, would retain discretionary ability to keep, or discharge, individuals. Senators such as Adams, Hill, Hughes, La Follette, Lodge, and Norris voted nay while Andrews, George, Taft, Vandenburg, and Wheeler voted with Danaher. With this victory secured, Administration supporters turned to the Adams amendment, even though little time remained for that day's debate.[63]

In proposing an amendment to restrict reservists to duty within the "continental United States and Territories and possessions of the United States," Adams believed that Guardsmen and reservists should "be limited to service upon lands under the flag of the United States." Perhaps more importantly, he viewed the proposed amendment as safe-guarding Congress' war powers.[64] To Adams, granting the President or any other official power to send men to foreign lands surrendered that right.

Democrat John H. Overton of Louisiana, who had opposed neutrality revision but supported federalization, attacked the proposed amendment, asserting that the Constitution granted Congress the power to raise armies in any manner it saw fit. In his opinion, Congress could order to federal service the National Guard, lawyers, women, or any other group it desired, with no limitation of any kind. While Senator Adams maintained the Militia Clause limited Congress' authority, Overton followed Austin's argument of the previous day that the National Defense Act of 1933 changed the nature of the Guard when in federal service. He then took this view one step further to assert that the resolution actually drafted the military force known as the militia. "Congress," he told the Senate, "may do so without being guilty of any unjust discrimination. It may draft, muster into the service, and designate as part of the Army, the militia and the organized Reserves."[65]

Democrat Claude Pepper of Florida gained the floor to attack the proposed amendment from a different angle. He had just returned from the hastily called Havana (Cuba) Conference of representatives of the United States and Latin American Governments, where, as a delegate, he heard the concerns of American states caused by pressures exerted by Hitler to turn those nations away from the Allies.[66] Pepper concluded that Axis propaganda had caused worry in governments of South America that the United States lacked the ability in men and material to defend the hemisphere. He warned that passage of the amendment would create greater doubt among other nations concerning America's resolve to defend the hemisphere. Pepper and Hill reminded the Senate of Senate Joint Resolution 271, passed on June 17 (the day France capitulated), which stated that the government and people of the United States would not recognize transfer of land in the Western Hemisphere from one non-American nation to another. Approving the Adams amendment, Pepper contended, would send a message to the world that the United States uttered such words but would not back them."[67] Pepper felt the Senate needed to act and in acting show more than "half-hearted determination."[68] Surprisingly, Pepper's appeal was one of the few references to the foreign impact of the bill.

After Pepper, Tom Connally, Texas' junior senator attacked the amendment, taking up Overton's argument that Congress could indeed order out the Guard without violating the Constitution. He interpreted Congress' power under the Militia Clause to discipline the militia as enabling it to mobilize the National Guard of the Several States for one year of training. Jumping to the constitutional powers of the President and from the Militia clause to the 1933 National Defense Act, Connally agreed that as commander-in-chief the President could send U.S. military forces anywhere. The joint resolution itself, Connally stated, actually limited the President's power. Connally stated: "it says that the troops we are now drafting may not be sent anywhere except to places mentioned. It does not give any added authority."[69]

Connally's rather jumbled use of the Militia Clause, the powers of the President, and the National Defense Act attempted to paint SJR 286 as a moderate piece of legislation, which was exactly what Stimson wanted to project. By placing such limitations on how long and where mobilized reservists could be used, the Secretary of War hoped to win over fence riding senators who might vote with the isolationists. As the day ended, it became obvious to every one that the bill would pass and that only one point of contention really existed: that of the power of the President. The wounds of too many old political battles borne by some, such as Gillette, and the ingrained philosophy of non-intervention for Adams, Wheeler, and others prevented them from trusting Roosevelt with more power. Most had fought against his increased powers over the economy and feared that he was leading the nation to war. Aware of the opposition's dislike and distrust for the President, Administration supporters prepared to raise the issue of trust during the next days's debate, but to their advantage.[70]

After Connally finished his attack on the Adams amendment, it became clear to Barkley that no vote was possible that day. Although he hoped to end the matter on August 7 and take up the Burke-Wadsworth bill the next day, Barkley decided it would take at least one more day. But he did not want to linger on a matter where victory was assured. Therefore, he moved that debate on the resolution end at four o'clock the next day with an immediate vote to follow. The opposition protested this attempt to limit debate, but did not have the votes to block Barkley. For his part, Barkley had to make sure all the bill's supporters were in the chamber for the next day's vote.[71]

On August 8, the day that marked the beginning of the first phase of the Battle of Britain, Barkley opened the debate by taking the offensive against the Adams amendment as a great hindrance to the President. Not only would it prevent the deployment of the Guard outside American territory but it would do the same to the Officer Reserve Corp, a completely federal force. Barkley declared that protecting the interest of the nation was the prime duty of the Senate. Hampering the President, as the Adams amendment proposed to do, would be similar to allowing a murderer into the very last room in ones' home before offering a defense.[72] Barkley concluding by stating: "it seems to me it would be folly by its adoption to serve notice on the rest of the world that all our pious resolutions in behalf of liberty, democracy, and American solidarity are of no more effect than if they had been adopted by a quilting league."[73]

Hill next took up the attack by employing his tactics of the previous day. He railed against the proposed amendment as a serious limitation on the ability of the Army to defend the nation. To his mind, once Guardsmen or reservists came into active federal service they left their former distinctions as state soldiers or private citizens behind and put on the mantle of a soldier in the Army of the United States. "Yet," he told the Senate, "we sit here today considering the proposition that we will call out the great Reserve force . . . then say to [them], 'You shall go so far, and no further, in the defense of our country.'"[74] He felt the amendment would seriously harm the effectiveness of the reserve as well as undercut Latin American confidence in the United States.[75]

To meet this verbal onslaught Gillette took up his arguments of the day before. Ignoring Barkley and Hill, he challenged claims made by Overton and Austin on August 7 that Congress could "draft" the Guard, pointing to the United States district court in Delaware's decision in *United States v. Stephens* stating that the Congress could call those state militias into service only under the Militia Clause and under very limited circumstances. Gillette then examined the National Defense Act of 1933 and its limitations. It created the National Guard of the United States, as an entity completely outside of the Militia Clause, that Congress could order to active service but only after declaring a national emergency. Gillette pointed out that Congress had not declared an emergency nor was training the true issue. By custom and law, training belonged to the states. The real purpose of the measure, he asserted, was active service, which he characterized as unfair to Guardsmen. He attacked federalization as being imposed "on a group of the most patriotic and finest young men the country affords . . . obligations which they are not imposing on the other citizens of the United States."[76] His main attack, however, targeted the discretionary powers the President would gain. Gillette told his colleagues that supporters of the measure proposed that the Senate "abdicate our power and confer on the President of the Unite States full power to go far beyond the present law, and order these men anywhere he sees fit, within the limitations of the joint resolution, not for training but for such purposes as he sees fit. Perhaps other Senators want to do it. If so, very well, I do not."[77] For those reasons he would vote for the amendment and against the measure.

Austin rejected the idea of unfairness by citing first the oath taken by Guardsmen and then court opinions. Upon entering the National Guard, each man took an oath to defend the United States and his home state "against all their enemies whomsoever."[78] The Senator contended that Guardsmen understood the ramifications of the oath they took, that in effect it made them members of the Army of the United States as well as state militiamen. Austin saw no reason in discriminating in their favor, as the Adams amendment would by excluding them from possible service throughout the Western Hemisphere. He countered Gillette by citing Judge Bradford's opinion in *United Stated v. Stephens*, stating that men called into federal service lost whatever state character they possessed and became part of the National Army. As further evidence, he cited the majority opinion in *Sweetser v. Emerson*, which held that Guardsmen who volunteered for state service only were not liable for discharge because of federal employment beyond the nation's borders.[79] However, Austin touched the real heart of the issue when he asked: "Are we going to paralyze the sovereignty of this country simply because we are unwilling to trust the President of the United States and Commander in Chief of the Army to exercise the authority contained in this proposed act?"[80]

Democrat Albert Chandler of Kentucky voiced the sentiments of some who favored the amendment when he stated that he trusted the President, but believed, as did Norris, that not every place in the Western Hemisphere deserved defending. He believed that if the measure were simply for training, then the nation possessed ample territory to train the Guard. If a danger arose Congress would certainly extend all necessary powers to the President.[81]

Arthur Vandenberg entered the debate briefly to echo Chandler's basic theme that the Guard could be trained on American soil. But more to his point, Vandenberg told the Senate that he would vote for the Adams amendment "because it is my view that if the necessity ever arises to send the National Guard outside continental United States, it is a decision in which the Congress should specifically participate."[82] However, he intended to vote for the measure with or without the amendment because it recognized the traditional peacetime method of preparing against emergency, and for that reason he would vote against a draft.[83]

In the closing moments of debate, Sheppard made a last appeal to his colleagues to defeat the amendment. He implored his listeners not to hamper the Army in defending the nation or in planning for that defense by placing limits on where it could serve. Delay in removing such a hindrance, even if only a day, might throw the advantage to any enemy. He also believed that any limitation, as Pepper had stated earlier, would destroy Latin America's confidence in the United States. Sheppard pleaded that defeat of the amendment would reinforce the United States' commitment to the hemisphere's defense.[84]

As four o'clock approached, the Senate suspended debate on the Adams amendment, but before voting on the question it agreed to one amendment without debate. Key Pittman, long known for his close ties to the President on foreign relations legislation, introduced an amendment allowing Guardsmen and reservists to resign from the service within twenty days of induction for reasons of dependents or their vital place in the economy. Although on the surface Pittman's amendment resembled Adams, it left the power to decide each man's case in the hands of the President, through the War Department. The proposal was well within existing plans as stated by Generals Marshall and Williams before the Senate committee and, therefore, suffered no opposition from the bill's supporters. By voice vote the Senate unanimously consented to the amendment.[85]

At last, the presiding officer called for a vote on the Adams amendment, which was defeated thirty-nine to thirty-eight. By one vote the Senate had rejected limiting reservists to service in the continental United Stated and its territories or possessions. Of those voting for the Adams amendment, seventeen were Democrats, eleven were Republicans, and three were Progressives.[86] With the Adams amendment out of the way, the Senate voted on the entire measure. By a vote of seventy-one yeas, seven nays, and eighteen not voting the Senate passed and sent to the House SJR 286. Two Republicans voted against the bill (Danaher and Nye) as did four Democrats (Bulow, Donahey, Gillette, and Holt). The remaining negative vote came from Farm-Laborist Lundeen. With the exception of Danaher and Holt, all opposition came from the Midwest. True to his word, Norris voted for the joint resolution, as did other prominent isolationists, such as Hiram Johnson, La Follette, Taft, Vandenberg, and Wheeler. But the Administration could not count on their support for the Burke-Wadsworth bill, which the Senate took up next.

THE HOUSE DEBATES

While the Administration welcomed the Senate victory, the narrow margin of defeat on the Adams amendment caused concern. Although dissident Democrats led the attack on granting Roosevelt authority to send troops outside the country, Republicans, too, vented their objection by voting with Adams. While committed to national defense, Republicans were wary of placing too much power in the President's hands, especially in an election year. In the House of Representatives the story would be different, where, unlike their strategy in the Senate, Republicans led the fight.

The Administration faced a House that had 169 Republicans elected in 1938 and thirty Democrats who "were largely or wholly disenchanted with the New Deal and fifty more were not at all enthusiastic."[87] The Administration and its supporters did not fear defeat on SJR 286, which had wide bipartisan support. They were concerned that a coalition of Republican and anti-New Deal Democrats could successfully attach an Adams-style amendment to the bill limiting reservists to service in the United States. Such an amendment would force the bill back to the Senate for reconsideration. The Administration feared that a second trip through the Senate might tip the balance. Therefore, the key strategy for Roosevelt's supporters was to limit debate as much as possible, thereby stifling any attempt to introduce an Adams-style amendment.

Roosevelt publicly tried to minimize the possibility of sending men outside American territory to undercut isolationist opposition. During a press conference Roosevelt was asked for a comment on the attempt to limit the Guard to American soil. The President responded by saying:

Of course the simple answer to it is this: In terms of betting odds, it is a hundred to one that they would never leave the Untied States or American possessions, but to restrict—but one little restriction of that kind might tie up something in a very great emergency.[88]

Although the House Military Affairs Committee officially received SJR 286 on August 12, it had studied Guard mobilization since HJR 555 in early June. Having carefully noted the Senate committee hearings and debates, the House Committee returned a report to the House in what appeared a matter of moments.[89] Yet the Committee version differed from the Senate's. While the Senate allowed Guardsmen to seek discharge because of dependents, the committee decided to automatically discharge any reservist with dependents without the individual seeking a release from duty.[90]

On August 14, the full House formed into the Committee of the Whole House to consider SJR 286 but with only a few hours of general debate. In a move to speed the bill through, Administration supporters enacted House Resolution 567, which limited debate to four hours. Democrat Andrew J. May of Kentucky, chairman of the Military Affairs Committee, took the floor as the joint resolution's sponsor. Explaining that the Military Affairs Committee considered the subject of federalizing the Guard since Generals Marshall, Williams, and Reckord testified on the earlier HJR 555. Their statements, together with similar testimony before the Senate committee, convinced them of the need for the bill. The Committee also supported the Senate's ideas of protecting jobs and felt that alarming conditions in the Western Hemisphere warranted granting the President authority to deploy reserves within that limit. He also explained that the committee included a provision, similar to the Senate's, for releasing men who had dependents or were vital to the economy within twenty days of induction. However, he did not describe the difference in the versions.[91]

As in the Senate, House opponents centered on three major themes: Guardsmen had not contemplated being federalized for a year during peacetime and should be given a chance to resign; the Guard should not be sent beyond the limits of the United States or its possessions; and Congress had to guard against granting too much power to the President. As in the Senate, opponents of the bill knew they did not have the votes to defeat it. Their only hope revolved around forcing changes that would return the bill to the Senate where an Adams-styled amendment might pass. To counter the possibility of a vote on opposition amendments that day, most Democrats absented themselves from the chamber. In the event of a call for a vote, May could call for presence of a quorum and, lacking one, delay any action.

Republican Charles A. Halleck of Indiana took the floor as the first major opponent of the bill. Noted for being a conservative, "scrappy, [and] highly partisan Republican," he bitterly opposed the New Deal and actively supported Willkie as the best chance to defeat Roosevelt.[92] Halleck, who opposed SJR 286 but probably believed it would pass, opened the opposition's attack by raising the issue of the unfairness of SJR 286 to Guardsmen. He believed that no one could have foreseen the possibility of being ordered to active service for a year in other than an emergency situation. He quoted one unnamed Guard officer as saying:

If the guard is mobilized without a chance for resignation of officers who have a profession to look after or a job which no one else can fill, it is going to create a severe hardship on them. . . . I never would have kept up my commission if I had known I might be mobilized in peacetime just to fill in a gap resulting from failure to expand the Regular Army.[93]

Halleck could find no such declaration, and no reason for one.

Republican Earl C. Michener of Michigan agreed with Halleck that no emergency existed in spite of Roosevelt's letters to Congress. Following Danaher's stand in the Senate, Michener stated that the law allowed for the ordering of the Guard only when Congress had declared an emergency. Without such a declaration, any act inducting the Guard, even for training, was illegal. Michener believed the terms of enlistment that each Guardsman signed were binding contracts between them and their government. He considered induction in peacetime without an emergency declaration, or an attempt to change the existing law to allow involuntary induction, a serious breach of those contracts. Michener proposed an amendment to allow Guardsmen to resign. This would preserve the contract by allowing only those who volunteer to remain. "Then," he stated, "there will not be a compulsory thing about the bill."

May challenged this view throughout the running debate. He began by stating that the committee had no way of determining what each man thought when he joined the Guard. The committee assumed that each man was intelligent, patriotic, and "joined with the expectation of meeting any emergency that might arise."[94] A Guardsman might be called by his governor to put down insurrection or disturbances. "Consequently," May quipped, "the gentleman [Michener] will have to know that when a man joined the National Guard he did it like the man who gets married—'for better or for worse' [laughter]; and that he is subject to call at any time by the President of the United States when the Congress declares an emergency."[95] As far as living up to the letter of the National Defense Act, May considered the language of the bill tantamount to declaring an emergency. Democrat Charles I. Faddis of Pennsylvania added his voice to May's by stating: "the fact that Congress has made these appropriations, thus giving notice that there is an emergency."[96]

Republican Noah M. Mason of Illinois turned the attack to the second main issue of debate—the President's authority to send inducted Guardsmen and reservists outside the nation's boundaries. As with many in the House, he approved of the bill to provide needed training; however, he could not support sending "the boys to South America" under the label of training, which could "be done much better on United States soil. . . . This bill takes in the whole Western Hemisphere, and that takes in more than simply training."[97]

Other representatives added their voices to Mason's. Carl Hinshaw of California also objected to the prospect of sending reserve troops outside American territory, believing any step necessary to repel an attack or defend the Monroe Doctrine would bring, at the least, an emergency declaration or a declaration of war. He favored the bill as far as training, but believed that the ability to send troops throughout the hemisphere invited trouble from abroad. "It is folly," he stated, "and an invitation to disaster to pick a fight, certainly a year before you are ready to even decently protect yourself."[98] Republican J. Thorkelson could find no constitutional authority for Congress to allow the President to send the Guard from American soil. Citing the Militia Clause limitations, he concluded that without threat of invasion such an action would be unconstitutional. Additionally, he believed that if Germany hesitated to invade Britain across a mere twenty-two miles of water, it was certain they could not invade the United States.[99]

Republican William J. Miller of Connecticut supported the idea of training the Guard, as did Mason and Thorkelson. Miller knew that placing untrained men in combat could lead to disaster. And he had no doubt that the majority of Guardsmen wanted the training. Yet he could not support the possibility of sending the Guard to South America. He believed that in the event of an emergency, Congress could assemble in thirty-six hours for a vote on needed measures. He backed up these beliefs by submitting an amendment to limit the Guard to training on American soil.[100]

May responded to Miller that the committee examined the request for the provision carefully and concluded that the President needed the power to send the Guard outside the country. He contended that restricting the President's authority over the Guard might allow a foreign power to conquer Mexico or Canada. Democrat R. Ewing Thomason of Texas, strongly backing this provision, took up Pepper's argument from the Senate. He argued that striking the Western Hemisphere provision would invalidate the Havana agreement and encourage Hitler.[101]

At that point, opponents moved to their third major point—guarding against the President's encroachment on Congressional controls over the military. The issue was highly partisan. Most Republicans attempted to steer clear of the appearance of political feuding, others did not. Although most members favored ordering the Guard to duty for training, others considered giving Roosevelt authority to send men to foreign lands without further consulting Congress a step toward tyranny. Republican Robert F. Rich of Pennsylvania stated that he did "not want to grant to the President of the United States such authority that he might declare a national emergency to exist and then set himself up as a dictator."[102] He would not "grant such power to anyone, regardless of whether he may be a Republican or a Democrat."[103] Republican Clare E. Hoffman of Michigan pulled no punches. He accused Roosevelt of using the legitimate purpose of giving the Guard training as a guise to get the United States involved in the war. In a reversal of the Army's rationale for using the Guard, Hoffman propounded his belief that Roosevelt would dispatch the Guard to South America, where Germany possessed spheres of influence. There the Guard would become involved in fighting and would need support from the Regular Army. As for Roosevelt's assurance that the odds were 100 to 1 against sending the Guard to South America, Hoffman stated: "Unfortunately, as we have learned to our sorrow, the President's word is worthless."[104]

Thomason attacked Rich and Hoffman's view as giving the issue a "political aspect."[105] He told the House:

We must lodge authority somewhere. I feel very deeply about this matter and this is no time for politics, this is no time for partisanship. [Applause] This is the time when every one of us should rise to the support of our democratic institutions. I do not want to put the consideration of this bill on the basis of politics or partisanship.[106]

But politics was a major factor in the debate. With no vocal Democratic opposition to any section of the bill, it became obvious that only a small number of strongly anti-Roosevelt Republicans stood in the way of passage.

General debate ended after four hours, as Resolution 567 demanded. Unlimited debate then commenced on a series of amendments offered by members who, in general, supported the measure but objected to certain provisions. The House quickly defeated an amendment by Republican Frederick C. Smith of Ohio, which limited the President to ordering into service only those Guardsman who gave their consent. Democrat Sam C. Massingale of Oklahoma introduced an amendment that would immediately honorably discharge any member of the Guard under the age of eighteen. The proposal sparked heated protests from several ardent bill supporters.

Democrats Wadsworth and Alfred L. Bulwinkle of North Carolina, and Republican Walter G. Andrews of New York, claimed that the law already forbade federal recognition to Guardsmen under eighteen, automatically eliminating them from the call. May and Faddis objected to granting an honorable discharge to youths who joined through false statements of age. Republican Francis Case of South Dakota defended granting honorable discharges on the grounds that a youth of less than eighteen years old could join a unit only if a recruiter turned a blind eye. He thought it unfair for Congress to punish those who enlisted for patriotic reasons by giving them less-than-honorable discharges (called a "Blue" discharge because of the distinctive blue paper it was printed on). The latter argument seemed to reflect the majority's will, and Massingale's amendment passed by a vote of 93 to 58.[107]

Next the House considered Miller's amendment to restrict reserve units to the continental limits of the United States, its island possessions including the Philippine Islands, the Panama Canal Zone, and Alaska. Immediately, members renewed the debate that had ended less than an hour before. Republicans attacked the prospect of sending the National Guard to Central or South America. Mason once again declared his support for a training bill but not for sending troops abroad. Republican Roy O. Woodruff of Michigan doubted Congress' right under the law to enact such legislation because it had not declared an emergency. Hinshaw opposed granting the President the power "to order the National Guard to go anywhere in the Western Hemisphere for any purpose, regardless of what the Congress and the people of the United States may then think about it."[108]

Faddis was the main opponent of the amendment during the closing moments of the day's debate. He denounced the amendment as a serious hindrance to national defense and harmful to the Monroe Doctrine, telling the House that time was the "essence of any movement to protect the integrity" of the United States or any nation.[109] Defending the Monroe Doctrine meant being able to move swiftly. Accepting the proposed Miller amendment, he stated, would discourage South American nations while at the same time encouraging the aggressive activities of totalitarian powers. "If we are to quibble," he stated, "or play politics over such matters, we are setting our feet in the same road which France trod. That road leads to national impotence and to destruction."[110]

Several times during the exchange that day May unsuccessfully attempted to limit debate on amendments. As the day neared an end, and with many supporters of the bill out of the chamber, May moved that the Committee of the Whole House rise. He then added: "I want to serve notice that if there is not a quorum here tomorrow morning there will be a roll call."[111] May intended to have all the amendment's opponents on hand to defeat Miller's proposal and, if possible, to bring the entire matter to an end.

Three hundred and sixty members of the House sat in the chamber on August 15 as May moved that the House form into the Committee of the Whole. The chairman of the Military Affairs Committee seemed determined to defeat Miller's amendment and push the measure through. Two pro-administration Republicans, Andrews and Wadsworth, began the day's debate by sternly attacking the proposed limitations on the Guard. Andrews argued that because the increase in the Army came largely through the use of reserve officers, Miller's amendment threatened to cripple the Army by restricting the Guard and reserves with the result that no regular Army units could leave United States' soil without first removing all its reserve officers and men. Andrews called this "a process which would cut down the size and effectiveness of the force that could be employed."[112] Miller rejoined that he would later offer an amendment that would limit only the Guard.[113]

Although Miller's proposal may have weakened opponents' argument, it did not disarm them. Wadsworth gained the floor and attacked from a different angle. The co-sponsor of the pending Selective Service bill, argued that the proposal violated the "spirit and intent of the National Defense Act of 1920," reminding the members that during the Great War the Guard had been drafted as part of the militia and then was looked down upon by Regulars.[114] After the war, Guardsmen (the NGA) requested that if called upon again, the law should grant them status equal to the Regular Army. Out of this request, Wadsworth told them, Congress created the Army of the United States, "its officers and men . . . automatically and instantly Federal Soldiers."[115] Passing Miller's amendment meant abandonment of the National Army concept. To illustrate the danger of again splintering the Army, Wadsworth recounted how New York militiamen, restricted by the Militia Clause, failed to support regular troops during the 1813 battle of Queenston Heights. They refused to cross into Canada believing that they could legally repel an invasion but not participate in one. The result was defeat, and a generation of acrimony. Wadsworth suggested that the proposed amendment might have the same effect in an emergency. Beyond the restricting of the National Guard, he challenged the idea that Congress could react rapidly to a crisis, called upon it to make up its mind on using the Guard before any emergency. As he put it: "And are we to say that in that event we must convene the Congress, introduce a bill, have hearings on it, bring it to the floor, and debate it to determine whether or not half the Army of the United States can be used to meet the emergency; I hope not!"[116]

As supporters of the amendment began to rise in its defense, May attempted to cut off debate. Bender objected to May's tactics while Farm-Laborist Vito Marcantonio and Republican Harry N. Routzohn found no need for haste and defended the right of each member to speak. Routzohn unleashed perhaps the bitterest attack on May and the Administration. He denied aspersions cast by May, Faddis, and others that supporting the amendment amounted to playing "a sordid game of politics."[117] Routzohn wondered if the reverse were not true. He believed the Democrats in Congress blindly followed the President's lead without knowing what Roosevelt promised to Britain or Latin America. "Is it true," he asked May, "that the proponents of this amendment are playing politics; or are you, my Democratic colleagues, merely laying a smoke screen to hide the politics that are behind your opposition thereto?"[118]

May attempted to counter the stinging Republican invective by charging that political motives lay at the bottom of their objections to the bill. The Republicans had issued a statement in January 1939 to the effect that the Army had to be ready to defend the hemisphere. May read the statement into the record.

Our Military Establishment must be adequate to carry out the obligations so clearly implied in the Monroe Doctrine—the obligation to prevent the extension of foreign political domination through military action in the Western Hemisphere. This may well be considered as part of the supreme obligation to defend the continental United States.[119]

He then suggested that it seemed that in August 1940, some Republicans wished to repudiate this statement by preventing the formation of an adequate military establishment.

Though not answering May directly, Bender and Hinshaw pressed their point that the final decision of whether or not to send United States forces outside the country should be retained by Congress. Bender concluded the case for the proposed amendment by saying: "Let us not create an emergency through any action we may take on this measure at this time."[120]

Democrat Sam Rayburn of Texas closed effective debate on the amendment, by rhetorically questioning the amendment while stating his support for the measure. The nation had spent billions on planes, ships, and arms. "Are we," he asked, "going to have an army to use these instruments or not?"[121] The nation had increased the size of the National Guard with men who knew they might be called into federal service. Rayburn asked, "Are we going to build up the National Guard under the law . . . to preserve, protect, and defend the interests of this country?"[122] He told his fellows that Congress "resolved with the other countries of the Western Hemisphere that if they are attacked or if we are attacked our interests are mutual."[123] And then asked, "Are we going to say within less than two weeks after the conclusion of these conversations and . . . agreements that we will not use . . . soldiers . . . to carry out what we have agreed to?"[124] As to the power of the President, he stated that it did not matter whether Congressmen loved or hated Roosevelt. Since any President, reckless or unpatriotic enough, could plunge the nation into war, with or without Congress' consent, pending legislation did not matter. Therefore, he called for the amendment's defeat.

Clifton Woodrum, chairman of the Committee of the Whole House, sounded the gavel as Rayburn finished, declaring time had expired on the proposed amendment. He called for a vote and on a division found 108 ayes and 159 noes. Miller asked for tellers. May and Mason totaled the votes once more, finding 110 ayes and 210 noes. Woodrum declared Miller's amendment rejected. With its defeat went the last major obstacle to the bill.[125]

Following the defeat of Miller's amendment, Republican John M. Vorys of Ohio introduced an new amendment supported by those who opposed the "conscriptive" nature of the bill. It allowed Guardsmen to resign without seeking consent from the President or state governors. It quickly came under attack from Faddis and Wadsworth. Resurrecting the issue proved of no real value for Vorys and his followers. By a vote of 122 to 68, Administration supporters defeated the proposal.

In the closing minutes of debate Rich made one last try to curb any expansion of presidential powers by proposing an amendment which read: *"Provided,* That this resolution shall not be construed as granting to the President any additional powers not herein specifically granted."[126] Although it was ill-defined, Rich viewed the amendment as a step against Roosevelt establishing a dictatorship in the United States. Evidently his fellow representatives did not agree, for without debate they rejected the proposal.[127]

Woodrum then called for a final vote, this time on the measure itself. Few doubted the measure would pass, for even many of those who wished to limit the President's powers had spoken favorably of the measure as a whole. By an overwhelming vote of 342 to 34, the House passed a slightly modified Senate Joint Resolution 286. Unlike the Senate, the majority of Representatives who voted against the bill were Republican. Of the thirty-four negative votes, twenty-eight came from Republicans, five from Democrats, and one from Farm-Laborist Marcantonio.[128] The bill then returned to the Senate for consideration of differences.

CONFERENCE AND COMPROMISE

On August 19, the Senate took up the House version. Sheppard disagreed with amendments proposed by the House and called for a conference committee. By this method, he hoped to work out differences between the two versions without reopening the Senate debate on the authority of the President to send Guardsmen outside the country. The Senate agreed with Sheppard and appointed him, along with Democrats Robert R. Reynolds, Thomas of Utah, and Sherman Minton of Indiana. Senate Republicans on the Committee were Austin of Vermont, Styles Bridges of New Hampshire, and Chan Gurney of South Dakota. House members proved just as determined to retain their amendments and appointed May, Thomason, Democrat Dow W. Harter of Ohio, Andrews, and Short as their half of the conference committee. All members of the Conference Committee had voted for the bill and against the Adams and Miller amendments.

The Committee's August 20 report eliminated several of the House amendments while the Senate side agreed on another ten and agreed to allowing lieutenants and below to resign because of dependents, but only through usual channels. With both sides of the committee extremely favorable to the bill, little change actually occurred. By August 22, both houses of Congress had accepted the report and on August 26 the President Pro Temporary of the Senate and the Speaker of the House signed the bill. Roosevelt signed SJR 286 into law on August 27 as Public Resolution Number 96. The first, and easiest, portion of the Administration's conscription plan had passed. The larger fight was yet to begin. However, for the Guard, when the political debate ended, preparations for mobilization began.[129]

NOTES

1. U.S. Congress, *Congressional Record*, 76th Cong., 3rd sess., 1940, 86:9971.

2. Memorandum for R.F. from G.G.T., July 19, 1940; and Letter from Secretary of War Stimson to President Roosevelt, July 11, 1940, Franklin D. Roosevelt Papers, File 155 (Roosevelt Library).

3. U.S. Congress, Senate, Committee on Military Affairs, *Ordering Reserve Components and Retired Personnel into Active Military Service, hearings before the Committee on 'Military Affairs on SJR 286*, 76th Cong., 3rd sess., 1940, p. 1.

4. Ibid., 4.

5. Ibid., 6.

6. Ibid., 11-20.

7. Ibid., 21.

8. Ibid., 23.

9. Robert R. Palmer, Bell I. Wiley and William R. Keast, *The Procurement and Training of Ground Combat Troops* (Washington, DC, 1948), 91-92.

10. Ibid., 24.

11. Ibid., 24-25.

12. Ibid., 25.

13. Ibid., 30-31.

14. Ibid., 32.

15. Ibid., 30.

16. Ibid., 32.

17. Ibid.

18. Ibid.; National Guard Association, *Proceedings, 1940*, pp. 60-63 (National Guard Association Library).

19. Senate Report No. 1987, 76th Cong., 3rd sess., 1940.

20. Ibid.

21. "Public Opinion Poll," *Public Opinion Quarterly*, December 1940, pp. 716-717.

22. Summary sheet of a telegram from Hon. Burnet R. Maybank, governor of South Carolina, to President Roosevelt, June 2, 1940, Franklin D. Roosevelt Papers, National Guard File (Roosevelt Library).

23. Summary sheet of a letter from Hon. Herbert H. Lehman, governor of New York, to President Roosevelt, June 3, 1940, Roosevelt Papers, National Guard File (Roosevelt Library).

24. Summary sheet of a letter form Hon. Carl E. Bailey, governor of Arkansas, to President Roosevelt, June 20, 1940, Franklin E. Roosevelt Papers, National Guard File (Roosevelt Library).

25. Ibid.

26. Proclamation dated July 22, 1940, Alabama State Archives, Adjutant General File No. 2 (Montgomery, AL).

27. Letter to President Roosevelt, June 3, 1940, Roosevelt Papers, National Guard File (Roosevelt Library).

28. Telegram to President Roosevelt, June 4, 1940, Roosevelt Papers, National Guard File (Roosevelt Library).

29. "Mobilizing Guard Generally Favored by Press," *The United States News*, July 26, 1940, p. 29.

30. Ibid.

31. Ibid.

32. Ibid.

33. U.S. Congress, Senate, Committee on Military Affairs, *Ordering Reserve Components and Retired Personnel into Active Military Service, hearings before the Committee on Military Affairs on SJR 286*, 76th Cong., 3rd sess., 1940, p. 21; *New York Times*, July 7, 1940, p. 17.

34. Letter from Major General Roy D. Keehn to General Marshall, July 12, 1940, Bland, ed., *Marshall Papers*, II, 267.

35. Letter from Mr. Michael Desmond to Mr. Steven Early, Secretary to the President, August 10, 1940, Roosevelt Papers, National Guard File (Roosevelt Library).

36. National Guard Association, *Proceedings, 1940*, p. 36 (National Guard Association Library).

37. Ibid.

38. Cole, *Roosevelt and the Isolationists*, 393.

39. Ibid., 319.

40. U.S. Congress, *Congressional Record*, 76th Cong., 3rd sess., 1940, 86:9835-9837.

41. Wheeler, *Yankee from the West*, 17-22.

42. U.S. Congress, *Congressional Record*, 76th Cong., 3rd sess., 1940, 86:9838.

43. Ibid.

44. Ibid., 9841.

45. James T. Patterson, *Mr. Republican: A Biography of Robert A. Taft* (Boston, MA, 1972), 196.

46. U.S. Congress, *Congressional Record*, 76th Cong., 3rd sess., 1940, 86:9848.

47. Ibid.

48. James T. Patterson, *Congressional Conservatism and the New Deal* (Lexington, KY, 1967), 50, 271.

49. Pogue, *Ordeal and Hope*, 27-28.

50. U.S. Congress, *Congressional Record*, 76th Cong., 3rd sess., 1940, 86:9848.

51. Divine, *The Illusion of Neutrality*, 277.

52. U.S. Congress, *Congressional Record*, 76th Cong., 3rd sess., 1940, 86:9849.

53. Ibid.

54. Ibid., 86:9856.

55. Ibid., 86:9855-9857.

56. *New York Times*, August 7, 1940, pp. 1, 2; "Public Opinion Poll," *Public Opinion Quarterly*, September 1940, p. 551; Cole, *Roosevelt and the Isolationists*, 379.

57. U.S. Congress, *Congressional Record*, 76th Cong., 3rd sess., 1940, 86:9966.

58. Ibid., 86:9967.

59. Ibid., 86:9969.

60. Leuchtenburg, *Roosevelt and the New Deal*, 266-267; Sherwood, *Roosevelt and Hopkins*, 177.

61. U.S. Congress, *Congressional Record*, 76th Cong. 3rd sess., 1940, 86:9971.

62. Ibid., 86:9977.

63. Ibid., 86:9990

64. Ibid.

65. Ibid.

66. Roosevelt included several members of Congress from both parties in the delegation to the Havana Conference to give it a bipartisan flavor. No treaty resulted from the meeting. Instead the representatives agreed to the Act of Havana as an executive agreement that "authorized any American country to take over and administer any European colony in the Western Hemisphere if it were threatened by change of sovereignty." It also stated that "any attempt on the part of a non-American state against the integrity or inviolability of the territory, the sovereignty, or the political independence of an American state shall be considered as an act of aggression against the states which sign this declaration." By those two provisions the United States hoped to cement hemisphere solidarity and shore-up sagging Latin American confidence in the United States' will to defend the hemisphere.

By placing the Act of Havana in the form of an executive agreement Roosevelt and Hull could bypass any isolationist opposition to the collective defense portion of the act. See Langer and Gleason, *Challenge to Isolation*, 688-702; Cole, *Roosevelt and the Isolationists*, 362; Hull, *Memoirs*, I, 813-830.

67. U.S. Congress, *Congressional Record*, 76th Cong., 3rd sess., 1940, 86:9993.

68. Ibid., 86:9994.

69. Ibid., 86:9996.

70. *New York Times*, August 8, 1940, p.1.

71. U.S. Congress, *Congressional Record*, 76th Cong., 3rd sess., 1940, 86:9998.

72. Ibid., 86:10049.

73. Ibid., 86:10050.

74. Ibid., 86:10054.

75. Ibid., 86:10054-10055.

76. Ibid., 86:10058.

77. Ibid.

78. Ibid.

79. Ibid., 86:10059-10060.

80. Ibid., 86:10060.

81. Ibid., 86:10061.

82. Ibid., 86:10062.

83. Ibid.

84. Ibid., 86:10063.

85. Ibid., 86:10066.

86. Ibid., 86:10066-10067.

87. Patterson, *Congressional Conservatism*, 290.

88. *Presidential Press Conferences*, XVI, 105; *New York Times*, August 10, 1940, p.1.

89. U.S. Congress, *Congressional Record.*, 76th Cong., 3rd sess., 1940, 86:10344.

90. Ibid., 86:10066, 10344.

91. Ibid., 86:10344-10345; *New York Times*, August 13, 1940, p. 10.

92. Alfred Steinberg, *Sam Rayburn: A Biography* (New York, 1975), 316.

93. U.S. Congress, *Congressional Record*, 76th Cong., 3d., sess., 1940, 86:10347.

94. Ibid., 86:10347.

95. Ibid.

96. Ibid.

97. Ibid., 86:10352.

98. Ibid., 86:10361.

99. Ibid., 86:10362.

100. Ibid.

101. Ibid., 86:10353-10354.

102. Ibid., 86:10351.

103. Ibid.

104. Ibid., 86:10358.

105. Ibid., 86:10352.

106. Ibid., 86:10353.

107. Ibid., 86:10365-10369.

108. Ibid., 86:10373.

109. Ibid., 86:10372.

110. Ibid.

111. Ibid., 86:10374.

112. Ibid., 86:10429.

113. Ibid.

114. Ibid., 86:10430.

115. Ibid.

116. Ibid.; *New York Times*, August 16, 1940, p. 6.

117. U.S. Congress, *Congressional Record*, 76th Cong., 3d. sess., 1940, 86:10432.

118. Ibid.

119. Ibid., 86:10434.

120. Ibid., 86:10435.

121. Ibid.

122. Ibid.; *New York Times*, August 16, 1940, p.6.

123. U.S. Congress, *Congressional Record*, 76th Cong., 3rd sess., 1940, 86:10436.

124. Ibid.

125. Ibid.; *New York Times*, August 16, 1940, p. 1.

126. U.S. Congress, *Congressional Record*, 76th Cong., 3rd sess., 1940, 86:10447.

127. Ibid..

128. *New York Times*, August 16, 1940,. p. 1.

129. U.S. Congress, *Congressional Record*, 76th Cong., 3rd sess., 1940, 86:10461, 10528, 10760-10763, 10791, 10952, 11088; H.R. Rep. No. 2874, 76th Cong., 3rd sess., 1940. See also *New York Times*, August 21, 1940, p. 1; August 23, 1940, p. 1; August

24, 1940, p. 1; August 29, 1940, p. 1.

6

Mobilization

"Join the Guard and go with the boys you know!"
—Guard recruiting slogan.[1]

INDUCTION PLANNING

When Marshall testified at the July 30 Senate Military Affairs Committee hearing, he had already spent three weeks preparing detailed procedures for inducting the Guard. By July 22, plans specified which units the Army would federalize in the first increment, their training stations, and their housing needs; corps area and army commanders knew which units would train at their camps. For planning purposes, the Adjutant General of the Army dispatched letters a week later to all army and corps area commanders, setting Monday, September 16, for induction of the first increment of Guardsmen.[2]

On August 8, before the Senate concluded its debate on SJR 286, the Adjutant General sent all army, corps, and department commanders a tentative mobilization plan. Based on G-3 studies, it provided each Guard unit at least ten day's notification before induction, a time believed by planners to be sufficient for the men to settle their affairs. After induction, Guard units would remain at home stations for up to seven days and then depart for Army training camps. Assuming Congress passed the Guard bill by September 1, the Army planned to have the first increment of Guardsmen arrive at their camps by the end of September, which would leave them up to twenty days to reorganize before receiving the first influx of selectees, if the Selective Training and Service bill passed.[3]

As debate in both houses of Congress progressed and it became clear to Marshall that some form of exemption was inevitable, he directed General Williams, Chief of the National Guard Bureau, to formulate a plan to discharge men along expected Congressional guidelines. Following War Department guidance, the Guard had already discharged many men with dependents and other acceptable exemptions. Therefore, the Guard was ready to adapt existing plans to meet Congressional criteria for releasing men. Thus, when the bill passed with the anticipated exemptions, most exempted Guardsmen had already left service, their places filled by new recruits.[4]

INDUCTION

President Roosevelt federalized the first increment of Guardsmen on September 16, the day the Selective Training and Service Act of 1940 became law after heated debate.[5] Executive Order 8530 inducted the Thirtieth Division (North and South Carolina, Tennessee, and Georgia); the Forty-first Division (Idaho, Montana, Oregon, Wyoming, and Washington State); the Forty-fourth Division (New York and New Jersey); and the Forty-fifth Division (Oklahoma, Colorado, Arizona, and New Mexico). It also ordered coastal artillery units and observation squadrons to report to their armories and await orders. In all, 63,646 officers and men, many of whom had just returned from the 1940 summer maneuvers, responded to the order.[6] The remaining 140,840 Guardsmen waited for federalization. Yet there were manpower shortages. Each Guard division had an authorized peacetime strength of 22,000 men, however, a division counted itself lucky to have half that number. At 10,000 men, most Guard divisions entered federal service under a severe handicap—a lack of experienced men. The exemption policy had cut the Guard nearly in half. As men of experience were replaced by eager but green, recruits, Guard units floundered during maneuvers, a point not overlooked by the Army or the press.[7]

Both the Guard and the Army suffered shortages in weapons and equipment. During the summer of 1940 maneuvers units substituted sticks for machine guns, stove pipes for artillery pieces, trucks masqueraded as tanks, and light observation planes played the part of bombers. When the first increment of Guardsmen entered active service they found such conditions unchanged. Some Guardsmen even declared the situation worse. Much of their equipment came from Army stocks manufactured for the Great War and had been used by the Civilian Conservation Corps, and for many, even obsolete equipment could not be found.[8]

In accordance with General Staff plans, Guardsmen spent the first ten days of active duty at local armories, usually taking breakfast at home. During the day men drilled, loaded trucks with equipment, underwent medical examinations, and filled out a myriad of forms. Because few units owned kitchens, at noon, Guardsmen dined in local cafes at government expense. At night, those who lived nearby returned to their homes because as most armories lacked enough space to bed a complete unit.

Despite the confusion of first days, units assembled, packed their equipment, and transported themselves (by one method or another) to training camps. The Thirtieth "Old Hickory" moved to appropriately named Fort Jackson, South Carolina, while the Forty-first "Sunset" Division traveled to Camp Murray, Washington. New York and New Jersey's Forty-fourth Division traversed the short distance to Fort Dix, New Jersey. Men from the southwest's Forty-fifth "Thunderbird" Division made their way to unfinished Camp Barkeley, Texas. Coast Artillerymen manned at harbor defenses from Fort Williams, Maine, to Camp Hulen, Texas, and from Fort Worden, Washington, to Camp McQuaide, California. Although Guardsmen were somewhat prepared to enter the camps, the camps were ill-prepared for them. Fort Dix had barely enough barracks for 1,500 men, but the Forty-fourth numbered 10,882. Tents over wooden platforms provided "temporary" shelter for most of the division. Temporary, however, soon became standard for most of the Guard.[9] Major Hal L. Muldrow of the Forty-fifth later recalled the supply system during the cold days of late 1940 at the division's "temporary" base, Fort Sill, Oklahoma:

They issued overcoats in bales. They'd throw them out and a man didn't know if he was getting Size 14 or 44. And we had men who had to wear their civilian shoes for several months because the shoes provided by the Army initially were all the medium size.[10]

Bill Mauldin, wartime cartoonist and member of the Forty-fifth Division, found Fort Sill a virtual sea of mud. In his book *The Brass Ring* he noted that "it is nearly always muddy where infantry is, no matter how normally dry the climate."[11]

On October 15 the second increment of Guardsmen entered Federal service, consisting of the Twenty-seventh "Orion" Division (New York), the Thirty-second "Red Arrow" Division (Michigan and Wisconsin), the Thirty-seventh "Buckeye" Division (Ohio) plus observation squadrons, artillery units, and unattached infantry brigades. In all, 38,588 men joined an already overtaxed system. The third and fourth increments of November brought in yet another 33,000 Guardsmen. By the end of November 1940, 135,500 Guardsmen were in federal service. The Army's support structure was visibly weakened by the sudden influx; however, it had yet another shock to endure.[12]

Just when camp conditions seemed at their worst, in November the first group of 13,806 selectees entered the Army, stressing the system further. By March 1941, the glut of selectees meant that no National Guard division in active service contained less than thirty-three percent selectees. The Thirty-seventh's situation was common to most Guard divisions. After only four months of federal service the division had received 9,857 draftees (fifty-eight percent of its total strength).[13] What few experienced Guardsmen remained were engulfed by both inexperienced Guard recruits and selectees. As a result, the Army returned units to basic training schedules to educate the green soldiers at the cost of "higher training of the National Guard organizations as combat units."[14] Yet filling existing Army and Guard units with draftees did not begin to absorb the thousands of young men coming into the service. As a result, the Army created new units and stocked the cadre with the only experienced men available: Guardsmen, reservists, and Regulars. As one Guard historian wrote: "It was not at all unusual for units to be levied on four or five times before being filled up [with selectees] for a final time and permitted to go overseas."[15] Draftees diluted Guard units until they remained tied to their home states by name alone; unit morale and proficiency plummeted.[16]

EQUIVOCATION OVER EXTENSION OF SERVICE

The first increment of Guardsmen had been in federal service a month when General Reckord, at the NGA's October 1940 convention, pointed out a flaw in General Staff plans: once Guard units completed their year's federal duty they would, presumably, return home. Beginning in September 1941, over 40,000 selectees would be forced to join other units as their host Guard units departed for home. Since the number of "orphaned" selectees would increase rapidly, Reckord told NGA members, the system as planned would not work.

The fact is that this important matter has not yet been thought through by those in authority in the War Department to the point where they have determined what is to be done at the end of this year [of training]. It almost makes you feel that they did not expect us to come home at the end of a year. At least, that is the way I feel. That may be only my personal reaction. Something undoubtedly will have to be done next spring when the new Congress convenes, with respect to this matter.[17]

Reckord was correct; the General Staff had failed to adequately consider the problem. The War Plans Division had concerned itself with devising plans and schedules for demobilizing Guard units at the end of the year but not with the consequences of their demobilization.[18] Even when the fate of the Guard surfaced at a December 13, 1940 staff meeting, General Staff planners did not treat the topic with urgency. As historian Mark Watson wrote:

Army and Navy estimates were then contemplating the possibility that America would be in the war by 1 April 1941. It does not appear that either of these extensions of service [Guard and selectees] was then being pressed as a specific plan; rather, that the possibilities were foreseen, and that routine Staff planning against the possible, rather than merely against the assured event, led to consideration of that contingency and how to handle it.[19]

The January 1941 American-British Conversations (ABC-1) set the agenda for American participation in the war. Defeating Germany was the first priority. The Victory Program, a series of studies prompted by ABC-1, estimated the United States needed a ground army of over eight million men with Regulars, reservists, and Guardsmen forming its nucleus. With war presumably only months away, the General Staff spent little or no time planning Guard demobilization.[20]

However, in early spring, the issue of releasing or retaining the Guard took on greater importance. Rumors of an Army plan to extend Guard service eventually reached Guard divisions, creating uncertainty that affected training and discipline in the units. Officers and men alike saw little use in hard training if they were to go home at the end of one year. Unsure of their fate and bombarded by the isolationist newspapers of William Randolph Hearst and Robert R. McCormick telling them there was no reason to keep the Guard in service, Guardsmen's morale declined. The sarcastic acronym "OHIO," for Over the Hill In October, began to appear around the camps.

The rumors reached print on March 7, when the *New York Times* reported that the War Department had requested an extension, a report it denied.[21] Public reaction came quickly. Marshall received several letters from concerned citizens. The Chief of Staff's reply to Reverend David P. Gaines's letter of March 8 typified his public stand on extension.

The press statement to which you refer in your letter of March eighth was made without any basis of authority, either from me or from the War Department. It has since been officially corrected.

The reasons you advanced against an extension of National Guard training time are those which prompted the War Department initially to limit this period to one year. Frankly, before making a final decision in the matter we propose to wait and see what world conditions are when the end of the training period now authorized by law approaches. It is our hope that Providence will so dispose events that we can follow our original plan to return the officers and men of the Guard to their civilian occupations after one year of active duty.[22]

Throughout March and April of 1941, Marshall made firm public statements that no War Department plan existed for retaining Guardsmen or draftees in federal service beyond the prescribed year, and he even promised that demobilized Guard divisions could return home with their newly acquired equipment. In April the Chief of Staff told members of the House Appropriations Committee that "The decision does not have to be made until about three months before the first units of the National Guard have completed 12 months of service. . . . Until that time we are going on the assumption that the National Guard will return to its home station at the end of 12 months."[23]

The news from Europe, North Africa, and Asia did not bode well for the Allies. Earlier victories against the Italians in Libya were undone when the *Afrika Korps*, under General Erwin Rommel, entered the battle in late March. The April 6 Nazi invasion of Yugoslavia and Greece expanded the war further. In Asia, Japan began the occupation of northern Indochina on August 22, 1940, thus squeezing off another source of supply to the Chinese. The United States promptly embargoed steel to Japan. While these and other events heightened interventionist concerns, isolationists concluded that Germany's preoccupation in the Balkans and North Africa made intervention in the Western Hemisphere unlikely; thus the need to keep Guardsmen and selectees in service was unnecessary—a theme soon repeated in the halls of Congress.

On May 5, the retention issue resurfaced. The *New York Times* published a story claiming the War Department had recommended the President extend the terms of service for Guardsmen and selectees. Unlike the press report of March 7, the War Department issued no denial. Eleven days later, Secretary of War Stimson, probably to test the political waters, fueled speculation when he intimated that the Administration might request an extension.[24] Yet the General Staff had no firm plan. Marshall wrote confidential letters to Major Generals George A. White (commander of the Forty-first Division), Edward Martin (Adjutant General of Pennsylvania and commander of the Twenty-eighth Division), and William S. Key (commander of the Forty-fifth Division) requesting their observations and advice on the Guard's reaction to an extension of service.[25] All three favored an extension but only for a specified length of time. White wrote to Marshall: "I believe that a Presidential request of Congress to extend the period of service of the civilian components will be accepted as the inevitable and only possible course."[26]

One month later, Roosevelt ended Marshall's public denials when he acknowledged to reporters that the War Department did have a report that called for an extension of service. However, the President did not receive Secretary of War Stimson's memorandum requesting an extension until June 20, two days before the Nazi invasion of the Soviet Union. Penned by the General Staff, Stimson's memorandum called for the removal of "legislative restrictions [which] seriously limit[ed] the employment of the Army."[27] The memo reminded Roosevelt that the acts bringing the reserves to active duty and establishing the draft limited these groups to service within the Western Hemisphere. These limitations, Stimson believed, placed the Army under a hardship.

No part of the Army is free from these restrictions. The strength of the National Guard includes 37% trainees, and 10% Reserve officers. Except in Air Corps units, 60% of the enlisted strength of the field forces of the Regular Army in continental United States are trainees, and 78% of the officers are from the Reserve Corps.[28]

The General Staff had foreseen the possibility of sending troops outside the hemisphere and had formed four task forces of one division each, plus air and artillery units, to meet contingencies. However, this system had its flaws. Well over ninety percent of the task force divisions officers came from the Reserve Corps, barred by Public Resolution 96 from leaving the hemisphere. Replacing reserve officers meant denuding every division in the Army of regulars. The divisions' enlisted ranks were similarly affected. Only one division consisted almost entirely of regular troops. "However, the other three task force divisions contain[ed], respectively, 3,000, 4,600 and 5,200 Selective trainees."[29] Thus no division could legally leave the Western Hemisphere. Stimson offered two possibilities for removing the restrictions, both involving Congress. First was a joint resolution declaring the national interest imperiled by the world situation. Under the Selective Training and Service Act once Congress declared the national interest imperiled draftees could be retained. Stimson would also add a clause to the resolution empowering the President to employ the nation's armed forces anywhere he believed necessary. His second remedy called for amending the two laws separately to remove the restriction. Stimson strongly recommended that Roosevelt urge Congress "to remove the legislative restrictions on the employment of our land forces."[30] Nearly a week later Roosevelt wrote to Stimson:

I have carefully read your memorandum of June twentieth in regard to the removal of legislative restrictions.

It is my belief that these restrictions should be removed by the Congress at the earliest possible moment.

In view of the fact that I am about to leave to try to get some strength back at Hyde Park for four or five days, would you be good enough to talk with the Speaker, Majority Leader McCormack, Chairman May, and Congressman Wadsworth; and from the Senate with Senators Barkley, Byrnes and possibly Walter George and Reynolds as to which method would be the easiest to handle in the two Houses?

Please go ahead and get some thing started as soon as you can.

F.D.R.[31]

However, Roosevelt did not formally ask Congress to extend the Guard, reserve, and draftees' term of service until July 21. Despite Stimson's urging, Roosevelt's message to Congress did not openly request the removal of restrictions on service outside the hemisphere. Instead, it focused on the possibility of an army melting away due to the release of the reserves and draftees.

It is true that in modern war men without machines are of little value. It is equally true that machines without men are of no value at all. . . . Within two months disintegration, which would follow failure to take Congressional action, will commence in the armies of the United States. Time counts. The responsibility rest solely with Congress.[32]

Although the Administration faced considerable opposition in Congress and a public willing to aid Britain but committed to keeping out of the war, it no longer had to fear the NGA. On July 15, Reckord dispatched a letter to Marshall lending unqualified support. Maryland's general also offered his formidable skills as a spokesman for the proposed legislation.

I am personally of the opinion the gravity of the present situation warrants the retention of the selectees as well as members of the National Guard.

If you feel I can be of any service to you when this subject is under discussion in Congress and that I can with propriety speak upon the subject to members of the Senate and the House, I will be glad to do so, and I am confident General Martin of Pennsylvania and others feel as I do and will be ready and willing to assist in any way you may desire.[33]

The Administration's time of indecision on retaining the Guard in service had passed. But the President and Congressional supporters had yet to face the isolationists in Congress and the American public.

AID SHORT OF WAR

The fight in Congress over the induction of the National Guard was only an opening round in Roosevelt's struggle to prepare the nation's armed forces. Soon after passage of SJR 286 the Selective Training and Service bill reached the floors of the House and Senate. The ensuing battle, documented in *The First Peacetime Draft*, drew even more attention from isolationists. During the debate over SJR 286, many Congressmen willing to federalize the Guard as a traditional means of raising manpower, drew the line at a peacetime draft. However, by the time Congress voted on the draft bill, the Administration had strong bipartisan support. Radio broadcasts and newsreels of the air battles raging over Britain, which came to a climax in early September, dramatized the peril of a world at war. Republican presidential hopeful Wendell Willkie had added his support to the draft bill during his August 17 nomination acceptance speech. As Hiram Johnson wrote to his son, Willkie's stand "broke the back of the opposition to the conscription law," removing the issue from election politics and greatly upsetting isolationist supporters.[34] Yet the mood of the nation was clear. Conscription's time had arrived.[35] Congress responded to the growing national consensus on the issue and, on September 14, 1940 passed the Selective Training and Service Act.[36]

Amid the political storms created by inducting the National Guard and establishing a draft, Roosevelt pursued his primary goal of aiding Great Britain. On May 14, 1940, newly installed Prime Minister Winston S. Churchill cabled Roosevelt requesting "the loan of forty or fifty of your older destroyers to bridge the gap between" what Britain had and those it planned to build.[37] Roosevelt refused at first, believing the matter a Congressional prerogative, which meant that no such "loan" could take place as long as nonintervention sentiments held sway over the nation and Congress. To justify giving Britain the destroyers, the Administration decided that the exchange of them for air and naval bases in British possessions would strengthen the nation's defenses. By mid-August, public opinion, undoubtedly influenced by General Pershing's August 4 radio address for destroyers-for-bases, favored the exchange.[38] Public acceptance and Attorney General Robert Jackson's August 27 opinion that the President could make an exchange without Congressional approval provided the ammunition Roosevelt required. By concluding the destroyer deal with an executive agreement, Roosevelt avoided a political contest with opponents in Congress. Despite Churchill's initial reluctance to frame the agreement as a swap of bases for destroyers, the Prime Minister and the President finalized the deal on September 3, 1940. As Roosevelt had expected, the exchange of old destroyers for bases in the Western Hemisphere left little maneuvering room for isolationists who had long proposed exchanging Western Hemisphere colonies for European debts. Thus, the destroyer deal provided visible aid for Britain and acquired desired bases in the hemisphere.[39]

Willkie expressed approval of the destroyer deal in a confidential letter to Lord Lothian, British ambassador to the United States, but he did not wish to make a public pronouncement. While the Republican challenger, like Roosevelt, believed Great Britain's survival was vital to American security, he did not want to see the United States enter the war. Leaving the Selective Service Act and the destroyer deal out of the campaign, he attacked Roosevelt for not rearming the nation soon enough. On foreign affairs Willkie stated that Roosevelt had "dabbled in inflammatory statements and manufactured panics."[40] As the campaign progressed, Willkie's attacks on Roosevelt took on a decidedly isolationist flavor. Historian Wayne S. Cole attributed this change in an otherwise internationalist candidate to pressure from isolationists and the desire to win the election.[41]

The President responded to Willkie's charges by short inspections trips to Army and Navy installations, which gave the impression of a strong rearmament policy. As for the charge of leading the nation to war, Roosevelt repeatedly stressed his desire to keep the country at peace. On October 30, just one week before the election, Roosevelt said: "And while I am talking to you mothers and fathers, I give you one more assurance. I have said this before, but I shall say it again and again and again: Your boys are not going to be sent into any foreign wars."[42]

On election day, November 5, most Americans supported Roosevelt for an unprecedented third term. As the Republicans took only ten states, the election seemed to validate the President's agenda and signal the ebb of isolationist tide. Yet Americans remained as opposed to intervention as before.[43]

In the midst of the election campaign, isolationists had formed a national organization to challenge the internationalists. During the summer of 1940, a young graduate student at Yale University, R. Douglas Stuart, began organizing the America First Committee to oppose United States intervention in the war. Stuart won the support of General Robert E. Wood, Chairman of Sears, Roebuck and Company. On September 4, the day after the announcement of the destroyer deal, the fledgling organization launched itself onto the national stage. Publicly, the Committee backed no presidential candidate, but as the campaign progressed, America First became a bastion for isolationists and non-interventionists who could not support either candidate. It quickly became a counter-force to William Allen White's Committee to Defend America by Aiding the Allies. Although the election validated Roosevelt's policies, the propaganda war between these organizations captured the public's attention. The isolationists had at last acknowledged their mistake of not organizing a national movement.[44]

While events in both Europe and the Far East affected American opinion, Europe was the major focus of concern from the nation and the Administration. Germany had forced the British from the Continent and occupied seven European countries. As Congress opened debate on the SJR 286 in early August 1940, the Royal Air Force and the *Luftwaffe* were engaged in mortal combat in the skies over Britain. As the Guard entered federal service, London endured the German Blitz, which lasted until May 1941. Although Hitler had canceled an amphibious invasion of the British Isles, this was not known to the world at large, and on America's election day Britain's fate remained unclear. Although most of her Army's heavy equipment was lost in France, Britain's forces in Egypt now engaged the Italians in a fight for North Africa.[45] At sea, Britain had lost millions of tons of shipping in the Atlantic to German submarines, which in April 1941, caused the U.S. Army to issue an order for American forces stationed on British islands in the Western Hemisphere to resist any Axis attacks. By May 1941, the War Plans Division concluded that the time to go to a war status had come, despite the unprepared nature of the Army.[46]

Besides military worries, Great Britain faced an economic crisis. The loss of so much war material in France and the expansion of the war had drained its coffers. On December 17, 1940, President Roosevelt responded to Britain's plight by proposing "'to eliminate the dollar sign' in aiding Great Britain."[47] Roosevelt's "lend-lease" proposal drew immediate fire from isolationists, including the America First Committee. Notables such as Colonel Charles A. Lindbergh, Alf M. Landon, historian Charles Beard and socialist Norman Thomas testified against House Resolution 1776 (HR 1776), the so-called Lend-Lease Bill. Isolationists pointed to Britain's victories against the *Luftwaffe* in skies over London, success against the Italians in North Africa, and the June 22 German invasion of the Soviet Union as evidence that there was no creditable threat to the United States. The President, however, successfully mounted his own campaign against opponents. Both houses of Congress passed HR 1776 by two-to-one margins, thus weakening organized isolationism still further.[48]

Although Roosevelt continued to consider Britain's resistance to the Germans a prime concern of American security, the growing world crisis forced him to consider preserving American preparedness by retaining Guardsmen and selectees beyond one year. Roosevelt waited until July 21 before formally requesting that Congress extend the provisions of both Public Resolution 96 and the Selective Training and Service Act of 1940. Unlike the support for both bills the year before, the American public was more evenly divided on the extension issue. Fifty percent polled favored keeping draftees, and thus the Guard, in service. Forty-five percent of respondents believed selectees should go home.[49]

Roosevelt's request opened the last comprehensive debate on Army manpower before America's entry into the war. It also risked his political standing. Overwhelmingly Americans favored aiding Britain, but they were less certain on the question of extending the terms of service.

EXTENSION LEGISLATION

Once Roosevelt openly supported extension, the War Department sent a draft resolution to Congress calling for a declaration of national emergency. Section 1 of the bill read:

Resolved by the Senate and House of Representatives of the United States of America in Congress assembled, That the national interest and welfare of the United States are gravely imperiled by the international situation; that a national emergency therefore exists; and the President is hereby empowered to employ the armed land forces of the United States in excess of those of the Regular Army in the national defense.[50]

By its wording, the War Department bill proposed extending the terms of service of the Guard, reserve, and draftees until six months after emergency ended. It also raised the number who could be called up at any one time, allowed the President to use retirees called to active service as he saw fit, and extended job protection to those inducted after May 1, 1940. Most importantly, the draft bill enabled the President to decide the final length of service and how to use the men. As one of the General Staff's Congressional liaison officers noted, many in Congress seemed terrified of the extension bill, believing "a vote for the bill would be political suicide."[51] Marshall had already tried to overcome some of the apprehension by impressing upon legislators the need for extension. However, Congress was unprepared to go as far as the Army or the President desired.

After hearing testimony from the Chief of Staff, the Senate Committee on Military Affairs retired to consider the War Department bill.[52] Political pressure from pacifists, isolationists, and anti-Roosevelt groups made accepting the Administration's proposal difficult. The bill returned to the Senate on July 28 resembled the War Department's draft in form, yet the substance had changed. Instead of declaring the existence of a national emergency, the Committee used the language of the Selective Training and Service Act of 1940: "That the Congress, acting in accordance with the provisions of section 3 (b) of the Selective Training and Service Act of 1940, hereby declares that the national interest is imperiled."[53] Thus, the Committee avoided using the term "national emergency," with all the powers it passed on to the President. However, by inserting the phrase "the national interest is imperiled," from the draft law, Congress could legally hold the draftees indefinitely without increasing Roosevelt's power. In section 2 of the Committee's version of the bill, the President gained authority to retain reservists, Guard units, and retired Army personnel for as long as the period of peril persisted. While this mirrored the War Department's bill, the Committee added a provision allowing Congress some power over how long the extension lasted. The Committee penned: "*Provided*, That the authority hereby conferred may be revoked at any time by concurrent resolution of the Congress."[54]

In section 3, the Committee addressed an issue the Army believed it had already covered in the 1940 Acts—deferment or release of men for hardship. In the intervening months, a public movement had begun for the release of men with hardships caused by Army service or of men over the age of twenty-eight. Although the Committee retained wording that gave the Secretary of War discretionary power over whom to release, it bowed, at least in form, to public opinion.[55]

In its last major divergence from the War Department's draft bill, the Committee refused to remove the cork from the manpower bottle without Congressional involvement. While section 6 of the Committee's bill removed the manpower limitation imposed by the Selective Training and Service Act (900,000 men), the Committee added a proviso requiring the Secretary of War to submit monthly figures on Army strength, placing the Administration on notice that it would closely watch the Army's size.[56]

On July 28, one week after Roosevelt announced support for service extension, Senator Elbert D. Thomas of Utah submitted the Senate Military Affairs Committee's report and its substitute bill, to the Senate. Only Democrat Robert R. Reynolds of North Carolina, the Committee Chairman, disagreed with the report.

While Senate leaders confidently predicted passage of the measure by a two-to-one margin, opponents gathered their forces. Senator Robert A. Taft joined the fray soon after Thomas reported the joint resolution out of committee. Although he did not oppose a form of Selective Service, he did oppose both the War Department's original draft bill and the Military Affairs Committee compromise bill. As a third alternative, Taft submitted his own plan for maintaining the Army's strength. It called for increasing the Army's strength above the 900,000 limit imposed by the Selective Service Act. As new men entered the system, 75,000 men a month would leave the Army after completing a year's training. Taft had submitted his proposal to Marshall, who rejected it as not meeting the Army's needs. Not satisfied with Marshall's rejection, Taft planned to fight for his bill on the Senate floor.[57]

As Thomas delivered the compromise bill to the full Senate, the Administration ran into trouble in the House Military Affairs Committee. In an effort to rush the bill to the full House, Congressman May attempted to limit the testimony of opposition witnesses. Representative Dewey Short of Missouri shouted his objection to May's tactics. "Talk about 'railroading'" said Short. "They will hear about this on the floor."[58] Representative Short's protest, echoed by Massachusetts Republican Charles R. Clason, forced May to allow additional testimony from groups such as Mothers of the U.S.A. that were committed to the extension bill's defeat.[59]

On Monday, July 28, Administration supporters in the Senate wanted to rush the extension bill through, possibly debating the bill on Thursday. However, they altered their plans on Tuesday after Senator Burton K. Wheeler announced that extension opponents had decided not to use the filibuster or other delaying tactics against the bill. As in 1940, they concluded that SJR 95 was unbeatable. Their best hope lay in narrowing the bill's focus and, thereby, Roosevelt's power. Administration supporters took the announcement as a signal to rush the bill to the floor on Wednesday instead of Thursday, they expected an even quicker victory.[60]

In the House Military Affairs Committee battle lines drew even tighter. Chairman May announced that the Committee had agreed to a compromise bill similar to the Senate's version, which he expected to report to the House on Wednesday. However, Representative Short told the press that he, and presumably others on the committee, supported extending the terms of service for reservists and the Guard but not for selectees. Short promised to fight reporting the resolution.[61]

On July 30 Senator Thomas opened the debate on SJR 95 by explaining each section and answering questions. Two hours into the general debate Republican Senator Charles W. Tobey of New Hampshire attacked the measure as unnecessary.

If the situation is so acute and the President has this intimate knowledge by which the Military Affairs Committee was so impressed, as it was impressed by General Marshall's testimony, there must be something the President knows and General Marshall knew and passed on to the committee that is "brass tacks" and arouses apprehension.

Why should not the Congress and the plain people of this country have a showdown in definite terms—epigrammatic language—of what the facts are, what the dangers are, which justify the statement of the President—"I believe, I know, it is much more serious."[62]

Having anticipated the opposition's strategy, Thomas responded that Germany was even more powerful at that moment than it had been in September 1939. Thomas told the Senate that as of July 16, the German army had 192 infantry divisions plus the armament production of Czechoslovakia, France, Belgium, and Denmark. Thomas believed that Germany had increased its motorized forces ten times, its infantry five times, and more than doubled the number of armored divisions. Germany's increase in military might, Thomas contended, threatened American interests.[63]

Although few senators were in the chamber during the exchange between Toby and Thomas, political observers believed that Thomas' impassioned plea "shoved the measure a long way toward passage in the Senate."[64] By the end of the day Senate leaders confidently stated that they could pass the measure before the weekend.[65]

Leaders in the House continued to couch their situation in positive phrases, yet their fight had not truly begun. Before the debate started in the Senate, the House Military Affairs Committee issued two reports on its compromise bill.[66] The majority report, delivered to the House by Committee Chairman Andrew J. May, followed closely the spirit, if not the actual wording of the Senate's compromise bill. Unlike the Senate, the House Committee included seven dissenters who issued a report questioning the threat to national interest and the immediate disintegration of the Army. They held that the nation was "incomparably stronger today than we were a year ago and it is obvious that each day as the warring nations spend their strength and become weaker, the United States each day is growing stronger."[67] They pointed to Winston Churchill's statement that England had broken German air superiority and that the Nile was "much safer" as evidence that the threat to the nation had decreased. They also pointed to the German invasion of Russia as another sign of diminished peril to national interests. Minority members feared that a declaration of national emergency and extending selectees' terms of service were only the first steps toward another American Expeditionary Force.[68]

In the second part of the minority report, dissenters disputed the idea that the Army verged on evaporation. The minority contradicted Marshall's statement that the Army would melt away by August 1. They pointed to the figures submitted by the Chief of Staff that the largest single release of selectees (153,159) would occur in March 1942. Before that time, many other inductees would have replenished the ranks. The minority suggested:

If the men are properly inducted, in a gradual, steady, and efficient manner, it could be so arranged that even a much smaller number would be prevented from leaving the Army in any one month. This would not destroy the Army nor would it imperil the Nation's defense. It would insure us a quick turn-over in our Army and it would give us many more trained men.[69]

Although the seven dissenting members of the House Committee discounted Marshall's advice and endorsed Senator Taft's plan, they could not agree to lift the limitation on the number of men serving at one time. Marshall had asked for an army of 1,700,000 men. The minority pointed out that 900,000 selectees could serve at one time, yet the Army had only 600,000 in uniform. Combining the regular Army, the Guard, reservists, selectees, and the Air Corps, the dissenters concluded that Marshall could have his Army by merely adding the 300,000 selectees provided for in the Selective Training and Service Act. However, they doubted the Army could adequately care for so large a force.[70]

While the minority rejected keeping selectees in service beyond one year, they supported the part of the proposed resolution that allowed retention of reservists and Guardsmen. The minority believed "Section 4 of the resolution should also be enacted since the retired personnel of the Regular Army are needed as much as the National Guard to train raw recruits and selectees."[71] The Army had thus won a portion of its goal before the measure reached the House floor. Retaining the Guard would not become an issue. However, because the two issues were linked under one resolution, retention of the Guard depended on passage of an extension bill. If the extension bill failed, the first Guard units would leave for home in the middle of September.

The Thursday, July 31, Senate debate opened with Senators Wheeler, Vandenberg, and Tobey launching attacks on the War Department, Hollywood, and Wendell Willkie. Vandenberg and Tobey denounced what they termed a campaign by the War Department to deny selectees, reservists, and Guardsmen their right to speak out on the extension bill. They charged that the Army prevented or threaten disciplinary action against servicemen who openly opposed the bill.[72] Senator John A. Danaher, ardent opponent of the Administration, speculated whether the Army would begin dissolving the next day, August 1, the date Marshall had suggested as the deadline for any decision on retention. He believed that "the leadership thought they would have us in the war by now, and that the question [of an extension] would be academic and never would arise."[73] Lister Hill of Alabama, who had battled Danaher on the Guard mobilization a year before, once again rose to defend the Administration. He stated that if the leaders had wanted to involve the nation in the World War they could have done so long before then. Hill told his fellow senators:

I will say that if the leaders had wanted to get the Nation into war, certainly any man who can see beyond his nose can see well enough to know that there would have been no difficulty about getting us into war. On the contrary, every effort has been made to keep us out of war; and, because these efforts have been made to keep us out of war, we are today not in war, but at peace.[74]

At the end of the day's debate, Administration supporters had lost much of their hope for the bill's early passage. Although they remained confident of its ultimate passage, opposition senators had clouded the issue with amendments.   Besides Taft's plan, opposition senators had inserted amendments to increase enlisted men's pay, release men twenty-eight years old and above, and to further restrict selectees' terms of service.[75]

Opposition stalling led the President and his supporters to search for a way to widen their base of support. As the week came to a close, an Administration surprise temporarily caught the opposition off guard. At the behest of the President, the Senate Military Affairs Committee agreed that Guardsmen, reservists, and selectees would be retained for only eighteen more months instead of "the duration" of the emergency or peril. Wheeler, retreating to the opposition's second line of defense, charged that any changes to the 1940 Acts constituted a breech of contract with the inducted men. Despite Wheeler's attempted to paint the measure as unfair, a definite time limit on extension brought wavering senators to the Administration's side.[76] The opposition had suffered a major blow.

On Monday, August 4, as the Senate renewed debate, the opposition continued their attack on the Administration. Senator Brooks told senators:

I speak today for the Taft amendment to limit the services of these men to 18 months. I do not believe we shall extend it at all except we are in peril. Why are we in peril? We are in peril because of the progress the present administration has made toward war. In every step they take they move first, and then they ask for authority.[77]

Senator Lee of Oklahoma responded to Brooks' charge that the President wanted the United States to enter the war by calling it "the rankest sort of demagoguery."[78] "I do not want war," he told the Senate. "I know President Roosevelt does not want war. I do not believe there is a Member of this body who wants war."[79] He went so far as to say that Hitler did not want war with the United States. Hitler, he contended, would rather conquer the world without a fight.

To infer that America is faced with danger today because of the policy of this Administration does not square with the facts. . . . So I say that if any action, or lack [of] action, on our part has brought us nearer to danger, it has been from following the policy of isolation.[80]

Despite the opponents' attacks, Administration supporters were able to limit debate on the Taft alternative plan to 1 P.M. on August 5. Since Senate leaders expected barely thirty votes in favor of Taft's plan, the

Administration's supporters expected to sweep through the other amendments and pass SJR 95 by late Tuesday or early Wednesday. Senate action on the Taft proposal prompted House leaders to initiate action on their version of the Senate compromise bill. The House Rules Committee cleared the bill's path to the House floor and allowed only two days' debate. However, House opponents, especially Hamilton Fish of New York, vowed a fight on the floor.[81]

The August 5 debate began as expected. Administration supporters easily defeated Taft's plan by fifty to twenty-seven (the opposition mustering three votes less than anticipated).[82] Yet soon after the vote, Administration support almost unraveled. Unknown to Senate Majority Leader Alben W. Barkley, several Democratic members of the Senate Military Affairs Committee had met with Senate Republicans and arranged a compromise limiting total service of draftees, reservists, and Guardsmen to two years, an extension of one year. By further lessening service time, the new coalition hoped to win additional bipartisan support in both houses.[83] Barkley, confused by the sudden change, spoiled their efforts when he gained the floor to "plead that Congress stand behind the President and the War Department in their request for a trained army and at least support the plan of the Military Affairs committee for extending [service] . . . by eighteen month to make it two years and a half."[84]

Senators Josh Lee and A. B. Chandler reacted angrily to Barkley's plea, since as members of the Military Affairs Committee, they had supported the one year compromise. With Barkley's refusal to agree to a one year extension, Lee and Chandler abandoned the compromise. Lee called for an "outright declaration of a state of national peril, with no limitation on the active service of the citizen soldiers."[85] Even Thomas of Utah, one of the bill's sponsor, stated that he would vote for the eighteen month extension, but added that he only mildly opposed a year's extension.[86] Barkley quickly shelved the debate on the extension bill, diverting the Senate's attention to other matters. However, the damage had been done. Efforts aimed to bring in uncommitted senators had almost split Administration support.

Administration ranks remained split as the next days' debate opened with a discussion on the one year extension plan. Barkley pressed for the Administration's eighteen month extension proposal. In a surprise move, isolationists leaders Wheeler, Danaher, and Clark joined in the chorus against one year extension. They had not changed their minds on the bill, but hoped that defeat of the one year extension would make the bill "unpalatable" to undecided senators. As a result, fifty senators voted against the compromise while only twenty-one voted for the one year extension.[87] Wheeler found himself, perhaps uncomfortably, on the same side as Hill and Barkley.

Having helped defeat the one year extension, isolationists then returned to attacks on the Administration. Alva B. Adams of Colorado attacked the Administration's claim that the nation's interests were imperiled. He denied that the Western Hemisphere was threatened and asserted that SJR 95 was part of a program by which "step-by-step the American people have been prepared emotionally and materially for war."[88] Danaher continued Adams' attack by quoting newspaper articles that noted the President's departure on a "carefree vacation," thus illustrating that if the President was off boating, no crisis loomed on the horizon.[89] Unknown to Danaher and many other Congressmen at the time, Roosevelt was aboard the USS *Augusta* heading to Argentia Bay, Canada for a meeting with Churchill, where they formed the Atlantic Charter.[90]

The isolationists, however, had already lost. In the final Senate vote on August 7, the Administration won with forty-five votes. Although opponents mustered only the expected thirty votes, they had forced the Administration to retreat from a declaration of national peril and an indefinite extension of military service for selectees, reservists, and Guardsmen.[91]

By the time Representative May, chairman of the House of Representatives Military Affairs committee and sponsor of the bill, introduced the measure to the House floor, battle lines had been drawn. As in the Senate, House opponents planned to attack Administration motives and the need for the legislation. Unlike the Senate, House opponents stood a good chance of defeating the measure. Two days before the bill reached the House floor, Majority Leader John W. McCormack reported "that forty-five Democrats were definitely opposed to the measure and thirty-five were undecided."[92] Opposition in the House, both Democrats and Republican, stemmed from an entrenched hatred of the President. Much to General Marshall's chagrin, Congressmen who personally favored the bill would not vote for it because of partisan politics. Indeed anti-Roosevelt feelings compelled Administration supporters to distance the President from the bill by thrusting into his place the Chief of Staff. Since Marshall had already taken the lead in the press and before Congressional committees, as Marshall's biographer Pogue noted, "Many of the doubtful congressmen were willing to back the resolution if he [Marshall] rather than the President would state the administration's case."[93] However, the Chief of Staff was not above reproach. Hamilton Fish called Marshall a good soldier, but then proceeded to cast doubt on his testimony before Congressional committees by suggesting that the loyal soldier followed the Secretary of War's lead.[94]

When debate opened on August 8, McCormack came to the Chief of Staff's defense, and thus to the defense of the bill, citing Marshall as the military authority requesting the extension. The House Majority Leader compared Marshall's dealings with Congress to those of General George Washington.

When I hear the utterances of those who, knowing nothing, laymen like me, would substitute their opinion for the opinion of the Chief of Staff, General Marshall, my mind goes back in history to the Revolutionary days. . . . We know that historians record that the Revolutionary War continued for 2 years longer than it would have if the

Continental Congress had accepted the re-commendations of the Chief of Staff in those days, Gen. George Washington. . . . Let us not be put in a position now, in this time of crisis to our Nation, of having it said in the future that this Congress refused to follow the recommendations of General Marshall, Chief of Staff of the United States Army.[95]

Representative Short, a dissident member of the House Military Affairs Committee, disputed Marshall's reputation, decrying "blanket and dogmatic statements" made by Roosevelt and Marshall of a national peril without offering evidence of its gravity.[96] Yet, Short believed that a crisis did exist large enough to warrant retention of draftees. He told the House that the Army had five times the number of men it possessed a year before and that since then England had increased its strength while Hitler's attack Russia sapped Germany military vitality. Short went on to state that keeping draftees in service beyond one year would weaken the forces already developed. "To prolong the period of service," he stated, "of the men now in the Army and to freeze them there would produce a static Army instead of a dynamic one."[97] Yet opponents did not press for the demobilization of Guard units or reservists at the end of one year. On the contrary, Short wanted to keep the Guard and reservists under arms as long as necessary.

We reject that part of section 2 of the resolution that would give the President power to continue in service these selectees, but we would give him the power to continue the National Guard, the reserve components, and the retired personnel of the Regular Army during the emergency he declared, provided you keep in that section of the provision that the authority of the President could be revoked by a concurrent resolution of Congress.[98]

Fish and Short's attacks on the Chief of Staff had little if any telling effect on the issue. A strong supporter of national defense, General Wood of the America First Committee (AFC) had already decided to remain silent on the extension bills and on Marshall's part in the bills' formulation. As Michele Flynn Stenehjem noted in *An American First*:

General Wood believed that the public would perceive the draft-extension question as one of defense rather than of foreign policy, and he therefore decided that for the AFC to stand in direct opposition to the army chief of staff would cause the public to doubt committee patriotism.[99]

Fish and Short, along with journalist John T. Flynn and Socialist Norman Thomas represented a minority in America First who tried to resist Wood's stand.[100]

Fish proposed yet another alternative to retaining draftees beyond one year the release of all married men; discharge of all draftees after one year of service, provided that no more than 45,000 could leave the Army at one time, and an Army limited to two million men. That limit, he hoped, would provide an adequate defense while preventing the formation of an army of intervention. Fish asserted his belief that the bill was:

part and parcel of a gigantic conspiracy which has for its main purpose our involvement in European, Asiatic, and African wars without the consent or approval of the Congress and the American people, who are overwhelmingly opposed to such action.[101]

May responded to Fish's charge of Administration warmongering by reiterating Marshall's statement that neither the Army nor the Administration had any intention of sending troops to Europe. Yet he backed away from any definitive statement that the Army would not go beyond American soil to protect the national interests, even to Dakar, Africa.[102]

As the House adjourned for the weekend, Administration supporters began lobbying Republicans likely to favor the bill while twisting the arms of undecided Democrats. Head counts revealed that the bill's supporters needed every vote they could muster. However, while counting noses, McCormack discovered that an eighteen month plan similar to the Senate version of the bill might pass the House. The *New York Times* reported "the fate of the bill probably would be determined by the votes of their large groups from New York City, Philadelphia and Chicago."[103]

Representative Short, also active over the weekend, announced to the press that the opposition planned to base their fight on two amendments, one to make service extension apply only to the National Guard and reserves, and second, to remove the phrase "the national interest is imperiled" from the preamble of the resolution. The Selective Training and Service Act of 1940 specifically stated that the government could only hold draftees beyond one year if the national interest was in peril. By deleting the phrase, opponents hoped to "remove the heart of the bill."[104] However, the Guard and reserve could still be held by the remaining sections.[105]

As the weekend ended, both sides claimed that they had made progress. On Sunday night, Democratic leaders told reporters that they had won over at least five, if not ten, undecided or opposition representatives. May still claimed that the bill enjoyed sufficient support to remove any time limit on the length of service, while Short said that only twelve Republicans would support the measure.

The death of Representative Albert G. Rutherford of Pennsylvania on Sunday caused an unexpected delay that allowed both sides to continue their arm twisting. Out of a meeting between Speaker of the House Sam Rayburn, Majority Leader McCormack, and members of the Military Affairs Committee came a decision that the bill's supporters would accept the eighteen month limitation, as passed by the Senate, and release all men from the Army whose business or dependents would suffer further from their absence. Unlike the Senate bill, the Committee's decision left no room for the Army discretion;

but, as in the Senate, House leaders hoped to win undecided votes by agreeing to the limitation.[106]

When debate resumed on Tuesday, House members spent much time in arguing minor side issues. On more important amendments, the opposition suffered one defeat after another. Short's attempt to gut the resolution by striking the "imperil clause" failed by a vote of 185 to 146.[107] Elston's amendment to keep the Army at 900,000 men met a similar fate.[108] Trying to at least limit the extension, Short offered an amendment allowing only twelve additional months of service but that also suffered defeat. The opposition could never muster the votes necessary to recommit the bill to committee, one last effort to delay the bill. When the final vote came on the resolution, the Administration won by the narrowest of margins, one vote. By a vote of 203 to 202 the House passed the measure and sent it to a conference committee to iron-out differences. One hundred and thirty-three Republicans and sixty-five Democrats opposed the bill while 182 Democrats joined by twenty-one Republicans stood behind the Administration. Immediately after the vote, May moved that the House set aside the just-passed resolution in favor of the Senate version, and also moved that the House language supplant the Senate's. The motion carried.[109]

Senate and House leaders jointly urged the Senate conferees to consider the two bills' differences. Failure to reconcile meant that a compromise version of the two resolutions would undergo yet another trip through both Houses. While the Senate was sure to pass the measure a second time, bill supporters could not risk a second round in the House.[110] Senate conferees relented and on August 15, accepted the House version. After both Houses accepted the final version, Roosevelt signed it into law on August 18.[111]

Although the opposition lost the contest, many believed that they had won a victory. They had forced the Administration to back away from an unlimited extension and had curbed the language of the bill to the extent that no "emergency" existed, only that the interests of the nation were "imperiled." In their opinion the difference of words marked a decline in the President's powers. The narrowness of the vote in the House encouraged Burton Wheeler; the Administration could not expect to pass a war declaration short of an all out attack.[112]

TROUBLE WITH THE GUARD

While the Administration faced trouble with Congress, the Chief of Staff confronted restlessness in the Guard. Despite NGA support of the extension bill, relations between the Army and the Guard had worsened since the passage of SJR 286. Even before the 1940 mobilization started in earnest, Guard leaders, Reckord in particular, braced for a renewal of the old feud. Although speaking of the Selective Training and Service Act of 1940,

Reckord, at the September 1940 AGA meeting, reflected the Guard's mood when he told the assemblage: "It was only because of the necessity which confronted us at the time of great emergency that I felt we had to lay down and let the old steam roller run over us and grind a bill out."[113]

But Reckord stood his ground on two issues: the fate of Guard officers and the integrity of Guard units once they entered federal service. Although he agreed with the removal of incompetent officers, he and many other NGA members had vivid memories of the wholesale removal of Guard officers during World War I. On September 4, 1940 Reckord, determined to forestall any reoccurrence of that experience, wrote to General Marshall on the subject.

First, I feel that no attempt should be made to send officers of high rank to schools, but rather that they be left in their official capacity to assist in the training of the divisions. I cannot help but recall the terrible experiences had by some officers in the World War, where these men, who desired to serve their country, were ruthlessly thrown aside as of no value when they had served practically their entire lives with the idea of being of some value should war ever come. I, myself, attended the famous Patsy Dugan school at Fort Sam Houston, which was nothing more nor less than an elimination contest. It is my humble opinion that inefficient officers can be discovered and eliminated without the necessity of any such ruthless treatment as was experienced by many in the World War.[114]

Marshall was particularly sensitive to Guard feelings on this matter. His three year tour of duty with the Illinois National Guard made him aware of Guardsmen's attitudes toward the Army. The preceding year had reinforced Marshall's earlier experience; during the budget fight, Reckord showed the NGA had political power and would use it. As a result, the Chief of Staff moved cautiously in removing Guard officers, but he did not shrink from the necessity of removing an officer, even in the face political opposition. Marshall biographer Forrest C. Pogue recorded the repercussions of one general's removal: "General Marshall received a protest from the entire congressional delegation from the general's home state."[115] He defended the decision as protecting many of their constituents, members of the division, while they sought to protect only one man, the general. Marshall told the Congressmen: "I am not going to leave him in command of that division. So I will put it to you this way-if he stays, I go, and if I stay, he goes."[116] The resolve of the delegation wilted in the face of Chief of Staff's determined stand; the general was removed.

Although Marshall exercised cautious judgement when removing Guard officers, NGA leaders viewed other regular officers as conducting a vendetta against the Guard. Lieutenant General Lesley J. McNair, General Headquarters (GHQ) Chief of Staff, quickly became the NGA's major villain; he was no friend of the NGA and made no attempt to win its favor.[117] At his direction, Guard officers were removed from their divisions, in what seemed to the Guard, wholesale numbers. Although usually replaced by reserve officers, Guardsmen quickly accused the Army of removing their officers in order to promote Regular officers. In June 1941, Marshall moved to quell the Guard's growing ire by proposing the creation of a "group of prominent active and retired officers to advise the Secretary of War on officer removal."[118] The Advisory Board, as it became known, followed the Chief of Staff's intention of making use of Guard and reserve officers not considered fit for combat duty but still useful to the service. By reclassifying relieved officers Marshall and the Board preserved potential talent while weeding out unfit commanders. It also avoided open political warfare.[119]

In his attempts to maintain peace within the Army of the United States, in several cases the Chief of Staff actively sought Guardsmen to fill posts vacated by relieved Guard officers. Marshall's policy found expression in an October 23, 1941 letter to Lieutenant General Ben Lear of the Second Army.

In considering the capabilities of a National Guard officer to command a National Guard unit, it is not believed that we should compare him with the best available Regular Army officer. Rather we should consider, in my opinion, whether or not the National Guard officer is capable of discharging the duties of the position in a creditable manner. If he can qualify under that standard, I feel that the National Guard officer should be selected.[120]

If no Guardsman proved qualified even under the relaxed policy, Marshall then allowed the placement of a qualified Regular or reserve officer in a Guard unit. But such replacement officers had to meet stringent standards.[121]

Despite Marshall's almost kid-glove treatment of officer replacement, the Guard retained a resentment for the alleged ill treatment of its officers long after the war was over. In 1953, for example, Major General Ellard A. Walsh, then president of the NGA, vented some of his rage by telling the NGA: "They [Guard officers] were relieved on any pretext, and sometimes on no pretext at all. In one instance a directive was issued by a high headquarters to relieve every National Guard officer and replace him with a Regular officer."[122]

Yet Guard officers fared as well, and sometimes better, than their Regular Army counterparts. Of twenty-one Guard generals who entered federal service in 1940 only Major General Robert S. Beightler remained at the head of his division, the Thirty-seventh Infantry, at the close of the war. However, nine Guard generals were in service in 1945. Of 273 Guard colonels who entered federal service before the war, 148—54.2 percent—remained on active service in 1945. Regular Army generals and colonels did not fare as well. Of twenty-one similarly ranked regular Army generals in service during 1940, five remained on active duty at the end of the war, and only thirty-nine percent of 1940 regular Army colonels remained in uniform on V-J Day. Although most inducted Guard general and field grade officers did not remain with their units, statistics showed that mobilization improved a Guardsman's chance of advancement. By war's end, 75,000 enlisted Guardsmen (a quarter of the Guard's 1940 strength) had become officers.[123]

The second major issue that troubled Reckord and the NGA was the loss of unit identity once inducted into the Army of the United States. Guard leaders who had been through the chaotic shuffling of units during World War I continuously sought legislative protection from a future dismemberment of Guard units. During the debate on the National Defense Act of 1920 Guard leaders sought a protective amendment from Congress, but obtained only a statement from Congress that Guard units should remain intact when federalized. No Congressional mandate compelled the Army to leave Guardsmen, or Guard units, in their original structure. In 1933, the NGA lobbied for the creation of the National Guard of the United States, believing that by forming a federal reserve, Guard units would remain indivisible.[124] However, even with this solution NGA leaders continued to worry that the Army would once again break up federalized Guard units.

Marshall knew of the NGA's concern and, on October 22, 1940, made a special point of reassuring NGA leaders that the National Guard would not lose its identity.[125] However, once the Guard entered federal service the Army converted or renumbered units at a rapid pace. In essence, the Army carried out a modification of its December 1939 Guard reorganization plan. The plan, which General Blanding projected as requiring years to complete, reached fruition in less than one.[126]

One of the first changes occurred to the Guard's four cavalry divisions, which the 1939 plan slated for reduction to regiments. In late 1940, the Army converted them into field, coastal, and anti-aircraft artillery regiments virtually overnight. Nearly 12,000 men suddenly went from horseback to 105 millimeter or 20 millimeter guns, leaving many of them bewildered. New missions and new equipment required the retraining of former horsemen, many of whom did not fire live rounds before America entered the war. The 200th Coast Artillery (formerly the New Mexico 111th Cavalry) was lucky enough to fire twelve demonstration rounds before shipping out to the Philippines and its rendezvous with tragedy. Other Guard units suffered similar shocks of sudden transformation. The New York Tenth Infantry became the 106th Infantry while portions of the original 106th transformed into the 186th Field Artillery and the 101st Military Police Battalion. Guardsmen's morale suffered as a result of these radical changes.[127]

The Army's renumbering and shuffling of Guard units added to Guardmen's ill feelings. In many cases, units of the various state Guards had similar numbers. For example, both Virginia and Maryland (as did most states) maintained First Infantry Regiments. When the War Department ordered the renumbering of Guard units to remove any possibility of confusion, the First Virginia and the First Maryland infantry regiments became the 176th and the 115th Infantry, respectively. In other instances, units were torn from their parent division and merged with other orphan units to form new formations. As in World War I, renumbering and reorganization clouded unit histories and traditions, thus causing confusion and hard feelings among Guardsmen toward the Army; many units with histories dating to before the Civil War vanished.[128]

Marshall had not lied to the Guard during his October 22, 1940 address. Primarily, the Army attempted to plug gaps in the nation's defense structure, using Guard units as raw material to meet the those needs. However, beneath this reason lay a fundamental difference between the Guard and the Army's interpretation of section 1 (c) of the Selective Service and Training Act of 1940, the Guard's so-called protective clause negotiated between Reckord and Grenville Clark.

(c) The Congress further declares, in accordance with our traditional military policy as expressed in the National Defense Act of 1916, as amended, that it is essential that the strength and organization of the National Guard as an integral part of the first-line defenses of this Nation be at all times maintained and assured.[129]

The General Staff believed section 1 (c) applied only when the states controlled the Guard, not while federalized. Assistant Chief of Staff Brigadier General Frank Andrews wrote:

The apparent intent indicated by the inclusion of the above [Section 1 (c)] in the legislation for selective service is to assure that upon completion of one year's active service National Guard units will return to their respective states and that the National Guard of the United States will continue as a reserve component of the Army of the United States.[130]

General Andrews' interpretation was partially correct. Congress, at the Guard's insistence, intended to protect the Guard once it left federal service. However, the NGA desired, and thought it had achieved, more. The NGA leadership intended the protective clause of the Selective Service Act of 1940 to preserve the Guard's integrity while federalized. General Andrews interpretation of section 1 (c) failed to take such goals into account, resting on the belief that the term National Guard referred to the Guard in its state status. The result of the Army's interpretation of the protective clause was a Guard reorganized by converting units, leveling units to provide cadres for new units, and removing some of its officers. Officers of the Guard angrily remembered the Army's acts of 1940-41 for decades.[131]

The Army's troubles with the Guard did not stop with officers. The Guard came into federal service with roughly half of its strength composed of green recruits. Their shortcomings became apparent rather rapidly. However, as already noted, once the issue of extending their term of service came to the fore, training efficiency declined. In a July 30, 1941 letter to Guard division commanders, Marshall noted that some Guard divisions had attained a high level of development, however, others lagged far behind. He noted the lack of discipline as the major problem, writing: "The standards of discipline are too low and reflect the unwillingness of leaders who knew their subordinates in civil life to hold them to strict compliance with military orders."[132] Marshall used this reason as one justification for reclassifying some officers and transferring others. A survey conducted in 1942 among Guardsmen supported Marshall's veiled contention that politics in Guard units created lower levels of discipline in the Guard's ranks, revealing that fifty-two percent of respondents thought that promotions in the Guard came through "bootlicking or politics." When given the same survey, only twenty-seven percent of Regular Army privates gave the same response.[133]

Yet Marshall's July letter to division commanders failed to mention other roots of lax discipline in the Guard's ranks. A month before releasing the letter to division commanders, Marshall sent a memorandum to the Secretary of War pointing out the effect that no decision about retention had on Guardsmen. On the whole, Guardsmen were willing to continue in service but sought some word on their future. Without a decision they could not make arrangements about family, jobs, or education. The result of the Administration's indecision was frustration and a decline in military efficiency. As the possibility of release from federal service came closer, officers and men increasingly saw little need for more training. The Guard leadership's attitude was identical to that of the Chief of Staff. Marshall's memo to Stimson borrowed heavily from a report submitted by General Williams, Chief of the National Guard Bureau.[134] Congress' extension of the Guard's term of service alleviated this particular problem; however, the damage had been done.[135]

DEMOBILIZATION PLANS

Even as Congress began to address the issue of retaining the Guard and selectees in federal service, the General Staff laid plans to return these men to civilian life. On the day that Marshall stated that the army would melt away, August 1, 1941, the Secretary of War directed the dispatch of a letter that contained instructions for the demobilization of Guard units if Congress did not pass the extension bill. While its passage rendered these instructions void, demobilization planning continued.[136] Three months after Congress passed the bill, Marshall met with General Staff planners on the issue of releasing the Guard units. Colonel Karlstad presented G-3's plan for demobilizing the Guard. In essence, the Army would "progressively" release federalized units at "monthly increments in such a way that there [would] always be available a minimum of 14 trained divisions."[137] Guard units would pass into an inactive status stripped of all but those weapons and equipment necessary for training. Once selectees completed training, the

Army would assign them to Guard units near their homes. General Marshall seemed to approve of the plan and even remarked that it might "be wise to utilize [the] defederalized strength to create two more armored divisions."[138] However, Brigadier General Mark W. Clark, General McNair's assistant, stated that GHQ opposed the reduction of active divisions, especially "in a manner which would cause an unfavorable reaction by our associates [meaning the Guard]."[139] Marshall foresaw no difficulty with moving the Guard to an inactive status. The Army would base release of the Guard on the idea that it was "simply passing to a reserve status and could be activated within the time that it might be necessary to use them."[140]

General Clark proposed a different plan for both expanding the Army and releasing the Guard from federal service. Plans formulated at GHQ called for a battle-ready force of fourteen divisions composed of men with three or more year's of enlistments. Selectees would form an additional ten to fifteen divisions, and after training with these for six months, selectees would move to "additional reserve units for the balance of their Selective Service training."[141] Unlike G-3's plan, Clark's presentation did not include the Guard as a reserve force.

The Chief of Staff agreed with the first portion of GHQ's plan; however, he did not accept the idea of transferring selectees to reserve divisions during the balance of their training. He believed that once selectees completed their training they should return home, possibly to reserve divisions. "The Chief of Staff also indicated that if the international situation did not indicate the utilization of ground troops by February 1942, that [the Army] should commence setting up this reserve."[142] Marshall directed G-3 and GHQ to confer on their plans and come up with another solution.[143] The Japanese attack on Pearl Harbor a month later rendered both G-3 and GHQ's plans obsolete, America had joined the war. Guard units entered combat in the Philippines on December 8, 1941. Guard divisions and smaller units served in virtually every major action of the war. Casualties amounted to 10,009 killed and 30,686 wounded in the Pacific, while 27,520 men died and 120,369 were wounded in Europe. Guard units received 148 Distinguished Unit Citations while individuals earned fourteen Medals of Honor, fifty Distinguished Service Crosses, forty-eight Distinguished Flying Crosses, and 500 Silver Stars. The demobilization plans, however, remained available for post-war use, and the basic problems revealed in the debates and policies of 1939-41 would re-emerge in the Korean War and in the early 1960s.[144]

NOTES

1. W. D. McGlasson, "Mobilization 1940: The Big One," *National Guard*, September 1980, p. 10.

2. Memorandum for the Chief of Staff from G-3, "Induction of certain National Guard Units into Federal Service," July 22, 1940, George C. Marshall Papers, xerox item 1906 (Marshall Library); Adjutant General's Office Letter, "Induction of certain National Guard Units into the Federal Service," July 30, 1940, call number 222.13, United States Air Force Historical Research Center, Maxwell Air Force Base, Alabama.

3. Adjutant General's Office Letter, "Tentative Mobilization Plans," August 8, 1940, National Archives, RG 165, AG 381; Memorandum for the Adjutant General, August 2, 1940, George C. Marshall Papers, Xerox Item 1901 (Marshall Library).

4. Memorandum for the Chief, National Guard Bureau from the Chief of Staff, August 6, 1940, George C. Marshall Papers, Microfilm reel 25, Item 907 (Marshall Library); War Department, *Annual Report of the Chief of the National Guard, 1941*, pp. 15-19.

5. For a full account of the debate over the Selective Training and Service Act of 1940 see Clifford and Spencer, *Peacetime Draft*, 174-234.

6. War Department, *Annual Report of the Chief of the National Guard, 1941*, p. 83.

7. Ibid., 11; *New York Times,* August 7, 1940, p. 3; Watson, *Chief of Staff,* 209.

8. Ibid.; McGlasson, "Mobilization 1940: The Big One," *National Guard*, September 1980, p. 14.

9. This situation ran counter to G-4's stated policy that Guard units should be "ordered into the Federal service only after proper housing is available." See Memorandum for the Chief of Staff from Brigadier General F. N. Andrews, September 17, 1940, George C. Marshall Papers, Box 82, File Folder 27 (Marshall Library).

10. McGlasson, "Mobilization 1940," *National Guard*, September 1980, pp. 12-17.

11. Bill Mauldin, *The Brass Ring: A Sort of a Memior* (New York, 1971), 83.

12. War Department, *Annual Report of the Chief of the National Guard, 1941*, p. 84.

13. Ibid., 29.

14. Ibid., 29.

15. McGlasson, "Mobilization 1940," *National Guardsmen*, September 1980, p. 18.

16. This was true of the Thirtieth Division, which was raided for cadres to the point of repeating basic training. The bitter feelings this created among the Guard officers was evident years after the war. See Henry D. Russell, *The Purge of the Thirtieth Division* (Macon, GA, nd).

17. National Guard Association, *Proceedings, 1940*, p. 58 (National Guard Association Library).

18. Demobilization Plans, September 20, 1940, National Archives, Record Group 165, OCS 21116-13.

19. Watson, *Chief of Staff*, 215.

20. Weigley, *The American Way of War*, 316-317; Greenfield, ed., *Command Decisions*, 40-42.

21. *New York Times*, March 7, 1941, p. 1 and March 8, 1941, p. 6.

22. General Marshall to The Reverend David P. Gaines, March 11, 1941, George C. Marshall Papers, Box 77, File Folder 22 (Marshall Library).

23. Watson, *Chief of Staff*, 216.

24. *New York Times*, May 5, 1941, p. 10, and May 16, 1941, p. 14.

25. General Marshall to Major General George A. White, May 16, 1941, George C. Marshall Papers, Box 77, File Folder 22 (Marshall Library).

26. Letter from Major General George A. White to General Marshall, May 29, 1941, Bland, ed., *Marshall Papers*, 508; Editor's notes, Bland, ed., *Marshall Papers*, 508.

27. Memorandum for the President from Secretary of War Henry Stimson, June 20, 1941, Marshall Foundation National Archives Project, Reel 115, Item 2674 (Marshall Library).

28. Ibid.

29. Ibid.

30. Ibid.

31. Ibid.

32. Rosenman, ed., *The Public Papers and Addresses of Franklin D. Roosevelt, 1941 Volume*, 272-273.

33. General Milton Reckord to General Marshall, July 15, 1941, George C. Marshall Papers, Box 82, File Folder 28 (Marshall Library).

34. Cole, *Roosevelt and the Isolationists*, 395.

35. A Gallup poll taken between June 27 and July 2, 1940 revealed that American men between the ages of twenty-one and twenty-five supported the idea of a draft by fifty-two to forty-eight percent. Less than a month later a wider based poll placed the percentages at 67 for and 33 against a draft. These percentages held true for all age brackets and remained stable during the debate on Burke-Wadsworth. See Gallup, *The Gallup Poll*, I, 231, 234, 236.

36. The Senate passed the bill on August 28 by a vote of fifty-eight to thirty-one. On September 7 the House passed the bill by a vote of 263 to 149. One week later, September 14, both houses accepted the conference committee's report, thus leaving it to the President to make it law. See Clifford and Spencer, *The First Peacetime Draft*, 174-225.

37. Francis L. Loewenheim, Harold D. Langley, and Manfred Jonas, eds., *Roosevelt and Churchill: Their Secret Wartime Correspondence*, 94-95.

38. A public opinion poll discovered that the nation favored a destroyer deal on a sixty-forty split. See Gallup, *Gallup Poll*, I, 237-238, 240.

39. Cole, *Roosevelt and the Isolationists*, 373; Warren F. Kimball, *The Most Unsordid Act: Lend-Lease, 1939-1941* (Baltimore, MD, 1969), 68.

40. Johnson, *The Republican Party and Wendell Willkie*, 122.

41. Cole, *Roosevelt and the Isolationists*, 396.

42. Ibid., 400.

43. Gallup asked Americans throughout the spring and summer of 1940 if given the opportunity would they vote to enter the war or stay out. Opinion help steady with eighty percent of the respondents voting to remain out of the war. Gallup, *Gallup Poll*, I, 270-290.

44. Michele Flynn Stenehjem, *An American First: John T. Flynn and the America First Committee* (New Rochelle, NY, 1976), 13-23.

45. Italy invaded Egypt on September 13, 1940 with five divisions.

46. Watson, *Chief of Staff*, 382-390.

47. Cole, *Roosevelt and the Isolationists*, 411; Kimball, *The Most Unsordid Act*, 91-150.

48. Kimball, *The Most Unsordid Act*, 151-229; Wayne S. Cole, *Lindbergh and the Battle Against American Intervention in World War II*, 92-93.

49. Gallup, *Gallup Poll*, I, 291.

50. U.S. Congress, *Senate Report No. 595, Declaring the Existence of a National Emergency, and for other purposes*, 77th Cong., 1 sess., 1941.

51. Watson, *Chief of Staff*, 223.

52. Text of the War Department Draft Joint Resolution, Reel 115, Item 2674, Marshall Foundation National Archives Project (Marshall Library).

53. Ibid.

54. Ibid.

55. Ibid.; Watson, *Chief of Staff,* 226.

56. U.S. Congress, *Senate Report No. 595, Declaring the Existence of a National Emergency, and for other purposes,* 77th Cong., 1 sess., 1941.

57. Outline of Senator Taft's proposal sent to the Secretary of War by General Marshall, Verifax 2792, Marshall Foundation National Archives Project (Marshall Library); *New York Times,* July 29, 1941, p. 1.

58. Ibid, p. 10.

59. Ibid., July 29, 1941, p. 10.

60. Ibid., July 30, 1941, pp. 1, 9.

61. Ibid.

62. U.S. Congress, *Congressional Record,* 77th Cong., 1st sess., 1941, 87:6445.

63. Ibid., 87:6446.

64. *New York Times,* July 31, 1941, p. 10.

65. Ibid., July 31, 1941, pp. 1, 10.

66. Ibid., July 31, 1941, p. 10.

67. U.S. Congress, *House Report No. 1117, Declaring the Existence of A National Emergency, and For Other Purposes, HJR 222,* 77th Cong., 1st sess., p. 16.

68. Ibid.

69. Ibid., 17.

70. Ibid., 19.

71. Ibid.

72. U.S. Congress, *Congressional Record,* 77th Cong., 1st sess., 1941, 87:6497-6499.

73. Ibid., 87:6517.

74. Ibid.

75. Ibid., 87:6507-6519; *New York Times,* August 1, 1941, p. 8.

76. A point Major General George A. White had stressed in his May 29 letter to General Marshall.

77. U.S. Congress, *Congressional Record,* 77th Cong., 1st sess., 1941, 87:6668.

78. Ibid., 87:6669.

79. Ibid.

80. Ibid., 87:6670.

81. *New York Times,* August 5, 1941, pp. 1, 8.

82. U.S. Congress, *Congressional Record,* 77th Cong., 1st sess., 1941, 87:6741.

83. Ibid., 87:6749-6750.

84. *New York Times,* August 6, 1941, pp. 1, 9; U.S. Congress, *Congressional Record,* 77th Cong., 1st sess., 1941, 87:6750.

85. *New York Times,* August 6, 1941, p. 9.

86. Ibid.

87. U.S. Congress, *Congressional Record,* 77th Cong., 1st sess., 1941, 87:6832.

88. Ibid., 87:6822.

89. Ibid., 87:6826-6827.

90. Divine, *Reluctant Belligerent,* 137.

91. U.S. Congress, *Congressional Record,* 77th Cong., 1st sess., 1941, 87:6881.

92. Pogue, *Ordeal and Hope,* 153-154.

93. Ibid., 149.

94. U.S. Congress, *Congressional Record*, 77th Cong., 1st sess., 1941, 87:6908.

95. Ibid., 87:6914.

96. Ibid., 87:6919.

97. Ibid.

98. Ibid., 87:6920.

99. Stenehjem, *An American First*, 93.

100. Ibid.

101. U.S. Congress, *Congressional Record*, 77th Cong., 1st sess., 1941, 87:6908.

102. Ibid., 87:6916-6917

103. *New York Times*, August 10, 1941, p. 1.

104. Ibid.

105. Ibid.

106. Ibid., August 12, 1941, pp. 1, 14.

107. U.S. Congress, *Congressional Record*, 77th Cong., 1st sess., 1941, 87:7024-7043.

108. Ibid., 87:7069.

109. Ibid., 87:7074-7077.

110. On August 13, Taft, Johnson, Clark of Missouri, Danaher, and La Follette dropped all ideas of fighting the bill. They knew that they could not defeat the measure in the Senate and thus could not force the House to reconsider the bill. See *New York Times*, August 14, 1941, pp. 1, 14.

111. U.S. Congress, *Congressional Record*, 77th Cong., 1st sess., 1941, 87:7166, 7196, 7199.

112. *New York Times*, August 14, 1941, p. 1.

113. Derthick, *The National Guard in Politics*, 58.

114. Letter from Major General Reckord to General Marshall, September 4, 1940, George C. Marshall Papers, Box 82 File Folder 27 (Marshall Library).

115. Pogue, *Ordeal and Hope*, 100.

116. Ibid.

117. General McNair's dislike for the Guard came to the surface in 1944 when he wrote "One of the greatest lessons of the present war . . . is that the National Guard as organized before the war contributed nothing to National Defense." Even when commanding officers were replace McNair considered guard divisions inferior. See Holley, *General John M. Palmer, Citizen Soldiers, and the Army of Democracy*, 656.

118. Memorandum for General Haislip from General Marshall, April 19, 1941, Bland, ed., *Marshall Papers*, II, 480-481.

119. Watson, *Chief of Staff*, 244-245.

120. Ibid., 260.

121. Ibid., 261; Memorandum for the Adjutant General from Brigadier General Wade H. Haislip, September 22, 1941, Marshall Foundation National Archives Project, Reel 14, Item 484 (Marshall Library).

122. National Guard Association of the United States, *The Nation's National Guard* (Washington, DC, 1954), 41; Mahon, *History of the Militia and National Guard*, 162-163.

123. Mahon, *History of the Militia and Guard*, 186.

124. Derthick, *The National Guard in Politics*, 50-51.

125. Memorandum from C. M. Adams to General Marshall, October 22, 1940, George C. Marshall Papers, Box 77, File Folder 21 (Marshall Library).

126. See Chapter III, Planning for the Guard.

127. McGlasson, "Mobilization 1940," *National Guard*, September 1980, p. 20; War Department, *Annual Report of the Chief of the National Guard Bureau, 1941*, p. 15; Palmer, Wiley and Keats, *Procurement of Ground Forces*, 433.

128. War Department, *Annual Report of the Chief of the National Guard Bureau, 1941*, p. 15.

129. Memorandum for the Chief of Staff, Subject: Recommendations of Commanding General, Twenty-nineth Division, September 17, 1940, George C. Marshall Papers, Box 82, File Folder 27 (Marshall Library).

130. Ibid.

131. Derthick, *The National Guard in Politics*, 70, 77-81, 92-93.

132. Letter from General Marshall to General Reckord with copies sent to all National Guard division commanders, July 30, 1941, George C. Marshall Papers, Box 77, File Folder 23 (Marshall Library).

133. Samuel A. Stauffer, and others, *The American Soldier: Adjustment During Army Life* (Princeton, NJ, 1949), 268-269.

134. Memorandum for the Chief of Staff from Major General John F. Williams, May 17, 1941, Marshall Foundation National Archives Project, Reel 14, Item 484 (Marshall Library).

135. Memorandum for the Secretary of War from General Marshall, June 20, 1941, George C. Marshall Papers, Verifax 2792 (Marshall Papers).

136. Memorandum for the Adjutant General from Brigadier General Harry L. Twaddle, August 1, 1941, Marshall Foundation National Archives Project, Reel 14, Item 484 (Marshall Library).

137. Conference in the Office of the Chief of Staff, Subject: Retention of the National Guard, October 31, 1941, Marshall Foundation National Archives Project, Reel 14, Item 484 (Marshall Library).

138. Ibid.

139. Ibid.

140. Ibid.

141. Ibid.

142. Ibid.

143. Ibid.

144. R. Ernest Dupuy, *The National Guard: A Compact History* (New York, 1971), 122-123, 125-126; McGlasson, "Mobilization 1940," *National Guard*, 17; Mahon, *History of the Militia and National Guard*, 190-194.

7

Conclusion

No man should take up arms, but with a view to defend his country
and its laws: he puts not off the citizen when he enters the camp; but
it is because he is a citizen, and would wish to continue so, that he
makes himself for a while a soldier.

—Sir William Blackstone[1]

THE SUCCESSFUL LOBBY

In the mid-1960s, political scientist Martha Derthick examined the National
Guard Association's effectiveness as a political pressure group and concluded
that it was one of the most successful in the American political system.[2] One
may find proof of this thesis in American legal and military history, yet from
its beginnings the Association has pursued two divergent goals, which made
complete success impossible. The NGA attempted to keep the National
Guard closely aligned with its local political power base in the states while
pursuing a greater role in the national defense. Although some members saw
the dilemma in these conflicting goals, others, such as Milton A. Reckord,
believed that by aggressive lobbying and legal protection the Guard could
serve two masters. Through Reckord's skill, the NGA was able to win short
term political victories, such as federal funds, but ultimately failed in its long
term goal of maintaining Guard autonomy. Although for much of its
existence, the National Guard of the United States was able to serve two
masters, by the last decade of the twentieth century jurisprudence finally
caught up with reality and recognized the supremacy of the federal
government's control of the Guard.

What was impressive about the NGA, particularly from 1880 to 1940, was
a string of political victories that gained federal money but deterred the

formation of an effective federally controlled Reserve. However, each victory cost the Guard some of its autonomy. The 1903 Dick Act increased federal funding for the militia (the National Guard), but required the Guard, still very much a state agency, to submit to Army inspections and limited controls. Continuing its drive for a national role, the NGA and its supporters in Congress successfully opposed the 1912 War Department attempt to form a Continental Army. The NGA won another increase in federal support, but at the expense of even more control. In 1920, the Guard was once again on the defensive, fighting, not altogether successfully, the formation of a federally controlled Reserve. The Guard was able to keep the Reserve weak and disorganized, thus preserving the Guard's place, although there was now a competitor.

The Guard's crowning success came in 1933 with passage of a new National Defense Act. The NGA hoped to correct perceived flaws in the earlier acts, namely the Constitutional limitations on use of the militia. As the successor to the organized militia of the states, the National Guard could serve the nation only to repel an invasion, suppress domestic rebellions, and carry out federal law. While the federal government worried about the legal difficulties of using the Guard for national defense, especially outside the country, the NGA was concerned that constitutional restrictions might lead to the Guard's displacement by the Reserve. The World War I drafting of Guardsmen and the dismemberment of their units, allowed by the National Defense Act of 1916, lead the NGA on a long search for a legal solution that would protect the Guard's integrity as a federal reserve force. In the early 1930s, the NGA came up with a solution. Drafted primarily by General Reckord, the National Defense Act of 1933 created a new entity—the National Guard of the United States—which was entirely a federal creature, separate and distinct from the Guard's state role. Association leaders believed the dual status created by the Act satisfied their dual goals of state and federal service.

The first test of the 1933 Act began as Nazi columns smashed their way across Poland. Considering the European war a threat to American security, Army Chief of Staff General Marshall requested additional men and money for both the Regular Army and the National Guard. For those in the NGA who favored an expanded federal role, the European war offered a chance to further their goal. As the 1939 Baltimore convention demonstrated, enthusiasm in the NGA ranks overcame resistance from the Adjutants General--the main proponents of stronger state connections. When some members questioned the need to expand the Guard beyond state needs, General Reckord, the master lobbyist and an old proponent of an increased federal role, redirected the issue to emphasize federal responsibility for funding national goals of the Guard. Although the convention's decision did not end the decades-long debate over which path the Guard should take, by using the patriotic fervor of the moment Reckord won the membership to his side, accelerating the Guard toward an enlarged federal role.

One obstructionist challenged Reckord and the will of the NGA convention. General Haskell of New York threatened the tenuous truce between the Guard and the Army by objecting to the scheduled summer maneuvers. Although he publicly cited the need for more small unit training, his real reason stemmed from a desire to maintain state control over New York's troops. His stated objection did not, however, square with current experience. As the 1939 maneuvers demonstrated, the Guard desperately needed more large unit training, not less. Since Reckord was about to quietly challenge the Army's training schedule, he saw Haskell as challenging the NGA's chosen path. Reckord quickly mounted a congressional counteroffensive and successfully defeated the New York general. Having disposed of Haskell's challenge, and thereby sending a message to any other dissident Adjutants General, Reckord persuaded General Marshall to limit the training schedule and provide funds for the additional units.

But the victory that Reckord considered the most important came from Grenville Clark's civilian group, the Military Training Camps Association (MTCA), which he had battled off-and-on for nearly twenty years. Since the inception of the MTCA, the two organizations had viewed each other as enemies, occasionally trading threats. Both believed that political support for one threatened the other, a reasonable concern in the tight budget days of the 1920s and 1930s. As the war in the Europe expanded, and Roosevelt made no move to press for a conscription act, Clark and his followers initiated a draft bill. Reckord quickly recognized both the potential harm and the benefit implied in the Selective Service Bill. In his best style, he used the NGA's formidable reputation as a successful lobby to persuade Clark to insert a "protective clause" in the legislation, believing it kept the Guard safe from displacement by a draft-fed reserve. However, drift toward federal control of the Guard, encouraged by Reckord and elements of the NGA, led to control by the Army.

Despite the short term victories the NGA won between 1903 and 1940, the Guard suffered several failures, many long term, as a result its conflicting goals. Expansion in 1939 and mobilization in 1940 brought many of these failings to light; the first came disguised as a success. With the prospect of war in the offing, Guard recruiting quickly reached the level set by the War Department in October 1939, but the Guard leadership had failed to persuade many longtime Guardsmen of the need for federalization. This flaw became clear when mobilization became a certainty. In an attempt to mollify a jittery Congress, the Guard and the Army released men for economic, educational, and family reasons. While this move may have been inevitable, Guard leaders were wholly unprepared for the mass exodus that followed. Predicting that only a low percentage would leave the ranks, NGA officials were stunned when nearly half of its experienced men resigned. While the NGA leadership supported the mobilization, the enlisted ranks did not want to sacrifice a year of their lives for training. Although rapidly refilled with untrained volunteers and later by draftees, Guard divisions were ill prepared for active duty. Many of the trained men who remained after mobilization were taken by the Army to form new divisions. Seemingly oblivious to this trend, many Regular officers publicly criticized the Guard as unprepared. Having helped to create this situation, the Army, found confirmation of its decades-old opinion of the Guard and concluded that it was nearly useless unless directly under Army control.

THE CONGRESS

Congress in the autumn of 1940 and again one year later overwhelmingly supported the mobilization of the National Guard of the United States. The opposition that arose during the August 1940 debate over federalization and again in August 1941 over retention centered on distrust of Roosevelt. In the wake of Nazi aggression and growing tension in the Far East, Congress was willing to increase military spending, but it did not intend to grant the President additional power over the National Guard. Roosevelt's May 31, 1940 request for authority to federalize the Guard if an emergency arose while Congress was in recess met swift bipartisan opposition, compelling him to include limitations on the President's powers over the National Guard. As the battle of France reached its tragic climax, the Administration introduced Senate Joint Resolution 286 (SJR 286) and ran into the same obstruction. Congress would pass the bill only if the Guard deployment was limited to American territory and the Western Hemisphere.

By passing SJR 286 without declaring a national emergency, Congress had adopted an unintentional amendment to the 1933 National Defense Act. A year later it revalidated this change by retaining the Guard in service for another eighteen months. These modifications forever changed the nature of the federal-Guard relationship in ways not always pleasant for the Guard. The dual status created by the 1933 Act was intended by the NGA as a means to fend off the formation of an effective reserve and a way to eliminate a Constitutional hindrance. Congress, traditionally skeptical of a large standing Army, accepted the legal duality with the sole stipulation that it had to declare a national emergency before activating the National Guard of the United States. As the Senate and House debates of August 1940 demonstrated, many Congressmen showed a surprisingly good grasp of the nature of the Guard's dual status, reflecting their education at the hands of the NGA. As a result, they spent very little time on Constitutional constraint on the Guard. Indeed, Congress spent more time on compensation for Guardsmen than debating the propriety of using them. The debate revealed Congress' realization, perhaps for the first time, that the 1933 Act freed it to use the Guard as it pleased. Whatever limitations existed were self imposed and driven by political necessity, not mandated by the Constitution. Ordering the 1940 mobilization for training, Congress established its right under the Army Clause of the Constitution to take the Guard out of state control, even in peacetime. While SJR 286 went unchallenged by the states, because of the world crisis and the NGA's strong desire to go along with the Army's plan, it laid a dangerous trap for the states, which governors tripped fifty years later.

ROOSEVELT

What occupied Congress' attention during the debates in 1940 and 1941 was not its right to order the Guard to active service but the power it was about to bestow on the Chief Executive. Many Congressmen feared that unrestrained Presidential control over Guardsmen, reservists, and, later, draftees was a large step toward entering the war and establishing a dictatorship. Although a portion of this sentiment was genuine isolationism, or non-interventionism, the bulk of the charges leveled against Roosevelt were politically motivated.

Roosevelt's own motives and actions remain a mystery to students of the period. In the summer of 1989, Merlin Gustafson and Jerry Rosenberg wrote that a visitor to the Roosevelt Presidential Library would, upon entering, immediately face a large caricature of the President portrayed as a sphinx. The authors believed that after forty years of scholarship "this characterization remains appropriate."[3] Revisionist authors of the immediate post-war era such as Hamilton Fish, Charles Callan Tansill, Charles A. Beard, and Harry Elmer Barnes asserted that Roosevelt deceived the nation, entering the European war through the back door by goading Japan into attacking Pearl Harbor.[4] In *Roosevelt: From Munich To Pearl Harbor*, Basil Rauch attacked the revisionists, and Beard in particular, contending that Roosevelt had tried to build an international framework against the forces of aggression but was thwarted by the isolationists. Robert E. Sherwood echoed this point in *Roosevelt and Hopkins: An Intimate History*. Roosevelt, Sherwood maintained, avoided controversial foreign policy initiatives that could lead to a defeat, which even on a relatively small matter would irreparably damage future actions. Thus, the President made no move in foreign policy, unless he had the votes to carry it through.[5] With a more critical eye, historians such as William L. Langer, S. Everett Gleason, James McGergor Burns, and John Lewis Gaddis examined Roosevelt's policies before America's entry into the war. Although of differing opinion, their works contain a common theme: Roosevelt's policies were at times in error but not aimed at involving the nation in World War II. Nor, they concluded, was he "just a political opportunist."[6]

Robert A. Divine approached Roosevelt's motives and actions from a different perspective. From speeches, papers, and personal letters, Divine concluded that Roosevelt's publicly expressed hatred of war was genuine. Until Hitler broke the Munich Agreement, Roosevelt followed an isolationist path, abhorring the idea of sending Americans to die in another European war. After Munich, he reluctantly put on the mantle of the interventionist, concluding, as Divine asserted, that appeasement had "served only to postpone, not prevent, a major European war."[7]

Roosevelt's policies followed a simple path—bolstering European democracies best served American interests. Facing heated opposition from isolationists in Congress and a non-interventionist populace, Roosevelt hesitated to press for increased aid to the Allies and rearmament at home until public opinion favored it.

In their work on the 1940 Selective Training and Service Act, historians J. Garry Clifford and Samuel R. Spencer suggested—almost in passing—that Roosevelt hesitated to support a draft and federalizing the Guard because he saw no immediate need for them. His priority, they suggested, was to provide aid to the Allies, namely the destroyer deal and later Lend-Lease. Roosevelt eventually supported both the Guard call up and the draft, but only after sufficient public support developed.

Each school of thought found in Roosevelt's actions evidence to support their theory. His aid to the Allies, naval protection for convoys, and occupation of Iceland were all acts that removed the United States from neutrality to co-belligerency. However, his policy contained shades of classical isolationism. Roosevelt expected the Allies to fight the war while the United States provided the material and kept its forces within the uncertain bounds of the Western Hemisphere. As Robert Sherwood noted, Roosevelt was a Navy man who:

did not look very far beyond the bridgeheads secured by Marines: however, he knew what the essential bridge-heads were—the British Isles, France, the Iberian Peninsula, the North and West Coasts of Africa and, in the Pacific, the Netherlands East Indies, the Philippines and the Marianas.[8]

Yet beyond material aid, any help lent by the U.S. Navy ended at the imaginary line separating the Western and Eastern hemispheres. With the Navy and the belatedly strengthened Air Corps, Roosevelt felt no urgent need to divert energies to increasing an Army he did not immediately intended for use. Despite the urging of Marshall, Stimson, and the interventionists—until the fall of France—Roosevelt made only grudging moves toward improving the Army, and even then he proceeded slowly. Whether the ferocity of the German attack in the West changed his mind about strengthening the Army, as Sherwood intimated, or he wanted to be prodded into action by the public remains unresolved. Roosevelt remains the sphinx. However, when examining the evidence in the case of Guard mobilization one must conclude that until the Germans ripped through the Allies, Roosevelt did not seriously consider using land forces.[9]

THE ARMY

The Army, too, hesitated when it came to the use and future disposition of the Guard. General Marshall, long acquainted with the political power of the NGA, took what he considered prudent, although politically risky, steps toward making the Guard an effective adjunct to the Army. As soon as war broke out in 1939, he asked Roosevelt to authorize substantial increases in the Guard. Marshall undoubtedly expected to run afoul of the NGA because he had asked for troops in excess of state needs without offering to pay for them. He won support for this move from Reckord and the NGA, but not before they pressed for federal funding. Politically more explosive was the War Division proposal to reorganize the Guard to meet the Army's needs without regard to its state mission, i.e. form units useless to the state. While Marshall (and even Chief of the National Guard Bureau General Blanding) saw the wisdom in the proposed realignment, he believed it would adversely alter the Guard-Army relationship. He was undoubtedly concerned about the political fight such a reform might cause and also its the cost to the Army. Greater reliance on the Guard as a federal reserve meant more federal money for its maintenace. In early 1940 Marshall had no reason to believe Congress would increase total military funding; rather, it seemed likely that Congress would simply re-slice the fiscal pie to make the Guard a real partner in national defense.

Furthermore, accepting the Guard as the primary reserve threatened to open the door wider to NGA interference without the Army gaining substantial control. This became evident during the mobilization. So as not to make himself vulnerable to charges of favoring Regular over Guard officers, Marshall took care to search for suitable Guardsmen to replace removed officers. However, in one instance Marshall threatened to resign when several Congressmen attempted to interfere with the removal of a Guard general. Confronted with a determined Chief of Staff, the Congressional delegation retreated, but the incident indicated that the Army's long-sought "control" over the Guard was not easily attainable. Yet once mobilization started, General McNair at General Headquarters initiated the very plan to reorganize the Guard that Marshall had hesitantly approved in 1939 for training purposes only. Painful as it was for both sides, the process of turning the Guard into a federally controlled reserve had begun.

Although continually scorned by professional soldiers for their lack of skill, Guardsmen, as a whole, acquitted themselves well in combat. Divisions and smaller units served in virtually every major action of the war, earning numerous unit and individual honors. However, the perceived Army abuses during the 1940 mobilization left the NGA leadership with a lasting hatred that eliminated whatever good will Marshall had built. General McNair's execution of the reorganization of the Army, considered a raid on Guard manpower by the NGA, and his 1944 assertion that the Guard added nothing to national defense, rekindled the NGA-Army feud. At the height of the war, the NGA began considering its postwar existence and pressed for a General Staff decision. Reckord in particular wanted a return to a small standing Army and an autonomous Guard fed by universal military training, a logical outcome of his dealings with Clark.[10] After the war, the NGA followed Reckord's lead by seeking even more federal funds without sacrificing autonomy.

In the postwar era, the NGA was successful, in many respects, in preserving the Guard's national role. In 1948, as the draft law expired and enlistments declined, the NGA secured $1,000,000 from Congress for recruitment. It also won a retirement pay program, death and disability benefits, active duty pay equal to that of the Regular Army, and the right to attend the Army's advanced military education programs. When in 1948, the Gray Board[11] recommended the merger of the Army and Air National Guards with their Regular counterparts, the NGA staged a massive lobbying effort in Congress, ultimately defeating the proposal.[12]

The Cold War, however, changed the nature of defense. With the Soviet army massed behind the Iron Curtain, deterrence required a larger standing army ready for immediate action, not one that took months to prepare. Readiness became the main issue for the Army as well as the reserves. As the Cold War progressed, the NGA's influence dwindled and that of its competitor, the Reserve Officer Association (ROA), increased. The NGA and the ROA went to verbal war over the provisions of the Armed Forces Reserve Act of 1952. Only intense lobbying enabled the NGA to incorporate many of its ninety-nine amendments into the legislation. By 1955, however, the decline was noticeable. In constructing the Reserve Forces Act, Congress supported the ROA by allowing it to recruit from the seventeen to eighteen year old age group, formerly a pool monopolized by the Guard, and required Army basic training for all reserve components, something the Guard had fought for years. However, the 1965 proposal advanced by Secretary of Defense Robert McNamara to merge the Army Reserve into the National Guard revealed the rise of the ROA and the NGA's slippage. Although the NGA supported the proposal, it drew vehement opposition from the ROA. ROA opposition, along with McNamara's attempts to rush the plan through Congress, led to its defeat.[13]

The Korean War revalidated the Guard and the Air National Guard as national defense assets. Guardsmen filled gaps in the Army created by post-World War II reductions. While most only served in the General Reserve, some saw combat. Yet the mobilization of one third of the Army Guard and three quarters of the Air Guard also revealed their lack of preparedness.

Poorly equipped and trained federalized units took months to reach acceptable readiness levels. Only two Guard fighter wings and divisions saw combat, and that nearly a year after fighting began.[14] Korea also marked a watershed in the use of the Guard as the primary source of early manpower for the Army. During the Korean War era the Army relied primarily on draftees and reservists; Guardsmen accounted for only one half of one percent of all the men serving. As early as 1940, Reckord foresaw the possibility of the draft, and a draft-fed Reserve, replacing the Guard as the first reserve. His dealings with Clark were an effort to fend off that development. However, Korea proved that the protective clause in the Selective Training and Service Act of 1940 was meaningless. The federal government could use the Guard as it wished.

In the aftermath of Korea the Guard went through a brief period of rebuilding; however, during the late 1950s and the early 1960s it was again allowed to fall into disrepair, as demonstrated during the limited call up for the 1961 Berlin Crisis. Two divisions, the Thirty-second Infantry and the Forty-ninth Armored, plus 264 separate units were federalized. Although some units were ready for active service in three months others were not prepared for duty when they were demobilized ten months later.[15]

The Guard's decline was abetted by congressional and executive neglect, but its image suffered more from its reputation as a haven for draft dodgers. Until 1958, Guardsmen were exempt from both the Selective Service System and Regular Army training. Recruits received most, if not all, of their training during week night (later changed to weekend drills). Fulfilling one's military obligation took no more time than one weekend a month plus two weeks a year. Even when the Guard was at last forced to send its recruits to basic training with the Army, it remained a less intrusive way to avoid the draft. Until the advent of the all volunteer force of the post-Vietnam War era, the image of the Guard as a haven for draft dodgers continued in the press and the public mind. In some ways this idea continues, as the 1988 vice-presidential campaign of Dan Quayle illustrated.

THE STATES

During the Vietnam War the Guard returned, if only temporarily, to more active state control. This development resulted not from any design by state or NGA officials but from the domestic unrest of the period. Governors in the early post-World War II era exercised decreasing control over troops. In most states they appointed the state Adjutant General, many times against the Army's better judgement, and "approved" training. The Army, however, set the agenda and paid the bills through the National Guard Bureau. But between 1970 and 1973 alone, governors called out the Guard to quell disorder on 203 occasions. President Lyndon B. Johnson, remembering the

1961 call up difficulties and not wishing to send "the wrong message" to the Chinese that the United States was escalating the war, declined to call up the Guard *en masse* and left it to act as an adjunct to state police forces.[16] The Tet Offensive in Vietnam and the North Korean seizure of the USS *Pueblo* forced President Johnson to mobilize 10,511 Air and 12,234 Army Guardsmen. However, few of these men reached Asia. Those who did usually served as fillers for Army units.[17]

The popular rejection of selective service in the post-Vietnam years and the resulting decline in the Regular Army, necessitated improvement in the reserve forces. The Guard and its competitor, the Army Reserve, took on an expanded role in deterring war in Europe. The Total Force concept of the Nixon Administration reasserted the national defense role of the Guard. After hesitant and limited use in Korea and Vietnam, the Guard became a key element in the Pentagon's war-making plans. Units were reorganized, as in 1940, to meet the new national demands with no regard to state commitments. In some cases they were virtually useless for traditional state duties—the state of Arkansas, for example, had no valid use for air assault troops or air defense fighters.

Guardsmen, too, were changing during this time. As the Vietnam War and the draft ended, so did the Guard as a haven from the Regular military. Recruiting became difficult; however, the type of men entering local units also changed. Many of them had prior military service, some in Vietnam, and brought a different attitude toward the regular Army. While Guardsmen of the Reckord-Walsh era (1942-1962) distrusted the Army, perhaps to an unreasonable degree, Guardsmen of the late 1970s and 1980s were Army trained and less wary of Army motives. By mission and temperament, the Guard was becoming an exclusively federal force.

THE LAW

Whatever remaining illusions of state control vanished during the Reagan Administration. Rather than challenging federal control over the Guard, the court cases pressed by Perpich and Dukakis with the support of other governors ended fictional state controls. Since World War II, the Pentagon had deferred to governors on Adjutant General appointments, even when candidates were unqualified, because of NGA and state pressure. The NGA under Walsh and Reckord was able to keep the Guard's dual nature and codify the power of governors in at least one regard—the approval of peacetime training. As long as governors cooperated with national defense training needs, both in and outside the country, the Pentagon was content to let the matter rest. Over time, however, Congress became less sensitive to the issue of the Guard's dual status, especially as the Total Force Team concept pushed the Guard further away from the state mission. In effect the

Guard was a federal force on loan to the states, bringing back into existence the pre-World War I War Department notion of a Continental Army.

An early example of the federal government's changing attitude toward the Guard came in September 1957 and should have served as a warning for governors. When Arkansas Governor Orville Faubus called up the Guard to prevent racial integration of Little Rock's Central High School, President Eisenhower federalized the entire 10,000 force, removing it from state control. Although caught in a dilemma of its own making, the Arkansas Guard obeyed federal orders.[18]

However, in training matters, governors quietly accepted the Army's control, surrendering the power granted them by the Militia Clause. By the early 1950s all that remained was the power granted by the 1952 Armed Forces Reserve Act[19] to veto Guard training outside the United States. In the 1970s and early 1980s, governors eagerly permitted "their" troops to participate in active duty European exercises. At times the competition for such trips between units bordered on political warfare, with the prize going to those with the better state house connections. Governors, however, failed to note that their power to approve overseas deployments came from Congress, who could just as easily take it away.

The three decade truce came to an abrupt end in 1985 when President Reagan began sending Guardsmen to Honduras. His intent was two-fold: to impress the Sandinistas with a show of force and to improve the image of the United States through humanitarian civic action programs. Opposed to the Reagan Central America policy, the governors of California and Maine exercised their rights under the 1952 Armed Forces Reserve Act and refused to allow state troops to participate.[20]

The Reagan Administration advanced legislation aimed at removing the governors' rights but quickly retreated under heavy political fire. However, the Administration was not long deterred. In 1986, Congressman Gillespie V. "Sonny" Montgomery of Mississippi proposed an amendment to the National Defense Authorization Act for fiscal year 1987, which prevented a veto of overseas training by "governors who, for political purposes, objected to the location where their National Guard units were being sent for routine peacetime training."[21] Montgomery said he did this, "with the Militia Clause of the Constitution in mind."[22] Passage of the Montgomery Amendment sent a message to the states that the federal government, which paid nearly 97 percent of Guard's expenses, controlled the National Guard and would use it whenever and wherever it wished.

The only course left for the governors was in court, however, precedent was against them. Citing the *Selective Draft Law Cases* of 1918, the National Defense Act of 1933, and legal scholars concerning the Militia Clause, the Eighth Circuit Court of Appeals ruled in *Perpich v. Department of Defense* that the Guard was an integral part of the national defense and as such Congress had "plenary and exclusive" authority over the Guard. Governor

Perpich appealed his case to the United States Supreme Court, citing the Montgomery Amendment's interference with the Militia Clause of the Constitution. In its June 11, 1990, opinion written by Justice John Paul Stevens, III, the Court held that Guardsmen wore three hats: as civilians, state Guardsmen, and members of the Army when on active duty. What veto authority the governors had over federally sponsored training came as "the product of political debate and political compromise" derived from the 1952 Act, not the Constitution. As a result, the Court concluded "that the Montgomery Amendment [was] not inconsistent with the Militia Clauses," asserting:

Neither the State's basic training responsibility, nor its ability to rely on its own Guard in state emergency situations, is significantly affected. Indeed, if the federal training mission were to interfere with the State Guard's capacity to respond to local emergencies, the Montgomery Amendment would permit the Governor to veto the proposed mission.[23]

However, Justice Stevens noted that if the states wished to avoid conflicts over state troops, they could "maintain at [their] own expense a defense force that is exempt from being drafted into the Armed Forces of the United States."[24]

Although the case dwelt on overseas training, *Perpich v. Department of Defense* forcefully asserted the federal government's supremacy over the National Guard. Governors were left with paper authority to train Guardsmen, but the training was scheduled and financed by Washington. On the other hand, the Court also upheld the state's right to use the Guard to maintain public order, but if the maintenance of public order conflicted with national goals—as they did in 1957 at Little Rock's Central High School—the state's authority evaporated. Thus, the Guard was a federal institution at all times, on loan as it were, to the states. The Continental Army of 1912, which the NGA had opposed, was now a legal establishment, due largely to the NGA's own actions.

Coming almost exactly fifty years after Congress authorized the mobilization of the entire Guard for one year's training, the Supreme Court's decision highlighted the important, if unseen, consequences of the 1940 expansion of federal power over the Guard. Intended by the Framers of the Constitution as a bulwark against the tyranny that a standing army might impose, the Guard was now a part of the establishment.

Federal control as a fact of life became clear less than two months after the Supreme Court's decision. The August 2, 1990 Iraqi invasion of Kuwait and the United State's susequent rapid deployment of forces to the Persian Gulf demonstrated the federal government's ability to use the Guard as it willed. While Guard support units were used extensively, combat forces were left conspicuously at home. Major General Robert F. Ensslin, Jr., NGA president, complained about the Pentagon's "'waffling' on deployment of Guard units into combat roles," but to no avail. As in 1940, the Regular Army complained that Guard combat units were not ready for immediate duty. In the wake of the Gulf War, Secretary of Defense Dick Cheney suggested the Guard's combat role should be reduced. Captain Jeffrey A. Jacobs, a reserve officer, suggested in the *Armed Forces Journal International* that the Guard should be permanently federalized. The NGA's weak voice during the crisis revealed the true impact of the Court's decision. There was not need to follow Jacobs' advice, the Guard was already under virtual federal control.[25]

If the NGA was unhappy with the results of mobilization in 1940, and the governors with the Court's decision in 1990, they should recall words written by historian Frederick Todd nearly fifty years earlier:

No longer is the Guardsman drafted into federal service, for he is already in; his unit need only be ordered to duty after Congress has declared a national emergency as it did in the summer of 1940.

Few people, not even all legislators, understand what this "federalization" really means or know the thought and effort which has gone into its development. Some, indeed, feel the Guard has been forced into a doubtful position. But to place all honor and credit where it is due, it must be recorded that it was Guardsmen who perfected and supported this legislation and who have entered into its first application with resolution and pride. If today there is dissatisfaction over the retention in service or other matters, it is not difficult to put one's finger on the real root of the trouble. It is the old story—the lack of a well thought out plan.[26]

In 1933, the National Guard Association laid out what it thought was a well made plan. The Guard would have a national role but at the same time retain its state connections. By 1940 the NGA was on the horns of a dilemma of its own making. Obstructing the General Staff's plans for national defense meant rejecting its national goals while supporting mobilization sacrificed the state mission. The NGA chose the national goal and forever changed the way the federal government viewed the Guard.

NOTES

1. Sir William Blackstone, KNT, *Commentaries on the Laws of England* (Philadelphia, PA, 1903), 320.

2. Derthick, *The National Guard in Politics*, 1.

3. Merlin Gustafson and Jerry Rosenberg, "The Faith of Franklin Roosevelt," *Presidential Studies Quarterly*, 19 (Summer 1989):559.

4. Hamilton Fish, *FDR: The Other Side of the Coin* (New York, 1976); Charles Callan Tansill, *Back Door to War: The Roosevelt Foreign Policy, 1933-1941* (Chicago, 1952); Charles A. Beard, *American Foreign Policy in the Making, 1932-1940* (New Haven, CT, 1946); Harry Elmer Barnes, *Perpetual War for Perpetual Peace* (Caldwell, ID, 1953).

5. Basil Rauch, *Roosevelt: From Munich To Pearl Harbor* (New York, 1967); Sherwood, *Roosevelt and Hopkins*, 132-133.

6. Randall Bennett Woods and John A. Cooper, "F.D.R. and the Triumph of American Nationalism," *Presidential Studies Quarterly*, 19 (Summer 1989):567.

7. Divine, *Roosevelt and World War II*, 25.

8. Sherwood, *Roosevelt and Hopkins*, 124-125.

9. Ibid.

10. Charles Joseph Gross, *Prelude to the Total Force: The Air National Guard, 1943-1969* (Washington, DC, 1985), 14-17.

11. A study group appointed by Secretary of Defense Louis Johnson and headed by Assistant Secretary of the Army Gordon Gray.

12. Mahon, *History of the Militia and National Guard*, 199-202.

13. Ibid., 210-211, 215-217, 232-233.

14. Ibid., 208-209.

15. Ibid., 228-229; Colby, *The National Guard of the United States*, XIII, p. 3.

16. William C. Westmoreland, *A Soldier Reports* (Garden City, NJ, 1976), 143, 193; Lyndon Baines Johnson, *The Vantage Point: Perspectives of the Presidency, 1963-1969* (New York, 1971), 149.

17. Mahon, *History of the Militia and National Guard*, 243.

18. Ibid., 224-226.

19. The 1952 Act also removed any stipulations on federalizing the Guard, a consequence of the 1940 mobilization. No longer would Congress have to declare a national emergency in order to use the Guard.

20. U.S. Supreme Court, *Rudy Perpich, Governor of Minnesota, et al., Petitioners v. Department of Defense, et al.*, June 11, 1990, p. 5.

21. Letter from Gillespie V. Montgomery, MC, to the Author, August 14, 1989.

22. Ibid.

23. U.S. Supreme Court, *Rudy Perpich, Governor of Minnesota, et al., Petitioners v. Department of Defense, et al.*, June 11, 1990, p. 7.

24. Ibid., 8.

25. Letter from Major General Robert F. Ensslin, Jr., to the Author with newspaper clipping, December 4, 1990; John G. Roos and Benjamin F. Schemmer, "Desert Storm Bares 'Roundout' Flaw but Validates Army Modernization Goals," *Armed Forces Journal International*, April, 1991, pp. 14, 35; Melissa Healy, "Cheney Would Reduce Reserve Combat Role," *Los Angeles Times*, March 14, 1991, p. 1; Jeffrey A. Jacobs, "Today's National Guard: Time to Federalize," *Armed Forces Journal International*, April 1990, pp. 55-58.

26. Frederick P. Todd, "Our National Guard: An Introduction to Its History," *Military Affairs*, V (Fall 1941), 170.

Bibliography

PRIMARY SOURCES

Manuscript and Archival Collections

Adjutant Gerneral Associaiton Conference Minutes, March 1940. National Guard Association of the United States Library, Washington, DC.

Adjutant General File, Alabama State Archives, Montgomery, AL.

Adjutant General's Office Letter, "Induction of certain National Guard Units into the Federal Service," July 30, 1940. United States Air Force Historical Research Center, Maxwell Air Force Base, AL.

Ensslin, Robert F., Jr., Major General, to Robert B. Sligh, 8 January 1991. Letter and newspaper clipping in the private collection of Robert B. Sligh.

Marshall, George C. Papers. George C. Marshall Library, Lexington, VA.

Marshall Foundation National Archives Project. George C. Marshall Library, Lexington, VA.

Montgomery, Gillespie V. MC, to Robert B. Sligh, August 14, 1989. Letter in the private collection of Robert B. Sligh.

National Guard Association Proceedings, 1939. National Guard Association of the United States Library, Washington, DC.

National Guard Association Proceedings, 1940. National Guard Association of the United States Library, Washington, DC.

Roosevelt, Franklin D. Papers. Franklin D. Roosevelt Library, Hyde Park, NY.

War Department, Record Group 165, National Archives, Washington, DC.

Watson, Edwing M. Papers. University of Virginia Library, Charlottesville, VA.

Government Documents

State Department. *Foreign Relations of the United States, 1937.* vol 5. Washington, DC, 1954.

_____. *Foreign Relations of the United States, 1938.* vol 5. Washington, DC, 1956.

U.S. Congress. *Congressional Record,* 76th Cong., 3 sess., 1940.

_____. *Congressional Record,* 77th Cong., 1st sess., 1941.

_____. *Hearing before the Joint Committee on the Investigation of the Pearl Harbor Attack,* 79th Cong., 1st sess. (Washington, DC, 1946), Part 15.

_____. House, Appropriations Committee. *Military Establishment Appropriation Bill for 1941, hearings before a subcommittee of the House Committee on Appropriations, H.R. 7805.* 76th Cong., 3 sess., 1939.

_____. House, Appropriations Committee. *Military Establishment Appropriation Bill for 1941, hearings before a subcommittee of the House Committee on Appropriations, H.R. 9209.* 76th Cong., 3 sess., 1940.

_____. House. *House Report No. 1117, Declaring the Existence of A National Emergency, and For Other Purposes, HJR 222,* 77th Cong., 1st sess.

_____. House. H.R. Rep. No. 2493, pt. 1, p. 2, 76th Cong., 3rd sess., 1940.

_____. House. H.R. Rep. No. 2493, pt. 2, p. 1, 76th Cong., 3rd sess., 1940.

_____. House. H.R. Rep. No. 2874, 76th Cong., 3rd sess., 1940.

_____. Senate, Appropriations Committee. *Emergency Supplemental Appropriation Bill for 1940, hearing before a subcommittee of the Senate Committee on Appropriations.* 76th Cong., 3rd sess., 1940.

_____. Senate. Committee on Military Affairs, *Compulsory Military Training and Service, hearings before the Committee on Military Affairs on S 4164,* 76th Cong., 3rd sess., 1940.

_____. Senate. Committee on Military Affairs, *Ordering Reserve Components and Retired Personnel into Active Military Service, hearings before the Committee on Military Affairs on SJR 286,* 76th Cong., 3rd sess., 1940.

_____. Senate. Senate Report No. 595, *Declaring the Existence of a National Emergency, and for other purposes, Senate Reports,* 77th Cong., 1st sess., 1941.

_____. Senate. Senate Report No. 1987, 76th Cong., 3rd sess., 1940.

U. S. *Constitution.* Art. I, sec. 7.

U. S. Supreme Court. *Rudy Perpich, Governor of Minnesota, et al., Petitioners v. Department of Defense, et al.,* June 11, 1990.

War Department. *Annual Report of the Chief of the National Guard Bureau, 1941.* Washington, DC, 1941.

Contemporary Articles

Colby, Elbridge and James F. Glass. "The Legal Status of the National Guard," *Virginia Law Review* 29 (May 1943):839-856.

"Calling of Guard Generally Favored by Press," *The United States News,* July 26, 1940, p. 29.

"Public Opinion Poll," *Public Opinion Quarterly,* September 1940, p. 551.

"Public Opinion Poll," *Public Opinion Quarterly,* December 1940, pp. 716-717.

Todd, Frederick P. "Our National Guard: An Introduction to Its History," *Military Affairs,* 5 (Fall 1941):152-170.

Newspapers

Army and Navy Journal, October 14, 1939–March 6, 1940.

Christian Science Monitor, February 20, 1987.

Los Angeles Times, March 14, 1991.

New Orleans Times Picayune, April 26, 1986–February 2, 1987.

New York Times, January 14, 1940–August 14, 1941; May 6 1986–August 5, 1987.

Providence (Rhode Island) Journal, December 12, 1988.

Washington Post, October 26–December 7, 1988.

Washington Times, May 7–December 15, 1988.

Memoirs, Reminiscences, Published Papers, and Contemporary Books

Bland, Larry I., ed. *The Papers of George Catlett Marshall: We Cannot Delay, July 1, 1939–December 6, 1941*. Baltimore, MD, 1986.

Complete Presidential Press Conferences of Franklin D. Roosevelt, Vol 15–16. 25 Vols. in 12. New York, 1972.

Hull, Cordell. *Memoirs of Cordell Hull*. 2 Vols., New York, 1948.

Johnson, Lyndon Baines. *The Vantage Point: Perspctives of the Presidency, 1963–1969*. New York, 1971.

Loewenheim, Francis L., Harold D. Langley, and Manfred Jonas, eds., *Roosevelt and Churchill: Their Secret Wartime Correspondence*. New York,, 1974.

Marshall, Katherine Tupper. *Together: Annual of an Army Wife*. New York, 1946.

Mauldin, Bill. The Brass Ring: A Sort of a Memior. New York, 1971.

Rosenman, Samuel, ed. *The Public Papers and Addresses of Franklin D. Roosevelt, Vol. IX*. 13 Vols. New York, 1938–1950.

Stimson, Henry L. and McGeorge Bundy, *On Active Service in Peace and War*. New York, 1948.

Westmoreland, William C. *A Soldier Reports*. Garden City, NJ, 1976.

Wheeler, Burton K. with Paul F. Healy. *Yankee from the West*. Garden City, NY, 1962.

SECONDARY SOURCES

Books

Adler, Selig. *The Isolationist Impulse: Its Twentieth Century Reaction*. New York, 1957.

Ambrose, Stephen E. *Upton and the Army*. Baton Rouge, LA, 1964.

Barnes, Harry Elmer. *Perpetual War for Perpetual Peace*. Caldwell, ID, 1953.

Beard, Charles A. *American Foreign Policy in the Making, 1932–1940*. New Haven, CT, 1946.

Bernardo, C. J. and Eugene H. Bacon. *American Military Policy: Its Development Since 1775*. Harrisburg, PA, 1955.

Blackstone, Sir William, KNT. *Commentaries on the Laws of England* Philadelphia, PA, 1903.

Clifford, J. Garry and Samuel R. Spencer, Jr. *The First Peacetime Draft*. Lawrence: University of Kansas, 1986.

Colby, Elbridge. *The National Guard of the United States: A Half Century of Progress*. Manhattan, KS, 1977.

Cole, Wayne S. *Roosevelt and the Isolationists*. Lincoln, NE, 1983.

_____. *Charles A. Lindbergh and the Battle Against American Intervention in World War II*. New York, 1974.

_____. *Senator Gerald P. Nye and American Foreign Relations*. Minneapolis, MN, 1962.

Conn, Stetson and Byron Fairchild. *The Framework of Hemisphere Defense*. Washington, DC, 1960.

Crossland, Richard B. and James T. Currie. *Twice the Citizen: A History of the United States Army Reserve, 1908–1983*. Washington, DC, 1984.

Derthick, Martha. *The National Guard in Politics*. Cambridge, MA, 1965.

Divine, Robert A. *Roosevelt and World War II*. Baltimore, MD, 1969.

_____. *Roosevelt and Isolationism in America, 1935–1941*. Ithaca, NY, 1966.

_____. *The Illusion of Neutrality*. Chicago, 1968.

_____. *The Reluctant Belligerent: American Entry Into World War II*. New York, 1979.

Dupuy, R. Ernest. *The National Guard: A Compact History*. New York, 1971.

Fish, Hamilton. *FDR: The Other Side of the Coin*. New York, 1976.

Frye, Alton. *Nazi Germany and the American Hemisphere, 1933–1941*. New Haven, CT, 1967.

Gallup, George. *The Gallup Poll: Public Opinion, 1935–1971*. 3 Vols. New York, 1972.

Greenfield, Kent Roberts, ed. *Command Decisions*. Washington, DC, 1960.

Gross, Charles Joseph. *Prelude to the Total Force: The Air National Guard, 1943–1969*. Washington, DC, 1985.

Hewes, James E., Jr. *From Root to McNamara: Army Organization and Administration, 1900–1963*. Washington, DC, 1975.

Hill, Jim Dan. *The Minute Man in Peace and War*. Harrisburg, PA, 1964.

Holley, I. B., Jr. *General John M. Palmer, Citizen Soldiers, and the Army of a Democracy*. Westport, CT, 1982.

Johnson, Donald Bruce. *The Republican Party and Wendell Willkie*. Westport, CT, 1960.

Jonas, Manfred. *Isolationism in America: 1935–1941*. Ithaca, NY, 1966.

Kimball, Warren F. *The Most Unsordid Act: Lend–Lease, 1939–1941*. Baltimore, MD, 1969.

Kreidberg, Marvin A. and Merton G. Henry. *History of Military Mobilization in the United States Army, 1775–1945*. Department of the Army, Washington, DC, 1955.

Langer, William L. and S. Everett Gleason. *Challenge to Isolation, 1937–1940*. New York, 1952.

Leigh, Michael. *Mobilizing Consent: Public Opinion and American Foreign Policy, 1937–1947*. Westport, CT, 1976.

Logan, John A. *The Volunteer Soldier of America*. Chicago, 1887.

Luechtenburg, William E. *Roosevelt and the New Deal*. New York, 1963.

Mahon, John K. *History of the Militia and the National Guard*. New York, 1983.

Matloff, Maurice and Edwin M. Snell. *Strategic Planning For Coalition Warfare, 1941–1942*. Washington, DC, 1953.

Maurer, Maurer. *Aviation in the U.S. Army, 1919–1939*. Washington, DC, 1987.

McCann, Frank D., Jr. *The Brazilian–American Alliance, 1937–1945*. Princeton, NJ, 1973.

McFarland, Keith D. *Harry H. Woodring: A Political Biography of FDR's Controversial Secretary of War*. Lawrence, KS, 1975.

Mosley, Leonard. *Marshall: Hero for Our Times*. New York, 1982.

National Guard Association of the United States, *The Nation's National Guard*. Washington, DC, 1954.

National Guard Bureau, *General Officers of the National Guard*. Washington, DC, 1963.

Neal, Steven. *Dark Horse: A Biography of Wendell Willkie*. Garden City, NY, 1984.

Nevins, Allan. *The New Deal and World Affairs*. New York, 1950.

Palmer, John M. *America in Arms: The Experience of the United States with Military Organization*. Washington, DC, 1941.

Palmer, Robert R., Bell I. Wiley, and William R. Keast. *The Procurement and Training of Ground Combat Troops*. Washington, DC, 1948.

Patterson, James T. *Congressional Conservatism and the New Deal*. Lexington, KY, 1967.

_____. *Mr. Republican: A Biography of Robert A. Taft*. Boston, 1972.

Pogue, Forest C. *George C. Marshall: Ordeal and Hope, 1939–1942*. New York, 1966.

Rauch, Basil. *Roosevelt: From Munich To Pearl Harbor*. New York, 1967.

Roosevelt, Elliot and James Brough. *A Rendezvous with Destiny: the Roosevelts of the White House*. New York, 1975.

Russell, Henry D. *The Purge of the Thirtieth Division*. Macon, GA, n.d.

Sherrill, Robert. *Saturday Night Special*. New York, 1973.

Sherwood, Robert E. *Roosevelt and Hopkins: An Intimate History*. New York, 1948.

Stauffer, Samuel A., and others. *The American Soldier: Adjustment During Army Life*. Princeton, NJ, 1949.

Steinberg, Alfred. *Sam Rayburn: A Biography*. New York, 1975.

Stenehjem, Michele Flynn. *An American First: John T. Flynn and the America First Committee*. New Rochelle, NY, 1976.

Tansill, Charles Callan. *Back Door to War: The Roosevelt Foreign Policy, 1933–1941*. Chicago, 1952.

Upton, Emory. *The Military Policy of the United States*. Washington, DC, 1917.

Watson, Mark Skinner. *Chief of Staff: Prewar Plans and Preparations*. Washington, DC, 1950.

Weigley, Russell F. *The American Way of War*. New York, 1973.

Wiltse, Charles. *John C. Calhoun: Nationalist, 1782–1828*. Indianapolis, IN, 1944.

Wiltz, John E. *In Search of Peace: The Senate Munitions Inquiry, 1934–1936*. Baton Rouge, LA, 1963.

Articles and Papers

Borg, Dorothy. "Notes on Roosevelt's 'Quarantine Speech,'" *Political Science Quarterly*. 72 (September 1957):405–433.

Brown, Richard C. "General Emory Upton–The Army's Mahon," *Military Affairs*, 17 (Fall 1953):125–131.

Cantor, Louis. "Elihu Root and the National Guard: Friend or Foe?" *Military Affairs*, 33 (December 1969):361–373.

Colby, Elbridge. "Elihu Root and the National Guard," *Military Affairs*, 23 (Spring 1959):28–34.

Furman, H. W. C. "Restriction on the Use of the Army Imposed by the Posse Comitatus Act," *Military Law Review*, 85 (Winter 1960):85–129.

"The Guard in Honduras," *Newsweek*, February 17, 1986, p. 36.

Gustafson, Merlin and Jerry Rosenberg. "The Faith of Franklin Roosevelt," *Presidential Studies Quarterly*, 19 (Summer 1989):559–566.

Jacobs, Jeffrey. "Today's National Guard: Time to Federalize," *Armed Forces Journal International*, April 1990, pp. 55–58.

McGlasson, W. D. "Mobilization 1940: The Big One," *National Guard*, September 1980, pp. 10–23.

Roos, John G. and Benjamin F. Schemmer. "Desert Storm Bares 'Roundout' Flaw but Validates Army Moderization [*sic*] Goals," *Armed Forces Journal International*, pp. 14, 35.

Stoler, Mark. "From Continentalism to Globalism: General Stanley D. Embick, the Joint Strategic Survey Committee, and the Military View of National Policy during the Second World War," *Diplomatic History*, 6 (Summer 1983):303–321.

"Supreme Court Rejects Dukakis Appeal, Upholds Montgomery Amendment on OCONUS Training," *National Guard*, June 1989, p. 10.

Woods, Randall Bennett and John A. Cooper. "F.D.R. and the Triumph of American Nationalism," *Presidential Studies Quarterly*, 19 (Summer 1989):567–581.

Index

Adams, Alva, 102, 104, 106-112, 119, 141, 142

Adams amendment, 104, 106, 107, 108, 111, 112

Adjutants General Association (AGA), 33, 54, 57, 60, 98, 146

Advisory Board, 147

Ainsworth, Fred C., 26

Air Corps, 12, 13, 16, 17, 62, 69, 100, 130, 139, 162

Air National Guard, 164

Alsop, Donald, 2

America First Committee, 104, 134, 143, 153

American-British Conversations (ABC-1), 129

American Expeditionary Force (AEF), 14, 138

American Legion, 22, 68, 77-80, 90

Andrews, Frank M., 52, 75, 78, 149

Andrews, Walter G., 60, 61, 70, 106, 115, 116, 118

anti-New Deal, 80, 81, 111

anti-Roosevelt Democrats, 81, 100

Argentina, 15, 102

Armed Forces Reserve Act of 1952, 164, 167, 168

Army Clause, 104, 161

Army Reserve 12, 13, 83, 164, 166

Austin, Warren R., 74, 102-104, 106, 108, 109, 118

Axis, 78, 106, 134

Babbit, Bruce, 2

Bailey, Earl E., 97, 120

Bailey, B. M., 55-57

Baker-March Bill, 27

Baltimore Convention, 29, 34, 41, 44, 45, 82, 153, 158

Barbour, Warren, 21

Barkley, Alben, 75, 85, 86, 105, 107, 108, 131, 141

Baruch, Bernard M., 10, 69

Beard, Charles, 134

Belgium, 67, 68, 71, 138

Berlin Crisis, 165

Blanding, Albert H., 43, 47-49, 59, 98, 148, 163

Borah, William, 6, 10, 20-22

Brazil, 15, 70, 72, 102

Brown, S. G., 43, 44

Buchanan, Kenneth, 48, 49, 64

Bullitt, William 7

Bulwinkle, Alfred C., 115

Bureau of the Budget, 43

Burke, Edward R., 80, 153

Burke-Wadsworth, 81, 82, 83-85, 87, 95, 101, 104, 107, 110

Calhoun John C., 14
Camp Barkeley, 127
Camp McQuaide, 127
Camp Murray, 127
Carnegie Endowment, 6
Case, Francis, 115
Chandler, Albert, 109, 141
Chicago Daily Tribune, 97
Chief of Naval Operations, 15
Chief of Staff: Marlin Craig 11, 15;
    Douglas MacArthur 6, 14, 15;
    George C. Marshall 6, 7, 11, 15-
    20, 25, 26, 28, 31, 32, 41, 43, 46,
    47, 49-55, 57, 58, 60-62, 68, 69, 71,
    72, 77, 80, 86, 94, 98-100, 129, 136,
    138, 142, 143, 145, 146, 147,
    149-51, 158, 163; Leonard Wood
    14, 26
China, 10, 78
Churchill, Winston S., 71, 80, 81, 133,
    138, 142
Civil War, 14, 23, 24, 149
Civilian Conservation Corps (CCC),
    15, 18, 71, 101, 126
Civilian Volunteer Effort, 75
Clark, Bennett C., 27
Clark, Grenville, 72, 79, 80, 83, 85,
    149, 159, 164, 165
Clark, Mark W., 151
Clason, Charles R., 137
Cold War, 164
Cole, Charles H., 19, 29
Collins, Ross A., 60
Committee to Defend America by
    Aiding the Allies, 104, 134
Congress 2, 6-13, 15-17, 19-24, 26-28,
    30-33, 41-44, 49-62, 70, 72-77, 80,
    81, 83-86, 93-97, 99, 101-109,
    112-17, 125, 126, 128, 130-36, 138,
    141, 142-45, 148-50, 158-64, 166,
    167-69
Connally, Tom, 107
Continental Army, 26, 95, 158, 167-68
Craig, Marlin, 11, 15
Crowder, Enoch H., 26
Culkin, Francis D., 61
Czechoslovakia, 11, 138

Dabney, W. D., 43
Dakar, Africa, 71, 144
Danaher, John A., 104-106, 110, 112,
    139, 141, 142, 155
DeLamater, Walter A., 44, 45, 53, 54,
    57, 58, 83, 98
demobilization, 105, 128, 129, 143,
    150-52
Denmark, 61, 62, 138
Dewey, Thomas, 81, 137
Dick Act of 1903, 25, 158
Dick, Charles, 25
Dixon, Frank J., 97
Dozier, James C., 29
Drum, Hugh A., 32
Dukakis, Michael, 1-3, 166

Eisenhower, Dwight D., 167
embargo, 8-11, 20-22, 100
Emergency Appropriations bill, 51, 56
Ensslin, Robert F., Jr., 168
Erickson, Edgar C., 56
Ethiopia, 9
Executive Council, 44, 49, 83, 98

Faddis, Charles I., 113, 115, 116, 118
Farley, Jim, 85
Faubus, Orville 167
federalize, 78, 84, 86, 87, 96, 104, 125,
    132, 160
Fish, Hamilton, 141-44, 161, 169
Fleming, Raymond H., 30, 98
Flynn, John T., 143, 153
Fort Dix, 127
Fort Jackson, 127
Fort Sill, 127
Fort Worden, 127
Forty-fifth Division, 126, 127, 130
Forty-first Division, 126, 127, 130
Forty-fourth Division, 127
Fortune, 5
France, 5, 7, 8, 10, 16, 18, 22, 67, 70,
    71, 78-81, 84, 106, 115, 134, 138,
    160, 162

Gallup, George, 21, 153
Garner, John 85

Garrison, Lindley, 26
Gasser, Lorenzo D., 17, 18, 43, 51, 52, 63, 64
General Headquarters (GHQ), 46-49, 58, 76, 146, 151, 163
General Headquarters Air Force, 73
General Reserve, 164
General Staff College, 48
General Staff, 14-20, 25, 27, 33, 34, 41, 42, 44, 46, 48, 49, 55, 57, 68, 71-73, 75, 78, 79, 83, 87, 126, 128-131, 135, 149, 150, 164, 169
George, Walter F., 74
Germany, 5-8, 14, 15, 20, 71, 73, 78-81, 87, 100, 101, 113, 114, 129, 130, 134, 138, 143
Gillette, Guy M., 102-104, 107-110
Grahl, Charles H., 83, 98
Gray Board, 164
Great Britain, 5, 7, 8, 14, 78, 87, 133, 134
Gullion, Allen W., 77

Halleck, Charles A., 112
Haskell, William N., 50, 51, 53, 55, 61, 71, 159
Havana, Cuba, 79, 106, 114
Hawaii, 12
Hay, James, 26
Hayden, Carl, 62
Hearst, William Randolph, 129
Hershey, Lewis B., 72, 83
Hill, Jim Dan, 3
Hill, Lister, 93, 105, 106, 108, 139, 141
Hinshaw, Carl, 113, 115, 117
Hitler, Adolf, 5-7, 11, 12, 16, 18, 20, 21, 61, 67, 98, 106, 114, 134, 140, 143, 162
Hoffman, Clare E., 114
Holt, Rush, 104, 110
Hooper, Stanford C., 87, 100, 101
Hopkins, Harry, 85, 161, 169
House Appropriations Committee, 29, 32, 42, 52, 57, 60, 129
House Joint Resolution 555, 75, 76, 78, 111
House Military Affairs Committee, 70, 75, 111, 137, 138, 143
House of Representatives, 16, 17, 20-22, 25, 26, 29, 32, 44, 47, 51, 55, 60-62, 76, 86, 110, 111, 113-19, 129, 132, 135, 141-45, 160, 167
House Resolution 567, 111
Houes Resolution 1776, 135
Hull, Cordell, 10, 67, 79, 85
Hull, John A. T., 24, 25

isolationism, 7, 8, 135, 161, 162
isolationists, 5-11, 16, 20-22, 32, 42, 62, 68, 69, 73, 76, 77, 80, 81, 87, 100, 107, 110, 130, 132-36, 141, 142, 153, 161, 162
Italy, 6, 9, 14, 153

Jackson, Robert, 133
Japan, 6, 10, 14, 78, 130, 161
Johnson, Edwin C., 95
Johnson, George W., 43, 44
Johnson, Herbert, 30, 31
Johnson, Hiram, 6, 10, 21, 22, 96, 110, 132
Johnson, Louis, 11, 51, 69, 90
Johnson, Lyndon B., 165, 166

Keehn, Roy D., 56, 98, 120
Kelly, Edward J., 85
Key, William S., 130
Knox, Frank, 20, 72, 81, 87
Korean War, 151, 164, 165

La Follette, Robert, 21, 106, 110, 155
Landon, Alf, 20, 81, 134
Latin America, 1, 7, 15, 68, 109, 117
Lawton, Samuel T., 31, 33
League of Nations, 6
Lear, Ben 147
Lee, Josh, 96, 140, 141
Legislative Committee, 28, 29, 44, 49, 56, 83
Lehman, Herbert, 96, 120
Lend-Lease, 134-35
Life, 85
Light, Gilson D., 30, 50, 126
Lindbergh, Charles A., 20, 69, 134, 153

Little Rock Central High School, 167-
    68
Lodge, Henry Cabot, Jr., 62, 106
Logan, John A., 14
Ludlow, Louis 42, 43
Luftwaffe, 20, 134, 135
Lusitania, 79

MacArthur, Douglas, 6, 14, 15
Marcantonio, Vito, 116, 118
Marshall, George C., 15, 72, 102, 111,
    137-39, 144; aid to the Allies, 51;
    appropriations, 16, 41-44, 52-53,
    59-62, 68-70 73, 73; career, 7;
    conscription, 79, 82, 84-87, 105;
    extension of service, 129-32, 135,
    142-43; Guard mobilization, 71, 73,
    75-79, 85-87, 93-94, 100, 110, 125,
    126, 164; preparedness, 11, 17,
    162; relations with Milton Reckord,
    52-54, 57, 159, 163; relations with
    the National Guard, 22-23, 27-29,
    31-32, 44-45, 52-54, 57, 146-51,
    163-64; training, 18-19, 46, 48-49,
    159, 163-64
Marshall, Katherine, 72
Martin, Edward, 28, 50, 53, 54, 83,
    130, 132
Mason, Noah M., 113, 115, 118
Massingale, Sam C., 114, 115
May, Andrew J.: 42, 75, 78, 111-18,
    128, 130-38, 142, 144, 145,
Maybank, Burnet R., 96, 120
McCormack, John W., 131, 142, 144
McCormick, Robert R., 129
McKinley, William, 24, 25
McNair, Lesley, 146, 151, 155, 163,
    164
Mexican War, 24
Michener, Earl C., 112
Military Training Camps Association
    (MTCA), 72, 76, 83, 159
Militia Act, 73
Militia Bureau (See also National
    Guard Bureau), 27
Militia Clause, 24, 27, 73, 103,
    106-108, 113, 116, 167, 168
Militia, 116, 158

Miller, William J., 113, 115, 116, 118,
    119
Minton, Sherman, 104, 118
mobilization, 3, 12, 14, 15, 17, 19, 46,
    70, 71, 73, 75-77, 79, 80, 82, 85,
    95, 97, 98, 104, 111, 119, 125, 139,
    145, 148, 151, 159-64, 168-69
Monroe Doctrine, 113, 115, 117
Montgomery amendment, 168
Montgomery, Gillespie V. "Sonny," 2,
    167
Moore, Richard C., 78
Morgenthau, 68, 69, 73, 75
Munich, Germany, 5, 7, 11, 21, 162,
    169

National Defense Act of 1916, 83, 149
National Defense Act of 1920, 27,
    116, 148
National Defense Act of 1933, 3, 13,
    26, 27, 33, 73, 83, 95, 96, 98, 102,
    103, 106, 107, 108, 113, 158, 160,
    167
National Defense Authorization Act
    (FY 1987), 167
National Guard Association (NGA),
    3, 7, 22-30, 34, 41, 44, 45, 48-50,
    52, 54, 56-58, 60, 61, 73, 82, 83,
    94, 96-99, 116, 128, 132, 145-49,
    157-61, 163-66, 168, 169
National Guard Bureau (NGB), 19,
    25, 31, 43, 44, 47-50, 52, 55, 56,
    58, 64, 75, 94, 95, 99, 126, 150,
    163, 165
National Guard, 1-3, 6, 7, 12-14, 16,
    17, 19, 20, 22-24, 27-32, 42-53,
    56-59, 61-62, 70, 71, 73-86, 93-99,
    102-109, 113, 115, 116, 117, 119,
    126-30, 132, 133, 139, 143, 144,
    146-51, 157, 158, 160, 163-65, 167-
    69
National Labor Relations Act, 96
National Rifle Association, 22, 28
NATO, 1
Navy Department, 7
Navy, 7, 15, 20, 51, 72, 79-82, 84, 101,
    128, 133, 162
Netherlands, 67, 162

Neutrality Act, 8-10, 20, 22
New Deal, 8, 21, 81, 85, 102, 110-12
Nixon, Richard M., 166
Norris George A., 21, 103, 106, 109, 110
North Korea, 166
Norway, 61, 62
Nye, Gerald P., 6, 9, 10, 21, 22, 110

O'Ryan, John F., 28, 70, 71
Officer Reserve Corps, 13, 27, 49, 104
Orange Plan, 14
Orr, Robert D., 2
Overton, John H., 106-108

pacifist, 5, 6
Palmer, John McAuley, 14, 28, 72, 79, 155, 156
Panama Canal, 12, 78, 115
Parsons, James K., 32
Pearl Harbor, 151, 161
Pepper, Claude, 106, 107, 109, 114
Perpich, Rudy, 1-3, 166-68
Perpich v. Department of Defense, 1, 167, 168
Pershing, John J., 6, 7, 18, 78, 133
Philippine Islands, 12, 93, 115
Pittman, Key, 11, 22, 110
Plattsburg Movement, 83
Plattsburg, New York, 79
Poland, 5, 7, 8, 11, 16, 18, 20, 21, 41, 45, 158
Powers, D. Lane, 59
protective clause, 159, 165
Protective Mobilization Force, 70
Public Resolution 96, 119, 131, 135

Quarantine Speech, 11
Quayle, Dan, 165

RAINBOW, 14, 16
Rayburn, Sam, 117, 122, 144
Reagan, Ronald, 1, 166, 167
Reckord, Milton A.: appropriations 59, 60, 61; Baltimore Convention, 29-33, 41, 45; career 28, 70, 157-58, 166; conscription, 82-84, 145-46, 149, 164-65; Guard mobilization,

95-97, 111, 1488; extension of service, 128, 132; protective clause, 149; relations with George Marshall, 52-54, 57, 159, 163; training plan, 29-33, 50, 61, 159
Red Plan, 14
Reserve Officer's Training Corps, 26
Reserve, 1, 12, 13, 24-27, 30, 31, 47, 49, 58, 73, 74, 76, 79, 80, 83, 93, 100, 103, 104, 108, 113, 115, 116, 119, 130, 131, 135, 143, 144, 147, 148, 149, 151, 158-60, 163-67, 169
Reynolds, Robert R., 118, 131, 136
Rich, Robert F., 114, 118
Ridgway, Matthew B., 71, 72
Rilea, Thomas E., 59
Roosevelt, Franklin D., 30, 79, 100, 102, 103, 110, 111, 112, 137, 142, 143; aid to Allies, 71, 117, 132-33; conscription, 80-82, 84-87; extension of service, 130-32, 135, 136 140, 145; foreign affairs, 6-8, 67, 162; Guard mobilization, 74-77, 86, 93, 97, 99, 114, 119, 126, 160; isolationists and, 8-11, 161; neutrality legislation, 9, 10, 20-22, 104; preparedness, 12, 16, 17, 18, 41-42, 68-73, 101, 162, 163; third term, 85, 101, 105, 134, 159
Roosevelt, Theodore, Jr., 79
Root, Elihu, 25, 26, 79
Routzohn, Harry N., 116
Russell, Richard D., 51, 56, 152

Salem (Mass) Evening News, 97
Secretary of War, 5, 11, 14, 16, 25-27, 29, 32, 42, 44, 51, 79, 81, 84, 86, 98, 99, 107, 130, 136, 142, 147, 150, 153, 154, 156
selective service, 79, 80, 83, 84, 86, 94, 96, 105, 133, 137, 149, 151, 159, 165, 166
Selective Draft Law Cases, 167
Selective Service Act, 136, 137, 145, 149
Selective Service Committee, 79
Selective Service System, 165
Selective Training and Service bill, 82,

101, 116, 125, 132, 159
Senate Appropriations Committee, 50, 51, 62
Senate Foreign Relations Committee, 11
Senate Joint Resolution 271, 106
Senate Joint Resolution 286, 93-96, 99-104, 107, 110-12, 118, 119, 120, 125, 132, 134, 145, 160, 161
Senate Joint Resolution 95, 137, 141, 142
Senate Military Affairs Committee, 84, 93, 125, 136, 140, 141
Senate, 44, 50, 51, 57, 60-62, 73, 75, 76, 84-86, 108, 109, 110
Sheppard, Morris, 93, 100-102, 109, 118
Short, Dewey, 137, 143-45
Smith, Frederick C., 114
Smith, Harold D., 43
Snyder, J. Buell, 29, 31, 32
Spanish Civil War, 10
Standing Liaison Committee, 15
Stark, Harold R., 72, 80, 82, 84
Stark, Lloyd C., 97
Starnes, Foster Waterman, 42
Stevens, John Paul Stevens, III, 168
Stimson, Henry L., 79, 81, 84-87, 93, 98, 107, 119, 130, 131, 150
Strong, George V., 46-49, 75, 78
Stuart, R. Douglas, 134
Supreme Court, 1, 2, 10, 100, 102, 105, 168
Sweetser v. Emerson, 109

Taber, John, 44
Taft, Robert A., 21, 74, 81, 101, 102, 106, 110, 120, 137, 139-41
Tennessee Valley Authority, 81
Terry, David D., 59
Tet Offensive, 166
Third Corps Area, 19, 32
Thirtieth Division, 126, 127
Thirty-second Division, 127
Thirty-seventh Division, 127
Thirty-third Division, 98
Thomas, Elbert D., 94, 105, 118, 136-38, 141

Thomas,Norman, 135, 143
Thomason, R. Ewing, 77, 113, 114, 118
Thorkelson, J., 113
Tobey, Charles W., 137, 139
Total Force, 166
Twenty-eighth Division, 130
Twenty-seventh Division, 70, 127

United States v. Gettysburg Electric R. Co., 105
United States v. Stephens, 108
Universal Military Training (UMT), 24, 26, 79, 103, 164
Upton, Emory, 14, 24
U. S. Army, 1, 3, 6, 7, 11-20, 23-34, 41-44, 46-58, 60-66, 67-73, 75-79, 82-86, 93-97, 100-104, 106, 108, 109, 112, 114, 116, 117, 125-31, 133-39, 141, 143-51, 158-69
USS *Augusta*, 142
USS *Pueblo*, 166
Vandenberg, Arthur H., 22, 74, 81, 109, 110, 139
Victory Plan, 129
Vietnam, 165, 166
Vorys, John M., 118

Wadsworth Committe, 28
Wadsworth, James W., 61, 70, 80, 81, 85, 115, 116, 118, 131, 153
Walsh, Ellard A., 30, 33, 58, 59, 83, 147, 166
War Department, 15-17, 26-29, 31, 32, 41, 42, 44-46, 49, 51, 53, 54, 55, 57-59, 62, 69, 70, 72, 73, 75, 79, 80, 84, 86, 93, 94, 96, 99, 104, 106, 110, 126, 128-30, 135-37, 139, 141, 148, 158, 159, 167
War Plans Division (WPD), 6, 16, 18, 19, 46-49, 63, 75, 76, 78, 128, 134
Ward, Orlando, 46, 69
Welles, Sumner, 72
Western Hemisphere, 6, 7, 15, 16, 53, 62, 72, 77, 80, 93, 96, 100, 102-104, 106, 109, 111, 113, 114, 115, 117, 130, 131, 133, 134, 142, 160, 162
Wheeler, Burton K., 6, 85, 87, 100,

101, 106, 107, 110, 137, 139-141, 145
White, George A., 130
White, Wallace H., 103
White, William Allen White, 104, 134
Wickersham, George W., 26
Wigglesworth Richard B., 44
Williams, John F., 52-55, 75, 94, 95, 97, 105, 110, 111, 126, 127, 150, 156
Willkie, Wendell, 80-82, 85, 112, 132, 133, 139, 153
Wilson, Woodrow, 26, 70
Wood, Leonard, 14, 26
Wood, Robert E., 134, 143
Woodring, Harry H., 11, 16, 17, 29, 31, 32, 43-45, 51, 61, 62, 69, 81
Woodruff, Roy O., 115
Woodrum, Clifton A., 44, 117, 118
Works Progress Administration 58
World Peace Foundation, 6
World War I, 5, 6, 8-10, 13, 14, 18, 26, 28, 70, 79, 80, 146, 148, 149, 158, 167
World War II, 3, 5, 7, 153, 161, 164-166

About the Author

ROBERT BRUCE SLIGH is historian at the Headquarters of the Twelfth Air Force (Tactical Air Command), Bergstrom Air Force Base, Texas. He is a graduate of Louisiana Tech University and Texas A&M University.